REALISM, IDENTITY
AND EMOTION

For Shelagh, Robert, and Holly

REALISM, IDENTITY AND EMOTION

Reclaiming *Social* Psychology

John D. Greenwood

SAGE Publications
London • Thousand Oaks • New Delhi

© John D. Greenwood 1994

First published 1994

All rights reserved. No part of this publication may be reproduced, stored in a retrieval system, transmitted or utilized in any form or by any means, electronic, mechanical, photocopying, recording or otherwise, without permission in writing from the Publishers.

Sage Publications Ltd
6 Bonhill Street
London EC2A 4PU

Sage Publications Ltd
2455 Teller Road
Thousand Oaks, California 91320

Sage Publications India Pvt Ltd
32, M-Block Market
Greater Kailash – I
New Delhi 110 048

British Library Cataloguing in Publication Data
Greenwood, J.D.
 Realism, Identity and Emotion: Reclaiming
 Social Psychology
 I. Title
 302

 ISBN 0–8039–8926–1
 ISBN 0–8039–8927–X (pbk)

Library of Congress catalog card number 93–087017

Typeset by Mayhew Typesetting, Rhayader, Powys
Printed in Great Britain by Redwood Books, Trowbridge, Wiltshire

Contents

Cyclops, if anyone ever asks you how you came by your unsightly blindness, tell them your eye was put out by Odysseus, Sacker of Cities, the son of Laertes, who lives in Ithaca.

Homer, The Odyssey, Book IX (E.V. Rieu translation)

Preface

In the past few decades much has been written on the social dimensions of identity (Breakwell, 1992; Yardley and Honess, 1987) and emotion (Franks and Doyle McCarthy, 1989; Harré, 1986a), and on their intimate relation to social discourse (Coulter, 1979; Shotter and Gergen, 1989). Much has also been written on the social dimensions of science (Barnes, 1982; Bloor, 1976; Latour and Woolgar, 1986), and social constructionism has been advocated as an alternative meta-theory for psychological science (Gergen, 1982, 1985; Potter and Wetherell, 1987). Unfortunately all too often these distinct intellectual developments have been conflated, with the consequence that many have come to treat a commitment to the social dimensions of identity, emotion, and science as tantamount to acceptance of social constructionist denials of the objectivity of psychological theories and their empirical evaluation. This is perhaps unsurprising, since many identity and emotion researchers do seem committed to some form of social constructionism, insofar as they hold that social discourse about identity and emotion plays an important role in the constitution of identity and emotion.

In this work I argue that there is no intrinsic relation between theories of the social dimensions of identity and emotion, and social constructionist denials of the objectivity of psychological theories and their empirical evaluation. I claim that identity and (at least some) emotions are socially constituted, but that this poses no threat to the objectivity of psychological theories of identity and emotion, or to the empirical evaluation of such theories. I argue that, while social discourse about actions and social relations does play a major role in the constitution of identity and emotion, social discourse *about identity and emotion* does not. The frequent and unfounded presumption that it does has been the source of much contemporary confusion in the theoretical literature on identity and emotion.

In the case of emotion in particular, the regular confounding of psychological theories of the social dimensions of emotion, and social constructionist denials of objectivity, has led to an unfortunate and unwarranted polarization of theoretical positions on emotion. Thus those of a hard-nosed empiricist persuasion tend to look to biology and physiology as the only source of a genuinely objective theory of emotions, emphasizing the biological continuity and universality of emotions and their modes of expression. Those researchers dissatisfied with the sterilities of empiricism, and impressed by recent analyses of the social dimensions of science, tend to deny that there are any independent and universal facts about emotions, and lay great emphasis upon the cross-cultural and transhistorical diversity of socially constructed theories of emotion.

There is, however, no reason, or rather no good reason, why this should be the case. In this work I aim to provide an account of psychological theories that enables us to recognize that it is an objective and empirical question whether identity and emotion are biological, psychological, or social in nature, and whether they are cross-culturally and transhistorically universal or socially diverse.

I do this by advocating and defending a *realist* account of the semantics of scientific theories – including psychological theories. I argue that what is objectionable about traditional empiricist meta-theory is not its insistence on the empirical evaluation of psychological theories – which is also mandated by realism – but its narrow and debilitating account of the semantics of psychological theories, in terms of 'operational definitions' and the like. In contrast, a realist account of the semantic autonomy of psychological theories (with respect to the empirical phenomena they are employed to explain) is theoretically liberating. I argue that realism can surmount all the traditional problems of empiricism, and can effectively resist recent relativist critiques of objectivity advanced by social constructionists.

In this work I try to illustrate the virtues of a realist interpretation of psychological theory by exploring the possibilities it allows for theories of the social dimensions of mind – focusing on theories of the social dimensions of identity and emotion. I argue that neither traditional empiricism nor social constructionism can – or does – recognize the social nature of identity and emotion. Both traditional empiricism and social constructionism either ignore the social dimensions of identity and emotion, or offer only impoverished accounts, by effectively restricting the social dimensions of identity and emotion to the social dimensions of our theories or discourse about identity and emotion. In contrast, I offer a theory of the social dimensions of identity and emotion – in terms of the pursuit of 'identity projects' within social collectives, and the evaluation of actions and social relations by parties to the conventions of social collectives – that documents those social dimensions of identity and emotion that are *independent* of our socially constructed theories and discourse about identity and emotion.

In doing so, I hope to demonstrate that one of the primary virtues of the realist account, in contrast to both traditional empiricism and social constructionism, is that it enables us to acknowledge the social dimensions of identity and emotion, while at the same time recognizing that they pose no threat to the objectivity of psychological theories of identity and emotion, or their empirical evaluation.

Although advocating a realist account of psychological theory as superior to traditional empiricist and social constructionist accounts, I make no claim that my own account of scientific realism is representative, or that my treatment of social constructionism is comprehensive. The forms of realism advocated in philosophy of science, for example, are so various that one recent commentator has characterized realism as 'a majority position whose advocates are so divided as to appear a minority' (Leplin, 1984: 1). There are also a good number of theorists offering accounts of the social nature of identity and emotion who characterize themselves as social constructionists, but who are not obviously committed to more radical relativist denials of the objectivity of psychological theories and their empirical evaluation (Averill, 1980; Coulter, 1979; Harré, 1983a).

Instead of attempting to advance definitive statements of these positions, in this work I try to offer an account of the semantics of psychological theories – which I call 'scientific realism' – that is superior to and less restrictive than traditional empiricist accounts, but which preserves the objectivity of psychological theories and their empirical evaluation. This account enables theorists to acknowledge the social dimensions of identity, emotion, and science, without abandoning these genuine theoretical insights to the more radical and relativist forms of social constructionism. This I hope will provide researchers with a conceptual framework within which psychological theories of the social dimensions of identity, emotion, and science can be more fruitfully developed.

Very many friends, colleagues, and students have influenced the final outcome of this work. They are too numerous to mention, but I am especially indebted to conversations and correspondence with Chong Kim Chong, Jeff Coulter, Kay Deaux, Ken Gergen, Garth Fletcher, Juliet Floyd, Steve Fuller, Jerry Ginsburg, Margaret Gilbert, Rom Harré, James and Diana Herbert, Joe Margolis, John Sabini, Paul Secord, Bill Shadish, and John Shotter. I am also grateful to Ziyad Marar, my commissioning editor at Sage, for his cheerful enthusiasm and support, and to an anonymous reader at Sage for his or her substantive and constructive suggestions.

Many of the arguments presented in this work have been appropriated or developed from papers published in *Theory and Psychology*, *New Ideas in Psychology*, *Journal for the Theory of Social Behaviour*, *Theoretical and Philosophical Psychology*, *Behavior and Philosophy*, *Philosophical Psychology*, *Social Epistemology*, and *Philosophy of the Social Sciences*, and papers presented at the International Conference on Self and Identity (University College, Cardiff, 1984), The American Psychological Association (New Orleans, 1989), the Research Conference on Identity (CUNY Graduate School, New York, 1990), the American Philosophical Association (New York, 1991), the Conference on Realism and Social Constructionism (University of Houston, 1991), the Southern Society for Philosophy and Psychology (New Orleans, 1993), and the Conference on the Development of Ideas in Psychology (City College, New York, 1993).

Research for this work was supported by a Creative Incentive Award from the City University of New York PSC-CUNY Research Award

Program, and a Rifkind Fellowship from City College, City University of New York. I here acknowledge my sincere gratitude to City College and the City University of New York for the intellectual opportunities they have afforded me over the past few years – including the opportunity to pursue the themes that comprise the present work.

Last, but certainly not least, I thank my longsuffering family for enduring my manic behavior throughout the extremely hot and bothered summer months in which the final version of this work was produced.

John D. Greenwood
New York

1
Empiricism

Psychological science, for most of its recent history, has been based upon the traditional empiricist account of science. The inadequacies of this account, which will be documented in this chapter, are nowadays generally recognized: the problem is what to put in its place. Of the various contemporary meta-theories of psychological science, *realism* and *social constructionism* appear to provide the most detailed alternatives to traditional empiricism. Both have been recently advanced and defended in mainstream psychology journals (Manicas and Secord, 1983; and Gergen, 1985, respectively), where the traditional empiricist account has also been defended (Kimble, 1989).

Psychological scientists are naturally reluctant to embrace social constructionism, given its denial of traditional scientific virtues such as objectivity. They are perhaps more inclined to embrace realism, but seem presently to misrepresent it as a brand of empiricism. In this work, and especially in the following chapter, I argue that realism provides an account of *psychological theory* that is both distinct from and superior to the account provided by traditional empiricism. This enables the realist to recognize the social dimensions of psychological phenomena such as identity and emotion, without embracing social constructionist denials of objectivity. This gives many psychologists what I believe they want from a meta-theoretical account of psychological science: a richer conception of psychological science and its potential that avoids the intellectual sterility of traditional empiricism but preserves the traditional virtue of scientific objectivity. I also claim that realism provides a *viable* alternative to traditional empiricism, by arguing that social constructionist critiques of objectivity have considerably less force than is regularly supposed.

Objectivity

Since objectivity is the main issue in many contemporary debates between empiricists, realists, and social constructionists, it may be useful to clarify in advance the types of objectivity that are at issue. Two primary conceptions of objectivity are defended or contested in these debates: namely, *linguistic objectivity* and *epistemic objectivity*. These forms of objectivity are attributed to – or it is denied that they can be attributed to – putative descriptions, either in science or everyday life.

A description is *linguistically objective* if it makes a claim about a putative entity and attributes properties to it; if it is true or false – or accurate or inaccurate[1] – according to whether the entity putatively described has or has not the properties attributed to it by the description. Descriptions are linguistically objective if they are true or false by virtue of independent facts about the entity they purport to describe; if the employment of the description – by actor or observer or social group or collective – is neither a necessary nor sufficient condition of the truth of the description. Descriptions are not linguistically objective if they violate any of these – essentially equivalent – conditions. Ordinary empirical descriptions employed in sentences such as 'the cat is on the mat' and 'all swans are white' are generally held to be linguistically objective. Such sentences are true if and only if there is in fact a cat on the mat and if in fact all swans are white: the employment of these descriptions does not make it the case that the cat is on the mat or that all swans are white.[2] The critical question for present purposes is whether putative theoretical descriptions of 'unobservables'[3] such as atoms and emotions are linguistically objective.

A description is *epistemically objective* if its truth or falsity can be rationally or empirically evaluated. Sentences employing mathematical descriptions – such as '2 + 4 = 6' – are epistemically objective because their truth can be rationally demonstrated via deduction from self-evident axioms and rules of derivation. Ordinary empirical descriptions such as 'the cat is on the mat' and 'all swans are white' are epistemically objective because their truth or falsity can be empirically evaluated by making the relevant observations of the cat (and the mat) and swans. Descriptions are not epistemically objective if their truth or falsity cannot be rationally or empirically evaluated: what types of description fall into this category is a matter of contention. The critical question for present purposes is whether putative theoretical descriptions of 'unobservables' such as atoms and emotions are epistemically objective: whether such descriptions are empirically evaluable.

Chapters 1–3 of this work focus on the question of the linguistic objectivity of theoretical descriptions; the question of their epistemic objectivity is addressed in Chapter 4. It is, however, important to recognize from the outset that the two questions are analytically distinct. Although many descriptions – such as ordinary empirical descriptions or mathematical descriptions – are generally held to be both linguistically and epistemically objective, the linguistic objectivity of a description does not entail or depend upon its epistemic objectivity. Thus one can consistently hold that certain religious claims such as 'God is jealous' are linguistically objective – the claim 'God is jealous' is true if and only if there exists an entity that has the traditional properties ascribed to God (omnipotence, omniscience, and the like) and is also jealous – but not epistemically objective, because there is no rational or empirical means of assessing its truth or falsity.

A common error of both empiricist and social constructionist accounts is to assume that linguistic and epistemic objectivity can only be achieved for putative theoretical descriptions of atoms and emotions if such descriptions are operationally defined in terms of the empirical phenomena they purport to explain. Thus traditional empiricists maintain that linguistic and epistemic objectivity is achieved – and can only be achieved – via the operational definition of theoretical psychological descriptions. Social constructionists deny that theoretical psychological descriptions are either linguistically or epistemically objective by denying that they are – and that they can be – operationally defined. According to the realist, this is a fundamental error: theoretical descriptions can be – and regularly are – both linguistically and epistemically objective, even though they are not operationally defined.

In this chapter I argue that traditional empiricism does not and cannot account for the linguistic objectivity of theoretical descriptions. In the following chapter I argue that realism can.

Meaning Empiricism

It is often said that one has to be an empiricist to be a scientist, and that a commitment to the 'principle of empiricism' is the hallmark of post-Galilean science. Thus, in order to be a scientific psychologist, one has to be committed to the 'principle of empiricism.' In one sense this appears to be true – almost trivially true – and innocuous. What may be termed *methodological empiricism* is the reasonable requirement that scientific theories be subject to empirical evaluation. In this sense commitment to the 'principle of empiricism' *is* the hallmark of post-Galilean science, in the sense that scientists practicing since the time of the 'scientific revolution' – unlike scientists who practiced during medieval times – have held that theories ought to be empirically evaluated and adjudicated. Few who believe that disciplines such as chemistry and psychology can be scientific would dispute this requirement, and certainly no realist would. In this respect all scientists are empiricists, or ought to be. Social constructionists – and relativists – do dispute this, but their disputation amounts to the claim that such disciplines are not really sciences at all, or at least not sciences as traditionally conceived.

However, not all interpretations of the 'principle of empiricism' are so innocuous. What may be termed *meaning empiricism* is the often avowed requirement that theoretical descriptions must be defined in terms of observables. This interpretation of the 'principle of empiricism' is perhaps most clearly expressed in the standard empiricist account of the semantics of scientific theories concerning 'unobservables' such as atoms and emotions. According to this familiar account, 'theoretical postulates' are devoid of meaningful content unless they are defined via 'correspondence rules' or 'operational definitions' in terms of lower-level laws relating observables, which such postulates are introduced to explain (Braithwaite, 1953; Hempel, 1965). Thus, for example, it is standardly held that the meaningful content of Bohr's theory of the atom is specified via correspondence rules relating the theoretical descriptions to the empirical laws governing the spectral emission lines for hydrogen and helium, which the theory was introduced to explain. According to this account, the 'observational level' of scientific discourse is held to confer meaning on the 'theoretical level' by a process analogous to capillary action, via an 'upward seepage' of meaning from the 'soil' of observational experience (Feigl, 1970).

This account is familiar to and enormously popular with psychologists, who almost ritually insist upon the 'operational definition' of 'intervening variables' or 'hypothetical constructs' in terms of empirical laws. It is claimed that theoretical descriptions of psychological phenomena must be defined in terms of antecedent environmental stimuli and consequent behavior:

> The great usefulness of the intervening variable approach is that it provides objectivity for unobservable mentalistic concepts. The . . . laws [relating environmental and biological antecedents and psychological phenomena, and psychological phenomena and behavior] tie them to observable antecedents and behavioral consequences. This permits entry into psychology of the topics the radical behaviorist would banish. (Kimble, 1989: 494–5)

The doctrine of meaning empiricism derives historically from the classical empiricist account of cognition. According to classical empiricists such as Locke, Berkeley, and Hume, concepts or 'ideas' are derived from sense experience, and words gain their meaning by association with concepts or 'ideas.' Classical empiricists assumed the homogeneity of sensation and cognition: cognitions were held to differ from sensations in degree but not in kind. Most classical and later empiricists treated cognitions or 'ideas' as 'copies' or 'fainter images' of sense-impressions. They were held to differ only in their degree of intensity, or 'force and vivacity' (Hume, 1739). Since they held that 'ideas' are images derived from sense experience, they naturally held that prior sensory experience of an X or its compositional elements is a necessary condition of having the concept of an X, and of the meaningful employment of any linguistic term to refer to any particular X. Thus a congenitally blind man was said to be unable to have the concept of a blue object, or to employ the description 'blue' in a meaningful way. Given this account, it was also natural to suppose that one could only meaningfully employ a theoretical description if one could provide an ostensive or operational definition of it. In later 'verificationist' accounts of factual meaning, this developed into the doctrine that a concept or its linguistic expression is meaningless unless it can be defined in terms of observable phenomena (Schlick, 1936).

That is, the standard empiricist account of theoretical meaning is based upon the assumption that theoretical descriptions can only be meaningful if they are operationally defined, since this is held to be the only way that they can satisfy the principle of meaning empiricism (in the assumed absence of the possibility of an ostensive definition of descriptions referencing 'unobservables' such as atoms or emotions).

Instrumentalism

However, although the standard empiricist account does maintain linguistic objectivity with respect to empirical law descriptions – such descriptions are held to be true or false according to whether the ascribed correlations hold or not – it does *not* maintain linguistic objectivity with respect to theoretical 'descriptions,' or does so only in the most impoverished sense.

For the empiricist account involves the explicit treatment of theories as intellectual *constructions*, in the sense in which such constructions are contrasted with ordinary descriptions. Indeed, in earlier versions of logical empiricism and positivism, theoretical 'descriptions' were characterized as 'logical constructions' that bring formal organization to a set of observational descriptions. Such theoretical 'constructions' were not held to describe anything other than the objects of the sets of observational descriptions to which they were supposed to bring formal unity; in particular, they were not held to describe putatively 'inferred entities' such as emotions or electrons:

> Given a set of propositions nominally dealing with the supposed inferred entities, we observe the properties which are required of the supposed entities in order to make these propositions true. By dint of a little logical ingenuity, we then construct some logical function of less hypothetical entities which has the requisite properties. This constructed function we substitute for the supposed inferred entities, and thereby obtain a new and less doubtful interpretation of the body of propositions in question. (Russell, 1924: 152)

The empiricist account provides an *instrumentalist* interpretation of theoretical 'descriptions': they are not held to make independently meaningful ascriptions of properties to postulated entities such as atoms and emotions. Rather they are treated as intellectual constructions that serve as linguistic instruments for the 'conceptual integration' of the empirical laws in terms of which they are defined (Hempel, 1965).

Theoretical 'descriptions' are not held to have any sense or reference independently of the empirical laws in terms of which they are – operationally – defined. They are not true or false according to whether there are phenomena which do or do not have the properties attributed to them by the theoretical 'descriptions' (such as electron spin or content of emotion). The truth or falsity of such 'descriptions' is – at least ideally – wholly determined by the truth or falsity of the descriptions of empirical correlations in terms of which they are defined. As MacCorquodale and Meehl put it in their characterization of 'intervening variables' in psychological science (reading 'validity' and 'correctness' as equivalent to 'truth'): '. . . the validity of the empirical laws is both necessary and sufficient for the "correctness" of the statement about the concept' (1948: 109).

In this limited respect theoretical 'descriptions' may be said to be linguistically objective. They do have truth conditions: namely, the truth conditions of the empirical laws to which they supposedly bring conceptual integration. They are not, however, linguistically objective *qua theoretical descriptions*, because they have no *autonomous* truth conditions: their truth conditions are entirely derivative of and parasitic upon – because they are identified with – the truth conditions of the descriptions of empirical correlations in terms of which they are defined. They make no existential claims about theoretical entities and make no attribution of properties to them. They are not putative descriptions of postulated theoretical entities such as atoms and emotions. Insofar as they serve any descriptive function at all, they serve as convenient *re*descriptions of empirical correlations.

> . . . these intervening variables serve as *economical devices* to order experi-mental variables in relation to the dependent variables. They are *'shorthand' descriptions*, and nothing more, of the influence on behavior of several independent variables. The *only meaning* possessed by these intervening variables is their relationship to both the independent and dependent variables (Kendler, 1952: 271; original emphasis).

Yet this account of the meaning of theoretical descriptions, which is held to be a primary virtue of empiricism, is the source of most of its problems.

Problems of Empiricism

Despite its popularity, the empiricist account of the semantics of theoretical descriptions has a number of serious problems. Although these are generally recognized by empiricists, they are also held to be tractable. In this section I argue that these problems are intractable and lethal to the standard empiricist account – the proposed and generally accepted 'solutions' to the problems are no solutions at all.

It is often held – and certainly held by empiricists – that in psychology and other sciences theoretical explanations proceed by the deduction of empirical laws or descriptions from theoretical descriptions (Braithwaite, 1953; Hempel and Oppenheim, 1948): 'A psychological theory puts a collection of concepts and their associated laws into a structure that allows the deduction of behavioral consequences. To show that a fact of behavior is deducible from a theory is what it means to explain that fact' (Kimble, 1989: 498)

Yet if the semantic contents of theoretical descriptions – or postulates – are to be identified with the semantic contents of the empirical laws in terms of which they are supposed to be operationally defined, it is hard to see how such theoretical descriptions could provide illuminating and non-vacuous explanations of empirical laws. If 'intervening variables' really are defined in terms of the empirical laws to which they bring conceptual integration, any putative explanation of empirical laws in terms of intervening variables would be viciously circular, since it would not embody any information not already contained in the statement of the empirical laws. Thus if 'schizophrenia,' for example, is defined in terms of a behavioral syndrome, it can hardly be advanced as an explanation of that syndrome. Kimble (1989: 495), for example, makes precisely this point in railing against pseudo-explanations that appeal to 'mere definitions,' but fails to see that it applies directly to his own account of explanation by deduction from intervening variable concepts, which he insists must be operationally defined in terms of observable independent and dependent variables.

On this account it is also hard to make sense of what seems to be a common enough fact of scientific life, namely that we are often faced with competing and inconsistent theoretical explanations of the same range of empirical phenomena. Thus, for example, (at least for some considerable period of time) the Ptolemeic geocentric theory, which claimed that the earth is the centre of the universe, and the Copernican heliocentric theory, which claimed that the sun is the centre of the universe, advanced competing explanations – via their ability to predict – of pretty much the same range of empirical phenomena: the observed motions of the planets from earth. Analogously, the particle theory of light, championed by the followers of Newton, and the wave theory of light, championed by Huygens and his followers, offered apparently different theoretical explanations of the same range of empirical phenomena: both theories predicted the laws of reflection and refraction, and of the rectilinear motion of light. Yet if, as the empiricist maintains, the content of theoretical descriptions is determined by operational definitions in terms of the empirical phenomena that theories purport to explain, there would seem to have been *nothing at issue* between the Copernican and Ptolemeic theories, or particle and wave theories of light. The contents of both theories must have been identical (if both were defined in terms of the same set of empirical phenomena).

This point has not been lost on some empiricists. In 1952 Kendler dismissed the apparent theoretical dispute between the followers of Hull and Tolman – concerning 'what is learned' through maze-running by rats – in precisely this fashion. The followers of Hull maintained that what is learned are stimulus–response connections, whereas the followers of Tolman maintained that what is learned are 'cognitive maps.' Yet since, according to Kendler, both theories accounted for the same range of empirical phenomena, and since, also according to Kendler, theoretical postulates or intervening variables must be operationally defined in terms of the empirical phenomena they purport to explain, the contents of both theories are identical: the theories are semantically equivalent. Consequently, Kendler argued that the apparent conflict between the theories was apparent only, and that the dispute about 'what is learned' was completely spurious, and a 'pseudo-problem':

> ... the construct of learning, whether it be conceived in terms of modifications in cognitive maps or S–R connections, does not refer to an object, thing, or entity as suggested by those who are concerned with the question of what is learned. These intervening variables possess no meaning over and above their stated relationships between the independent and the dependent variables. (Kendler, 1952: 271)

More recently, Anderson (1981) has suggested much the same with respect to apparently competing theoretical accounts of 'cognitive units' (in terms of concepts as opposed to propositions or schemata) which advance apparently competing explanations of the same range of empirical phenomena.

These sorts of consideration might lead one to question, and historically have led many to question, the utility of employing theoretical descriptions in science. The classic statement of this sort of doubt about the utility of theoretical descriptions is expressed in Hempel's account of the 'theoretician's dilemma' (1965: 186). Given the scientific empiricist account of theoretical descriptions, they would appear to be wholly redundant with respect to the explanation and prediction of empirical phenomena (identified as deductions of empirical descriptions in the standard empiricist account):

> If the terms and principles of a theory serve their purpose, that is, they establish definitive connections among observable phenomena, then they can be dispensed with, since any chain of laws and interpretative statements establishing such a connection should then be replaceable by a law that directly links observational antecedents to observational consequents. (Hempel, 1965: 186)

Radical behaviorists such as B.F. Skinner (1953, 1984) have grasped the nettle of this implication, and rejected theoretical descriptions putatively 'about' psychological states (and indeed any form of postulated internal states, including physiological states of the organism)[4] as circular 'explanatory fictions.' Skinner's anti-theoretical stance is soundly based upon the explanatory vacuity and redundancy of theories, *given this account of their semantics.*[5]

Intervening Variables and Hypothetical Constructs

However, few contemporary psychologists have been inclined to follow behaviorists down this radical road. Most have adopted a variant of Hempel's own solution to the 'theoretician's dilemma.' According to Hempel (1965), not all theoretical postulates are wholly defined in terms of the empirical laws to which they bring conceptual integration. Scientific theories are held to be best characterized as 'partially interpreted systems,' which can be further interpreted to generate novel empirical predictions.

The classic expression of this instrumental justification of theory with respect to psychological science is to be found in MacCorquodale and Meehl's (1948) distinction between 'intervening variables' and 'hypothetical constructs.' According to these authors, with respect to intervening variables, '. . . the statement of such a concept does not contain any words which are not reducible to the empirical laws' (p. 107). As noted earlier, intervening variables have no descriptive content independent of the content of the empirical laws they purport to explain: consequently 'the validity of the empirical laws is both necessary and sufficient' for the truth of intervening variable descriptions (p. 107). Hypothetical constructs, in contrast, involve 'words which are not reducible to the empirical laws.' Hypothetical constructs have descriptive content additional to and independent of the content of the empirical laws they purport to explain: consequently 'the validity of the empirical laws is not a sufficient condition for the truth of the concept, insofar as it contains *surplus meaning*' (p. 107, my emphasis). MacCorquodale and Meehl agreed that intervening variables are essentially redundant and eliminable, but argued that hypothetical constructs are essential in a developing science: the potential 'surplus meaning' of such constructs can be developed via further interpretation to generate novel predictions.

When this account of hypothetical constructs was first introduced, it was met with extreme skepticism. No-one had any idea what the 'surplus meaning' of hypothetical constructs amounted to, or where it came from: whatever it was, many thought it must be a bad thing, and ought to be eliminated from psychological theory (Marx, 1951; Kendler, 1952). Despite these initial misgivings, however, this account of the 'surplus meaning' of hypothetical constructs has come to be generally accepted, and provides the standard justification for the theoretical constructs of cognitive psychology (Lachman et al., 1979) and 'cognitive behaviorism' (Ledwidge, 1978), and is characteristic of more liberal conceptions of empiricist science. Thus Kimble (1989), for example, rejects the 'strict and restrictive' operational definitions of the behaviorist, arguing that most theoretical concepts are 'open' to further definitional development and, therefore, serve a useful scientific role.

However, despite the current popularity of this account, it does *nothing* to resolve the original problem about the explanatory vacuity of theoretical explanations. At any point in time, it is only the case that the semantics of theories are not exhaustively defined in terms of empirical laws. *They are not independently defined in terms of anything else.* The determinate content of any theory at any point in time is just the content of the empirical laws it is presently held to explain. The problem of how such theories could provide illuminating explanations of empirical laws remains as acute as ever.

Moreover, the idea that such hypothetical constructs usefully serve to guide and direct scientific development is a complete illusion. In order that a theory can generate novel empirical predictions, this account requires the creation of new operational definitions relating 'partially interpreted' or 'open' hypothetical constructs to novel empirical laws. However, at any point in time, the determinate content of such constructs is specified by operational definitions relating such constructs to previously established empirical laws. On this account then, *the only guide to the discovery and prediction of novel empirical laws is our knowledge of previously established empirical laws*. However, if this is the case, Skinner, for example, is quite correct to dismiss the logical apparatus of hypothetical constructs and operational definitions as redundant with respect to scientific development. Psychological science would develop just as well (or badly) by simply focusing on previously established empirical laws, since these form the *only* basis and guide for theory development according to the empiricist account of the semantics of theoretical descriptions.

The problem is essentially this: if theoretical descriptions are wholly or partially defined via operational definitions, it is hard to see how they can have the 'surplus meaning' required for non-vacuous explanation and theory development. MacCorquodale and Meehl were correct to insist that such 'surplus meaning' is required for non-vacuous explanation and theory development, but were at a loss to explain where this 'surplus meaning' comes from. One of the virtues of a realist account of scientific theories is that it does explain how it is possible for scientific theories to have semantic contents additional to and independent of the semantic contents of descriptions of the empirical phenomena or laws they purport to explain.

Referential Realism

Before we turn to a consideration of realism, however, a possible objection to these claims ought to be considered. It might be objected that many theorists – and many psychological theorists – do not treat either intervening variables or hypothetical constructs as merely 'economical redescriptions' of empirical laws, but rather, treat them as making reference to actual internal psychological (or physiological) states or processes that causally intervene between observable environmental stimuli and observable behavior – which are caused by environmental stimuli and which in turn cause observable behavior. On this account, hypothetical constructs are operationally defined as internal states that play these causal roles. Such an account is suggested by MacCorquodale and Meehl's claim that hypothetical constructs 'involve the supposition of entities or processes not among the observed' (1948: 106–7) and by Kimble's claim that sometimes the entities or processes putatively referenced by hypothetical constructs can be identified with neuro-physiological states or processes (1989: 496–7).

It is undoubtedly true that many psychological theorists have conceived of theoretical descriptions as putative descriptions of causally potent internal states, despite their rhetoric about 'economical redescriptions' or 'summaries' of empirical laws. Hull, for example, quite clearly conceived of 'habit strength' as referring to a causally potent physiological state of the organism, and Tolman seemed to have been in no doubt that 'cognitive maps' are neurophysiologically realized forms of spatial representation that direct and guide behavior, and that can be adjusted via learning. It is also quite clear that this is how theoretical constructs are conceived by many if not most contemporary cognitive, social, clinical, and developmental psychologists, who treat theoretical descriptions as making putative reference to internal states that are operationally defined as states that play a functional role in the causal processing of stimulus inputs and production of behavioral outputs. According to this account, for example, 'anger' would be defined as an internal state which is caused by familiar environmental stimuli (insults and the like) and which in turn causes familiar behavioral outputs (aggressive behaviors and the like).

However, this account of theoretical descriptions – which may be characterized as 'referential realism' or 'semantic functionalism'[6] – does nothing to resolve the original problems of the empiricist account. This account of the referential role of theoretical psychological descriptions inherits all the vices of standard instrumentalist accounts.

If theoretical psychological descriptions are defined in terms of internal states that cause certain behaviors – if the semantics of theoretical descriptions are determined by the causal explanatory propositions in which they figure – it remains very hard to see how theoretical references to psychological states could provide illuminating and non-vacuous explanations of human behavior. If a theoretical reference to schizophrenia is vacuous as an explanation of a behavioral syndrome when 'schizophrenia' is operationally defined in terms of that behavioral syndrome, it remains vacuous when 'schizophrenia' is defined as an internal state that causes that behavioral syndrome. It amounts to saying that the internal state which causes that behavioral syndrome causes that behavioral syndrome – no news to anyone. If 'anger,' for example, is defined as an internal state that causes aggression, a theoretical reference to anger cannot provide any illuminating explanation of aggression.

As in the case of the standard instrumentalist account, apparently conflicting theoretical explanations of the same range of behaviors (in similar stimulus situations) would in fact be equivalent in content, if the semantics of theoretical descriptions are determined by the causal explanatory propositions in which they figure. Theoretical references to causally potent internal variables would also appear to be redundant by Skinnerian reasoning parallel to his objection to instrumentally conceived theoretical descriptions:

> Unless there is a weak link in our causal chain so that the second link is not lawfully determined by the first, or the third by the second, then the first and third links must be lawfully related. If we must always go back beyond the

second link for prediction and control, we may avoid many tiresome and exhausting digressions by examining the third as a function of the first. (Skinner, 1953: 35)

Finally, on this account, the 'surplus meaning' of theoretical descriptions amounts to little more than existence claims about internal states, and it is hard to see how such claims alone could generate any novel empirical predictions.

If the referential role of theoretical descriptions was all that was at issue between realists and empiricists, then the differences between them would be minimal, and psychologists would be free to get on with their business and remain agnostic with respect to the reference of theoretical psychological descriptions, and the reality of postulated theoretical entities. The debate between realists and empiricists would reduce to a merely 'verbal' dispute (Nagel, 1961). Yet, as I will note in the following chapter, the real issue between realists and empiricists concerns the semantics of theoretical descriptions. According to a realist account, the semantics of theoretical description are independent of any empirical laws they may be employed to explain, or causal explanatory propositions in which they may figure.

Behavior and Metaphysics
All the problems discussed in the previous sections derive from the restrictive account of theoretical descriptions advanced by traditional and contemporary forms of empiricism. These are not the only problems of empiricism. There are two others, which both derive from misguided a priori assumptions about the subject matter of psychological science. These bear directly upon some of the issues discussed later in this volume.

The empiricist is correct to maintain that epistemic objectivity can only be achieved if theoretical descriptions can be empirically evaluated, but, as I will argue in the following chapter, is wrong to suppose that this requires the operational definition of theoretical descriptions. The empiricist also mistakenly assumes that epistemic objectivity can only be achieved by making psychology a science concerned with (the explanation, prediction and control of) 'observable human behavior': where 'behavior' is conceived and defined – ideally, at least – in terms of the observable physical movements of humans (and other animals).

However, this piece of rhetoric is belied by the explanatory practice of psychologists, who regularly advance explanations – which they take to be empirically grounded – of intentional and meaningful human actions such as acts of aggression, dishonesty, helping, suicide, obedience, and the like. These forms of action cannot be identified with forms of physical behavior individuated via their physical dimensions, since the same form of action may be manifested by means of a wide variety of physical behaviors (there are very many behavioral ways of being dishonest), and since identical forms of physical behavior may be the behavioral basis of a wide variety of different forms of action (for instance, raising an arm may be an aggressive action, an auction bid, an 'all-clear' signal or a salute to the Führer).

That is, many of the types of action that are regularly the object of psychological explanation are intentional behaviors or human actions: they are behaviors constituted as particular human actions by their purpose or intentional direction. Thus for example, diverse forms of physical behavior such as raising an arm, moving a switch on a shock generator, and tampering with a colleague's brake cable, are all constituted as acts of aggression by being intentionally directed by the agent towards the injury of another. This has the important consequence that researchers must establish that the intentional dimensions of behavior are instantiated in experimental and other empirical studies that are treated as empirical evaluations of psychological explanations of acts of aggression, dishonesty, helping, and the like. Unfortunately this is rarely the case, because of the traditional definition of the subject matter of psychological science as 'observable behavior' *simpliciter*.

The empiricist mistakenly supposes that epistemic objectivity is served by the traditional focus on 'observable behavior.' It is not. Only the *convenience* of the researcher is served. The researcher cannot afford to ignore the intentional dimensions of human behavior, because these dimensions are constitutive of the forms of action the researcher purports to explain. If, for example, researchers do not determine that subjects in experiments represent coins retrieved from the floor of a supermarket (dropped by researchers) as rightly belonging to another, researchers have no grounds for supposing that observation of such behaviors (e.g. Farrington and Kidd, 1977) provides any evidence in support of experimentally evaluated theoretical explanations of theft. If, for example, researchers do not establish that experimental behaviors of moving a switch on a shock generator are represented by subjects as directed towards the injury of others, researchers have no grounds for supposing that observations of such behavior provide any evidence in support of experimentally evaluated theoretical explanations of aggression. Unfortunately, researchers regularly advance explanations of theft and aggression based upon experiments in which little or no attempt is made to determine the intentional dimensions of the observed behaviors. In consequence, rather than promoting epistemic objectivity, the focus on 'observable behavior' *simpliciter* undermines it: experimental behaviors are left open to a wide variety of alternative (and competing) descriptions and theoretical explanations.[7]

The other problem with traditional empiricism is the variety of a priori constraints on the adequacy of theories associated with empiricism. One of these derives directly from the standard empiricist account of the content of theoretical descriptions, which restricts the possible and legitimate content of scientific theories to the content of operational definitions. The others derive a number of metaphysical principles, which, although they are not intrinsic to the standard empiricist account (or not obviously so), are clearly generally associated with it by those who practice psychological science. These include the principle of atomism – or the principle of individualism when applied to the social psychological domain; the principle of ontological invariance (in space and time); the principle of universal causal explanation; and the principle of explanatory reduction. The empiricist mistakenly supposes that commitment to these principles is intrinsic to a scientific approach to any subject matter, and significantly restricts the domain of potentially viable theories by treating conformity to these principles as a *criterion for the adequacy of theories.* Commitment to some of these principles – which will be explicated and discussed in the following chapter – has served some sciences well for certain historical periods, notably physics and chemistry from the seventeenth to the nineteenth century. However, commitment to these principles is not intrinsic to a scientific approach to any subject matter: few of these principles have any place in biology, and most of them have been abandoned by contemporary physics. Consequently, it is an open and empirical question whether any of these principles apply to the phenomena that form the subject matter of social psychological science.

Notes

1 I use the terms 'true' and 'accurate', and 'false' and 'inaccurate', interchangeably throughout this work as applied to descriptions. This is unobjectionable, I hope, given the modest interpretation of truth as correspondence – presented in Chapter 2 – to which the present work is committed. Also, for convenience, throughout this work I talk about the truth or accuracy of descriptions, although, strictly speaking, it is generally the truth or accuracy of *sentences* or *statements* or *judgments* in which such descriptions are employed that is at issue.

2 It may in fact be doubted whether there are any descriptions that are not linguistically objective, since, as noted in this chapter, sentences employing mathematical and religious descriptions, such as '2 + 4 = 6' and 'God is jealous,' are normally held to be linguistically objective. Judgments about how things appear to our senses, such as 'it feels warm in here' or 'it seems round to me' are often treated as possible candidates for judgments employing descriptions that are not linguistically objective. Judgments employing these descriptions might be said to be *linguistically subjective* insofar as the making of a judgment employing these descriptions appears to be a sufficient condition for the truth of the descriptions employed: judging that it feels warm or seems round to me may be said to make it the case that it feels warm or seems round to me (Greenwood, 1991b). However, we ought to distinguish the role of such judgments in *determining how* things feel or seem to me, and their role in *reporting* how things feel or seem to me (in reporting how I judge them to feel or seem to me). In their former – constitutive – role, such judgments are not linguistically objective because they are not – and do not purport to be – descriptive. In their latter role, they are employed as putative descriptions, and are consequently linguistically objective.

I recognize – in later chapters – that there are many linguistic forms that are not descriptive. I also suggest that linguistic objectivity *is an intrinsic feature of any description.* Thus, to deny that a putative description is linguistically objective is tantamount to denying that a putative description is in fact descriptive – which is precisely the critical strategy adopted by many social constructionist theorists (and the strategy usually adopted by those who deny that moral judgments are linguistically objective).

3 'Unobservable' is used here in the sense of unobservable *intersubjectively*. Thus, although it is sometimes held that the persons to whom psychological states such as emotions are attributed can observe their own emotional states, via some form of 'internal perception' (although this is in fact denied in Chapter 10), it is usually granted that such states cannot be observed by others – i.e. intersubjectively.

4 Thus Skinner (1938, 1974) is as critical of Pavlov as he is of Hull and Tolman with respect to the postulation of 'internal states.'

5 Skinner has other, very bad, reasons for holding this view. These are discussed in Greenwood (1989).

6 The term 'functionalism' is here appropriated from contemporary philosophy of mind and psychology, where it is frequently employed to characterize this semantic thesis (Lewis, 1972), sometimes also known as 'folk-psychological' functionalism (Bechtel, 1988). It should be carefully distinguished from the form of evolutionary psychology – sometimes called *functional psychology* – championed by psychologists such as Angell and Carr in the early twentieth century.

7 For a detailed discussion of these problems – and their resolution – see Greenwood (1989).

2

Realism

The general philosophical thesis of realism is an *ontological* doctrine to the effect that objects in the physical, social, and psychological world exist and have properties independently of our theoretical concepts of them and theoretical discourse about them (Bhaskar, 1975; Greenwood, 1989; Manicas and Secord, 1983). This general philosophical thesis is accepted by both scientific realists and traditional empiricists, and indeed by most ordinary folk, including children above the age of two.

It is, perhaps, not a particularly interesting thesis, far less a theoretically fertile one: it implies *nothing* about the particular ontology of the natural, social or psychological world. I only mention it in the first place to distinguish it from *scientific realism* – a semantic doctrine that presupposes, but is not identical to, ontological realism; and in the second place because some social constructionists and relativists (as well as philosophical idealists) contest it, or dismiss it as 'unintelligible.'

The fact that realists and empiricists jointly accept this ontological thesis no doubt partially accounts for the fact that scientific realism is often represented as a form of empiricism (or neo-empiricism). However, this is a mistake. Scientific realism maintains the linguistic objectivity of scientific theories that traditional empiricism denies. It is directly opposed to empiricist accounts of scientific theory.

Scientific Realism

Scientific realism is a *semantic* doctrine about theoretical descriptions. According to scientific realism, theoretical descriptions attribute properties to postulated entities such as atoms and emotions, and are true or false, or accurate or inaccurate, according to whether or not the postulated entities exist and have the properties attributed to them by theoretical descriptions. According to scientific realism, the semantics and truth conditions of theoretical descriptions are *independent* of the semantics and truth conditions of descriptions of the empirical correlations they are often employed to explain: they are not determined by operational definitions.

Scientific realism provides an account of the linguistic objectivity of theoretical descriptions: of how it is possible for theoretical descriptions of 'unobservables' such as atoms and emotions to be linguistically objective, despite the fact that they are neither ostensively nor operationally defined. According to scientific realism, theoretical descriptions in science attribute to postulated entities some of the properties of empirically discriminable systems, exploiting the semantics of our familiar descriptions of them. This form of theoretical modeling allows the scientist to exploit relations of analogy and metaphor based upon descriptions of empirically discriminable systems, enabling scientists to introduce novel but meaningful theoretical descriptions such as:

> electrical charge (on analogy with a charge of gunpowder), electric current (which flows), displacement current in aether (on analogy with electric current in conductors), curvature of space (on analogy with curvature of a sphere), and so on, by continuous steps to the most esoteric terminology of modern physics. (Hesse, 1976: 8).

The employment of theoretical models is not merely a useful heuristic device (Duhem, 1906), nor does a reference to them merely provide a psychological account of the psychological genesis of theories (Kendler, 1952). Analogies, as N.R. Campbell insisted:

> . . . are not 'aids' to the establishment of theories; they are an utterly essential part of theories, without which theories would be valueless and unworthy of the name. . . . It is often suggested that the analogy leads to the formulation of the theory, but once the theory is formulated the analogy has served its purpose and may be removed and forgotten. Such a suggestion is absolutely false and perniciously misleading. (1920: 129)

Theoretical models – in the form of analogies and metaphors – are absolutely essential to theories because they specify the autonomous semantics of theoretical descriptions, enabling theoretical descriptions to be linguistically objective: to make claims about postulated entities and their properties additional to the claims made by the empirical laws they purport to explain.

Thus Bohr's theory of the atom ascribes to atoms some of the properties of planetary systems (on a smaller scale): atoms are held to be composed of a nucleus of protons and neutrons that maintains electrons in orbits via attractive forces. The semantics and truth conditions of the theoretical descriptions of Bohr's theory are logically independent of the semantics and truth conditions of the empirical laws they were employed to explain, such as the spectral line emissions of hydrogen and helium.

The theoretical descriptions of Bohr's theory are *semantically autonomous* with respect to the descriptions of the empirical phenomena that they were employed to explain (in terms of the energy levels of electrons). Bohr's theoretical descriptions of the atom are linguistically objective: they make claims about the existence, composition, and structure of postulated theoretical entities. These claims are true or accurate if and only if atoms exist and have the properties ascribed to them by these theoretical descriptions: they are true or accurate if and only if there are atoms composed of a nucleus of protons and neutrons that maintain electrons in orbits via attractive forces.

This explains why many persons can and do understand the meaning of the descriptive claims of Bohr's theory – they understand, via the theoretical model, what it claims and what has to be the case for it to be true – without having the slightest inkling of the spectral emission laws the theory was introduced to explain. Many people understand the descriptive claims of Freud's theory of the unconscious but have little knowledge of the empirical phenomena – 'hysterical conversions' and the like – it was introduced to explain. Analogous points could be made about the descriptive claims of the Copernican theory, the Darwinian theory of evolution, and the Marxist theory of history. These 'thought experiments' (which are in fact regularly actualized when students are taught many scientific theories) demonstrate that theoretical descriptions are not operationally defined: for if they were, these theoretical descriptions would be meaningless to anyone lacking knowledge of their explanatory employment, which is plainly not the case.

It is of course true that scientific theories are usually constructed with the explanation of empirical phenomena in mind. Yet this social psychological fact about theory construction has no semantic implications: it is entirely consistent with the recognition of the semantic autonomy of theoretical descriptions. There is no reason in principle why Bohr's theory of the atom could not have been developed independently of any attempt to explain the Balmer series and other spectral emissions. It is just that there would have been little point in doing so. Nevertheless the situation is not unknown in science. It was quite clear what Dirac meant in 1928 when he postulated the existence of anti-particles – particles with the same rest mass and lifetime as elementary particles such as electrons, but with a different electric charge – long before such particles were appealed to in the explanation of quantum electrodynamical phenomena.

According to scientific realism, theoretical descriptions are semantically autonomous and – thus – linguistically objective. This analysis has a number of significant virtues. It accounts for the fact that most theories can furnish an illuminating and non-vacuous explanation of empirical phenomena, since they embody semantic content additional to and independent of the semantic content of the descriptions of the empirical phenomena they are employed to explain. Thus an account of the compositional elements and structure of atoms, and of the energy levels of orbiting electrons, can provide an illuminating and non-vacuous explanation of spectral emission lines. Analogously, the 'hopelessness' theory of depression (Abramson et al., 1989) provides an independently meaningful account of the content of agent representations that provides an illuminating and non-vacuous explanation of dysfunctional behaviors.[1]

Moreover, scientific realism can easily account for the fact that two (or more) theories can advance different (and competing) explanations of the same range of empirical phenomena (such as the Ptolemeic geocentric theory and the Copernican heliocentric theory, or the particle and wave theories of light): they have different semantic contents and truth conditions because they are based upon different theoretical models exploiting different linguistic analogies.

Scientific realism also explains how theories can be semantically developed to generate novel predictions, via the development of the theoretical model. Thus, Bohr's theory was developed – in the Bohr–Sommerfeld theory – by supposing that electrons are further analogous to planets insofar as they also rotate on their axes while traversing elliptical orbits ('electron spin'). This enabled the theory to explain the Zeeman effect and predict more complex spectral emissions.

This is also familiar enough in psychological science. Human psychological functioning or social interaction is theoretically described in terms of some of the properties of familiar systems, such as ball-bearings falling through Y-shaped pipes (Broadbent, 1957), digital computers (Newell et al., 1958), rule-governed games (Berne, 1970) or the scripted performances of the theatre (Goffman, 1959). Theories are developed by asking whether human psychological functioning and social interaction are analogous in additional respects to the familiar systems that provide the source of the theoretical model.

This general account applies equally to the semantics of our everyday and scientifically developed theoretical descriptions of psychological states: the sorts of states that are held to be processed in accord with the cognitive rules described in theoretical cognitive psychology, or implicated in the production of the rule-governed actions described by theoretical social psychology. Theoretical descriptions of psychological phenomena such as beliefs and emotions are modeled upon some of the properties of linguistic utterances. Linguistic utterances have a *sense* (a meaningful or semantic content) and a *reference* (they are about some particular or class of particulars). In ascribing psychological states to ourselves or others, we ascribe states with *intensional* (meaningful or semantic) contents related to *intentional* objects (the objects to which our psychological states are directed). Thus, for example, in ascribing to myself the belief that the Empire State Building is the tallest building in the world I mean that I represent the Empire State Building (the intentional object of my belief) *as* the tallest building in the world (the intensional content of my belief). In ascribing shame to another, I mean that she represents her action (the intentional object of her shame) *as* personally degrading and humiliating (the intensional content of her shame). Such descriptions are semantically autonomous: they are meaningful independently of any explanations of human behavior in which they may figure. They are linguistically objective: they ascribe representational properties to postulated theoretical entities, and are true or accurate if and only if a person represents a particular aspect of reality in the contentful way we ascribe to them.

There is nothing mysterious about this. The realist account of the semantics of theoretical descriptions is in fact entirely consistent with the principle of meaning empiricism: that all concepts are derived from sense-impressions or perceptual affordances, and that all meaningful descriptions are definable in terms of observables. Scientific realism simply exploits an oft-neglected feature of this principle: that novel concepts and descriptions of unobserved and unobservable phenomena can be constructed out of concepts and descriptions (or elements of them) which are themselves derived from observations – that are grounded in empirically discriminable features of reality. Thus, for example, given our empirical concepts and descriptions of 'light' and 'waves,' grounded in our empirical concepts and descriptions of ambient light and ocean waves, we can construct the novel concept of light waves, and meaningfully employ the theoretical description 'light waves,' even though we have never observed light waves (and even if, according to our theory, they are unobservable). In the words of the last great classical empiricist, Alexander Bain (1855: 578): 'the mind has the power to form new combinations or aggregates *different* from any that have been presented to it in the course of experience.'

The essential error of the empiricist account of the semantics of theoretical descriptions in terms of operational definitions lies not in supposing that theoretical descriptions must be defined in terms of observables per se, but in supposing that they must be defined in terms of the empirical laws they purport to explain – as in instrumentalist accounts – or in terms of the observable causal manifestations of the phenomena to which they purport to refer (that is, via their role in causal explanatory propositions) – as in referential realist or semantic functionalist accounts. According to the realist account, and consistent with the principle of meaning empiricism,[2] the semantics of theoretical descriptions are autonomously defined via theoretical modeling: this is the source of their 'surplus meaning.'

Theoretical Description and Causal Explanation

It is important to distinguish scientific realism from the doctrines characterized in the previous chapter as referential realism or semantic functionalism. According to referential realism or semantic functionalism, the semantics of theoretical descriptions are determined by the body of causal explanatory propositions in which they figure: theoretical psychological descriptions postulate internal states that causally intervene between observable stimulus inputs and observable behavioral outputs. As noted in the previous chapter, these sorts of doctrines inherit all the vices of traditional instrumentalist accounts, and have none of the virtues of scientific realism documented in this chapter. If, for example, 'anger' is defined, *inter alia*, as an internal state that causes aggressive behavior, a theoretical reference to anger cannot provide any illuminating explanation of aggressive behavior. In contrast, an explanation of aggressive behavior in terms of anger, when 'anger' is autonomously defined in terms of representations of offense against one's rights or dignity, does provide an illuminating – and non-vacuous and non-circular – explanation of instances of aggressive behavior.

These referential realist or semantic functionalist doctrines about the semantics of theoretical psychological descriptions are in any case intuitively implausible. I may understand the meaning of theoretical psychological descriptions such as 'shame,' and may correctly ascribe shame to a visitor from another culture who describes how she feels about her actions, even if I have not the slightest inkling of how persons in that other culture respond to shame. I may understand the meaning of theoretical psychological descriptions such as 'anger,' and may correctly ascribe anger to myself, long before I finally decide how to respond to it. I may understand the meaning of theoretical psychological descriptions such as 'grief,' and may correctly ascribe grief to a seven-year-old nephew who has been recently bereaved. Yet I may have no idea how young children tend to respond to grief consequent to bereavement, and might have to seek the advice of a child psychologist on that matter if I want to help him.

This is not to deny that theoretical references to psychological states such as beliefs and emotions can be employed to furnish causal explanations of behavior. Of course they can be and often are when we make *additional claims* about the causal role of psychological states in the generation of intentional human behavior. But the semantics and truth conditions of theoretical psychological descriptions are not to be identified with the semantics and truth conditions of the causal explanatory propositions in which they regularly figure. The semantics of theoretical psychological descriptions are logically independent of any causal explanations of behavior that theoretical references to psychological states may be employed to furnish.

This is surely how we would want it to be, since we want to preserve the theoretical possibility that there are psychological states that do not play a causal role in the generation of particular behaviors. Thus persons may ascribe to themselves the belief that their children deserve punishment for represented offenses. However, although their description of their psychological state may be accurate, their causal explanation of their violent actions by reference to this belief may be inaccurate. Their actions may require explanation in terms of the unconscious emotions of psychoanalytic theory, or in terms of the presence of precipitating 'violent stimuli' (Berkowitz and LePage, 1967).

We ought not to be misled by the fact, noted earlier, that theoretical descriptions are often introduced for the purpose of explaining a range of empirical phenomena: it does not follow that the semantics of theoretical descriptions are determined by reference to the empirical phenomena that they are introduced to explain. Since theoretical descriptions are semantically autonomous with respect to the empirical phenomena they are introduced to explain, knowledge of the causal explanatory propositions in which theoretical descriptions do figure is not a necessary condition of understanding such descriptions. People can grasp the meaning of the theoretical descriptions of Bohr's theory of the atom without having any inkling of the causal explanatory propositions concerning spectral emissions in which they figure. Analogously, the semantics of our theoretical descriptions of the elements documented by the periodic table can be – and frequently are – introduced to students by reference to the atomic composition and structure of the elements in terms of which they are individually defined. Once students have grasped the meaning of these descriptions, they then learn how the atomic composition and structure of the various elements referenced by such theoretical descriptions are causally implicated in the explanation of the diverse properties of the various elements.

This may also be precisely how our lay forms of theoretical psychological description are learned: that is, independently of their deployment in causal explanations of behavior. Although children and adults do employ theoretical psychological descriptions in the causal explanation of their own and others' behavior, this does not appear to be a developmental condition of our grasp of the semantics of such descriptions. By about the age of two or three most children have an extensive psychological vocabulary that enables them to attribute psychological states such as belief, fear, and anger to themselves and others (Olson and Astington, 1986), and this form of linguistic competence appears to be achieved *prior* to their grasp of the causal explanatory employment of such descriptions:

> Very young children can take a causal view of the world. As far as the behavior of people is concerned, they include as possible causes of behavior only concrete objects and events. Independently of this causal view, these children can also formulate representations of mental states. This power develops in parallel with the causal view.
> Around four years of age, these two independent capacities come together; children enlarge their notion of 'possible causes of behavior' to include mental states. From this point, mental states can be treated as both *causes* of behavior and *effects* of perceptual exposure to a situation. (Leslie, 1988: 37–48)

This empirical claim has itself been contested (Wellman, 1988). However, the very fact that it does appear to be a contestable empirical claim supports the realist account of the semantics of theoretical psychological descriptions. For if these descriptions were defined in terms of the causal explanatory propositions in which they figure, such a claim would be a contradiction in terms – which it seems plainly not.

There is no mystery in supposing that children can meaningfully employ theoretical psychological descriptions prior to their causal explanatory deployment. It only appears to be mysterious if one supposes that such descriptions can be meaningful only if they are ostensively defined via introspection, or operationally defined within a causal explanatory framework. Given familiar Wittgensteinian arguments against the possibility of 'private' ostensive definitions of psychological descriptions based upon introspection (Wittgenstein, 1953), the account of the semantics of such descriptions in terms of their causal explanatory role appears to be the only alternative:

> Mental terms do not get their meaning through introspection but as theoretical constructs that are part of a theory for predicting and explaining behavior. Mental states have the status of hypothetical constructs. They are not directly observable, need to be inferred, and provide advantages for predicting behavior. (Perner and Wilde-Astington, 1993: 139)

However, according to the scientific realist, these are not the only alternatives, and there is no special problem with respect to the semantics of theoretical psychological descriptions. We are not obliged to employ either an inner ostensive definition or causal analysis to account for the semantics of such descriptions. Since our psychological descriptions are linguistically modeled, we have all the semantic resources we require for psychological state descriptions when we have mastered the semantics of the names and predicates (and operators) of whatever language we use to describe the world. When we can articulate a description of a lake as frozen, we can attribute this directed representational content to ourselves and others: we can ascribe this belief about the lake to ourselves and others. When we can articulate an evaluation of our behavior as degrading and humiliating, we can attribute this directed representational content to ourselves and others: we can attribute shame to ourselves and others.

Testability and Theoretical Meaning
None of these scientific realist claims about the semantic autonomy of theoretical psychological descriptions are designed to deny that psychological states *are* causal intermediaries between environmental 'inputs' and behavioral 'outputs.' But a recognition of the causal potency of psychological phenomena does not entail any commitment to the thesis that the semantics of theoretical descriptions are determined by the causal explanatory propositions in which they figure, just as a recognition of the causal potency of physical particulars does not entail any commitment to the thesis that the semantics of theoretical descriptions in natural science – such as the descriptions of Bohr's theory of the atom – are determined by the causal explanatory propositions in which they figure. Only an empiricist commitment to some form of verificationism – that theoretical descriptions must be defined in terms of those empirical phenomena by reference to which they are empirically evaluated – would incline anyone to suppose otherwise.

This perhaps takes us to the heart of the matter. None of the above claims about the semantic autonomy of theoretical descriptions entail the denial of the principle of *methodological empiricism*: the requirement that theoretical explanations of empirical phenomena – in terms of atomic structure or contentful psychological states – must be empirically tested and verified before they can be accepted as adequate theoretical *explanations.* Yet the acceptance of this mundane requirement of empirical evaluation is entirely consistent with the recognition that theoretical descriptions can be meaningful – and true – prior to and independently of their explanatory employment and empirical verification. As Popper (1959, 1963) has always insisted, the meaning conditions of theoretical descriptions cannot be identified with their testability conditions. Many theoretical descriptions are advanced and understood by scientific communities long before researchers can develop adequate means of testing them or evaluating their causal explanatory adequacy. This was true of the Copernican theory, the theory of evolution, the 'big bang' theory, and numerous others.

The error of empiricist analysis is to suppose that the operational definition of theoretical descriptions in terms of the empirical phenomena they are employed to explain is required for the testability of such theoretical descriptions: that empirical predictions must be *directly deducible* from theoretical descriptions by virtue of their operational definition. Yet any semantically autonomous set of theoretical descriptions, in conjunction with causal hypotheses and other auxiliary assumptions, can generate testable predictions about empirical phenomena. *There is simply no reason to suppose that the semantic contents of such theories must be restricted to the contents of operational definitions.* The spectral emission laws do not define the content of Bohr's theory, and cannot be derived from Bohr's theoretical descriptions of the atom alone: many additional causal hypotheses and auxiliary assumptions are required.

It appears that cross-cultural psychologists are able to reidentify emotions such as anger and shame in different cultures by reference to their psychological contents, as involving some representation of offense and humiliation (Triandis, 1980). Yet predictions about the behavior of persons in such cultures cannot be derived from theoretical descriptions of such emotions alone, but must be derived from such descriptions in conjunction with auxiliary hypotheses about socially appropriate objects of emotion and local rules governing behavioral expression. Persons in different cultures are often angered by or ashamed of quite different forms of behavior (they recognize different forms of behavior as offensive and humiliating), and conform to quite different 'display rules' for the behavioral expression of these emotions (Ekman, 1980; Harris, 1989).

The empiricist restriction of the semantic contents of theoretical descriptions to the contents of operational definitions is unknown outside of psychological science, and does nothing to promote theoretical development within psychological science. On the contrary, by artificially restricting the contents of theoretical descriptions, it promotes only theoretical sterility.

The commitment to the doctrine of the operational definition of theoretical descriptions accounts for the impoverished nature of many theories within empiricist forms of psychological science. This is not to claim that all theories in psychological science are hopelessly impoverished. Substantive psychological theories have been advanced in contemporary cognitive, social, developmental, and clinical psychology, but only because – mercifully – many psychologists do not practice their rhetorical preachings about the operational definition of theoretical descriptions. I noted in the previous chapter that even behaviorists such as Hull and Tolman did not practice their instrumental preachings: both treated 'intervening variables' such as 'habit strength' and 'cognitive maps' as internal states that causally mediate between stimuli and responses. It may also be maintained that many cognitive, social, developmental, and clinical psychologists do not practice their operationalist preachings about theoretical descriptions – even when these are given a referential realist interpretation. It seems clear that many theoretical references to psychological phenomena such as 'serial memory search,' 'cognitive dissonance,' 'maternal deprivation,' and 'hopelessness' – and 'cognitive maps,' for that matter – are semantically autonomous with respect to the empirical phenomena they are employed to explain: their meaning and truth conditions can be understood without knowledge of their causal explanatory employment.

One general source of misunderstanding in this area is the frequent rhetorical confusion of *operational definitions* and *operational measures*: between definitions of theoretical descriptions, and accounts of specific empirical measures of psychological phenomena employed in particular empirical studies. That is, it is one thing to insist that empirical reports include descriptions of the empirical measures of anger, memory, and attitude-change employed in empirical studies of such phenomena. This is an eminently reasonable requirement. It is quite another thing to suppose that the meaning of theoretical descriptions of anger, memory, and attitude-change employed in such reports is determined by definitions in terms of such empirical measures.

If theoretical descriptions of anger, memory, and attitude-change employed in individual empirical studies really were defined in terms of the empirical measures employed in such studies, the terms 'anger,' 'memory,' and 'attitude-change' would have quite distinct meanings when employed in different studies. For example, the term 'anger' would have one meaning in studies employing physiological measures, a different meaning in studies employing behavioral measures, and a still different meaning in studies employing verbal report measures.[3] This would preclude the theoretical integration of knowledge gleaned about anger, memory, and attitude-change from these empirical studies, including the recognition that the results of one experiment replicate or contradict the results of another, when they employed different empirical measures.

As noted, many psychologists mercifully do not practice their operational preachings. Otherwise it would be hard to put together the sort of articles that appear in the *Psychological Review*. The theoretical integration and comparison of information gleaned from empirical studies of anger, memory, and attitude-change requires that researchers provide an account of the meaning and truth conditions of theoretical descriptions such as 'anger,' 'memory,' and 'attitude-change' that is logically independent of particular empirical measures of these phenomena employed in particular empirical studies. The reluctance of many researchers to provide such an account – to provide substantive theoretical accounts of psychological phenomena that are not tied to postulated neurophysiological structures or particular experimental measures – perhaps explains why it is so difficult to provide any form of theoretical integration or critical comparison of empirical studies in many areas of psychological research. This seems to be especially true with respect to empirical research on identity and emotion.

Truth, Correspondence, and Objectivity

A number of qualificatory comments concerning scientific realism are in order at this stage, to guard against likely misinterpretations.

In the first place, the doctrine of ontological realism is itself *ontologically neutral*, in the following sense: all it maintains is that whatever entities exist in the natural, social, and psychological world exist independently of our concepts and descriptions of them – it makes absolutely no commitments concerning the types of entities and properties that do exist. It is consequently non-commital with respect to all the important and substantive theoretical issues of whether social and psychological phenomena are atomistic or relational, individualist or social and so forth.

Scientific realism does of course *presuppose* ontological realism, but is also completely neutral with respect to the ontology of the natural, social, and psychological world. It assumes nothing and precludes nothing. It is a purely *semantic* doctrine that advances a thesis about the semantic autonomy of theoretical descriptions with respect to the empirical phenomena theoretical descriptions are employed to explain. The primary virtue of this account is that it enables us to understand how theoretical explanations can be genuinely explanatory (and fertile etc.), something that *cannot* be accounted for by traditional empiricist accounts. An additional virtue of this account is that, unlike traditional empiricist accounts, it sets no a priori limits on the contents of theoretical descriptions. It neither privileges nor prejudices any form of theory. In particular, it does not privilege the theories offered by professional psychological scientists, for example, over those advanced by lay folk. For the realist, the accuracy of any theoretical account can only be assessed via its empirical adjudication: whether the theories advanced by professional psychologists are superior or inferior to those offered by lay folk is, for the realist, an open and empirical question.

To maintain that the truth or accuracy of theoretical descriptions is a matter of empirical adjudication is not to claim that theoretical descriptions are empirically adjudicated via any form of comparison of such descriptions with theoretical reality. Scientific realism does not claim that theoretical descriptions are 'reflections' or 'maps' of reality: it does not postulate any mysterious relation of *resemblance* between our theoretical descriptions and the phenomena they purport to describe. The truth or accuracy of a theoretical description is not held to be a function of its ability to 'picture,' 'reflect' or 'copy' reality. This particular and peculiar concept of the truth or accuracy of theoretical descriptions has its origin in traditional empiricist accounts of the nature of language and concepts – in terms of 'images' derived from 'sense-impressions.' Only within this empiricist account does it make sense to ask – with Locke – whether our ideas qua images resemble the objects they are supposed to be images of.

However, this imagistic account of concepts has been abandoned by contemporary cognitive psychologists, who no longer identify concepts with images,[4] or claim that descriptions derive their meaning via association with images (Simon and Kaplan, 1989). This archaic imagistic account of concepts plays no role in a scientific realist account of the semantics of theoretical descriptions. For the scientific realist, the truth or accuracy of theoretical descriptions depends upon whether or not postulated entities exist and have the properties attributed to them by theoretical descriptions. For the realist, the *only means* of assessing their truth or accuracy is by reference to empirical predictions derived from them, in conjunction with causal posits and other auxiliary hypotheses.

It is true that scientific realism is committed to a *correspondence* theory of truth: theoretical descriptions are held to be true or accurate if and only if they correspond to independent features of reality.[5] Social constructionists and relativists often claim that this notion is 'unintelligible' or 'problematic' (Gergen, 1985; Shotter, 1992): 'the notion of a match between the ontology of a theory and its "real" counterpart in nature . . . seems to me illusive in principle' (Kuhn, 1970: 207).

The notion of truth as correspondence is of course mysterious if it is conceived in terms of some form of resemblance between theoretical descriptions and theoretical reality itself, given that they cannot be compared. Yet, as noted above, this conception forms no part of a scientific realist account of theoretical descriptions, and there need be no mystery here. In order to understand how theoretical descriptions can correspond or fail to correspond to reality, one does not need to understand or apprehend any mysterious relation of resemblance or isomorphism. All one needs to understand is *the meaning of particular theoretical descriptions*: for example, what it means to ascribe a double-helical structure to DNA, or shame to a person. Someone who understands the meaning of such descriptions – of the structure of DNA or the content of shame, for example – *automatically* recognizes what it means for such descriptions to correspond or fail to correspond to reality: it just means that there are or are not objects with the properties ascribed to them by these theoretical descriptions. Only someone who failed to understand the meaning of such descriptions – who failed to grasp the analogical or metaphorical relations appealed to by such descriptions – could find talk of their correspondence to reality unintelligible.

This is perhaps easier to recognize if we note that ordinary empirical descriptions are also true, when true, by virtue of their correspondence to independent features of reality. This does not mean that empirical descriptions such as 'the table is rectangular' or 'that man is bleeding' are true, when true, by virtue of any resemblance relation between empirical descriptions and reality: it just means that there are observable entities that have the properties attributed to them by such descriptions. In order to understand how this can be the case, one only needs to understand the meaning of empirical descriptions.

Truth by correspondence only appears problematic in the case of theoretical descriptions if one mistakenly supposes that it is based upon some form of mysterious resemblance relation, or if one lacks an explanation of how theoretical descriptions can be meaningful independently of, and in the absence of, any form of operational or ostensive definition. The great virtue of a scientific realist account of theoretical meaning is that it provides just such an explanation. According to this account, we can develop systems of meaningful empirical descriptions of intersubjectively observable phenomena – such as tables, trees, and tarantulas – because our empirical discriminations of a wide range of phenomena are in basic agreement (Hesse, 1974). This is what enables us to form conventions of linguistic usage and employ interconnected systems of symbols to descriptively characterize the intersubjectively observable world. By exploiting the semantics of our empirical descriptions via theoretical modeling, we can develop theoretical descriptions of postulated entities that are not directly discriminable via our perceptual apparatus.

It may be acknowledged, and can be acknowledged by the scientific realist, that the ways in which humans can descriptively characterize the world are ultimately delimited by the affordances perceptually discriminable by humans. Since these provide the ultimate empirical grounding of our descriptive semantics, they delimit the possibilities of human theoretical imagination: they delimit the combinatory and developmental possibilities of theoretical modeling via the exploitation of a semantics based upon them. We, as humans, can ultimately understand the world theoretically only in terms of *our* socially constructed theoretical descriptions based upon the perceptual affordances *we* can discriminate.

These are grounds for intellectual modesty insofar as they are grounds for a *global* relativism about scientific theories. Human scientists have no extra-empirical or extra-theoretical access to reality: they have no 'God's eye view.' All human theoretical knowledge is dependent upon our modes of empirical access to reality and our forms of theoretical description based upon them. In this innocuous and uncontentious respect it is analytically true that 'man is the measure of all things.'

These are not, however, grounds for denying the linguistic objectivity of theoretical descriptions: their truth or falsity is determined by independent features of reality. Nor are they grounds for a *local* relativism about scientific theories that denies their epistemic objectivity, via the claim – often advanced by social constructionists and relativists – that we can never have empirical grounds for preferring one set of theoretical descriptions over another (or others).[6]

This is not to claim that the linguistic objectivity of theoretical descriptions entails or ensures their epistemic objectivity. It does not: as noted in the previous chapter, questions about the epistemic objectivity of theoretical descriptions are independent of questions about their linguistic objectivity. Scientific realism provides an explanation of how theoretical descriptions can be linguistically objective, but it does not guarantee their epistemic objectivity.

Of course many scientific realists (myself included) are also committed to the epistemic objectivity of scientific theories: they believe that scientific theories can be empirically evaluated and that competing theories can be empirically adjudicated (we can have empirical grounds for preferring one set of theoretical descriptions over another, or others). However, the two questions are logically independent: it is quite possible to be a scientific realist and maintain the linguistic objectivity of semantically autonomous theoretical descriptions, while at the same time accepting social constructionist or relativist denials of their epistemic objectivity.

Thus one might consistently claim that Bohr's theoretical descriptions of the atom, or psychoanalytic theoretical descriptions of unconscious psychological states, are semantically autonomous and – thus – linguistically objective, while at the same time recognizing – perhaps grudgingly – that they cannot be empirically evaluated. That is, even if the relativist arguments (derived from post-empiricist philosophy of science) advanced by social constructionists did undermine traditional assumptions about epistemic objectivity in science in general or social psychological science in particular, they would not support social constructionist denials of the linguistic objectivity of theories in science in general or social psychological science in particular. However, these arguments do not in fact oblige us to abandon traditional assumptions about the epistemic objectivity of theoretical descriptions.

To suppose that scientific theories are linguistically objective, and that they can be epistemically objective, is not to claim that science is itself an 'asocial consequence of the operation of abstract systems' (whatever exactly that means), or that it is 'ordered and simple' (Potter, 1992:

168–9). Nor is it to assume that scientific knowledge is the intellectual product of the work of individual scientists. A scientific realist account of the semantics of theoretical descriptions and their empirical adjudication is also quite neutral with respect to the best theoretical account of science itself. A scientific realist can easily recognize that science is a historically located and evolving social phenomenon that is often messy and complex, populated by practitioners with varieties of interests and motives and rhetorical strategies, and that scientific knowledge is often the outcome of a set of integrated social actions and practices. According to the scientific realist, this may very well prove to be the best theoretical account of science. The scientific realist only denies that the social dimensions of science pose any intrinsic threat to the linguistic and epistemic objectivity of theoretical descriptions.

The realist can and does recognize that theoretical descriptions are socially constructed or created. Their meaning is not abstracted from observations of the phenomena to which they purport to refer, nor are they ostensively or operationally defined: their meaning is a product of conventions based upon theoretical modeling. For the realist, however, this poses no threat to their linguistic or epistemic objectivity.

The Aristotelean and Ptolemeic theorists did not derive their concept of circular planetary orbits from observations of the starry heavens – since planetary orbits certainly don't look circular from the earth. Rather they employed the socially prevalent concept of the circle as the most perfect geometric figure in reasoning that planetary orbits must be circular, for largely aesthetic cum religious reasons. Yet it remained an entirely objective question whether the solar system has the geometric dimensions described by the Aristotelean and Ptolemeic systems. Kepler worked for ten years trying to accommodate Brahe's sophisticated measurements of the orbit of Mars to the Ptolemeic system of circles and epicycles, and eventually gave up in disgust: he could not accommodate Brahe's empirical measurements of the orbit of Mars to the theoretical descriptions of Ptolemeic theory.

Watson and Crick did not introduce the theoretical descriptions of the double-helical structure of DNA to refer to something that they – and others – could directly observe, but jointly – or socially – constructed them. These theoretical descriptions – and their meaningful content – were social in origin. Yet this is entirely consistent with the recognition that Watson and Crick's theoretical descriptions of DNA are true or accurate if and only if DNA has the double-helical structure attributed to it by these theoretical descriptions: the recognition of the linguistic objectivity of such theoretical descriptions. It certainly does not oblige us to suppose, as many social constructionists and relativists avow, that DNA itself – as opposed to our theoretical descriptions of it – is socially constructed or created.

The theoretical descriptions of natural science are socially constructed. It does not follow, nor is it true to say, that the phenomena studied by natural sciences – such as DNA, sulfur dioxide, or electro-magnetic fields – have social dimensions. This is important to stress when we consider theoretical descriptions of psychological phenomena such as identity and emotion. Theoretical descriptions of identity and emotion, like other theoretical descriptions in natural and social and psychological science, are also socially constructed. Yet although, as I will argue in Chapters 6–9, identity and emotion may be said to have social dimensions, the social dimensions of identity and emotion are not a constitutive consequence of, and cannot be identified with, the social dimensions of our theoretical descriptions of them. In consequence, the claim that identity and emotion have social dimensions poses no threat to the linguistic – or epistemic – objectivity of theoretical descriptions of identity and emotion.

Atomism, Invariance, and Reduction

I have argued that a scientific realist account of psychological theory provides a much richer conception of the possibilities of psychological science than that envisioned by traditional empiricist accounts, without abandoning traditional assumptions about the linguistic and epistemic objectivity of theoretical psychological descriptions. This meta-theoretical perspective offers the researcher and practitioner a potentially rational justification for their best contemporary scientific practice. This perspective also enables us to recognize the social dimensions of identity and emotion documented in later chapters of this work. Since, according to the account developed, the social dimensions of identity and emotion are independent of the social dimensions of our theoretical descriptions of them, they pose no threat to the linguistic or epistemic objectivity of our theoretical descriptions of them.

However, although scientific realism does involve a commitment to traditional scientific virtues such as linguistic and epistemic objectivity, it does not entail any commitment to a number of metaphysical principles that are frequently associated or identified with a scientific approach, and that are regularly associated with – and endorsed by – traditional empiricist accounts of science. Specifically, scientific realism *does not entail any commitment to* the principles of atomism; of ontological invariance (in space and time); of the universality of causal explanation; or of theoretical reduction.

These principles are not intrinsic features of scientific thought: they embody certain assumptions about the properties of the *phenomena* studied by particular scientific disciplines, or about the form or content of particular theories advanced by particular scientific disciplines. Commitment to these principles has served physics and chemistry well for certain historical periods, but not biology. Although these principles are cornerstones of Newtonian science, most have been abandoned by contemporary physics. According to the scientific realist, it is an open and empirical question whether any of these principles are appropriate in psychological science, and to a scientific psychological analysis of identity and emotion.

According to the *principle of atomism*, the phenomena that are the subject matter of any scientific discipline can be individuated and exist independently of other phenomena to which they may be related. This principle is a cornerstone of Newtonian science, and underpins a great many highly successful theories, such as the atomic theory and the periodic table of the elements. It continues to dominate much physical science and many branches of psychological science.

Nevertheless atomism involves a commitment to a metaphysical assumption about reality that is not an intrinsic feature of scientific thought. Modern physics has remained successful while abandoning commitment to this principle: the nature of theoretical entities such as electro-magnetic fields and quarks is treated in contemporary physical theories as determined – at least in part – by their relational location. Thus it is an open question whether this principle applies to psychological phenomena such as identity and emotion. I will suggest in the following chapters that it does not: such phenomena are social and – thus – *relational* in nature.

It may be useful to illustrate the difference between atomistic and relational phenomena by reference to a few contrastive examples from the social and physical world. Judges and trials by jury are logically *relational* in nature, whereas water and tin are logically *atomistic* in nature. Water and tin – like most other physical phenomena – retain their identity in isolation from other physical particulars. Judges and trials by jury do not retain their identity in isolation from other persons (jurors, lawyers, and defendants) or other social entities (judicial, penal, and legal systems) to which they are constitutively related *as* judges and trials by jury.

It is important to distinguish this sense of relational identity from a quite different and logically atomistic sense that is commonly ascribed to many physical and social phenomena. The nature of many physical and social particulars is – at least partially – determined by the internal structural relations between their components. Thus the identity of water and tin is determined by their molecular composition and structure, and the identity of a trial by jury is partially determined by the relations between participants (between judge and defendant, judge and jury, and so on).

However, water and tin remain logically atomistic insofar as their identity as tin and water does not depend upon their relation to entities that are external or extrinsic to them. A trial by jury is logically relational in nature insofar as its identity as a trial by jury does depend upon its relation to social entities external or intrinsic to it (legal, penal, and judicial systems).

Part of the significance of characterizing identity and emotion as social is to indicate their relational nature. It is not to endorse any theory about their constitution by our socially constructed theories of identity and emotion: the relational natures of identity and emotion are independent of, and not constitutive consequences of, our theories about them. The meaning of theoretical descriptions in natural and psychological science is social and – thus – relational in nature. However, the (social) relational dimensions of identity and emotion are not a consequence of, and cannot be identified with, the (social) relational dimensions of our theoretical descriptions of them, any more than the relational dimensions of quarks or electro-magnetic fields are a consequence of, or are to be identified with, the (social) relational dimensions of our theoretical descriptions of them.

According to the *principle of ontological invariance* (in space and time), the phenomena studied by a scientific discipline can be reidentified across different regions of space and time. This principle is presupposed by the Newtonian theory of universal gravitation, and it seems clear that it applies to many of the phenomena studied by astronomy, sub-atomic physics and chemistry, such as planets, electrons, and acids. It seems equally clear that it does not apply to many of the phenomena studied by evolutionary biology and medicine, such as species and viruses. Thus it is an open question whether this principle applies to psychological phenomena such as identity and emotion. I will suggest in the following chapters that it may not: identity and emotion may very well vary cross-culturally and transhistorically.

According to the *principle of the universality of causal explanation*, properly scientific explanations are universal in scope: the same explanation applies to each and every instance of an event, regularity, or structure. This principle may be alternatively expressed as the principle of the singularity of causation: that every event, regularity or structure has (at least on some level of description) one and only one causal explanation. However, although this principle does appear to hold with respect to many phenomena, it does not appear to hold with respect to them all. Although there appears to be (ultimately) only one cause of death, rusting, and superconductivity, there appear to be a plurality of causes of some diseases (some cancers appear to be induced by external agents, others are the product of genetic inheritance). Thus it is an open question whether this principle applies to psychological phenomena such as identity and emotion. I will suggest in the following chapters that it may not.

According to the *principle of theoretical reduction*, theoretical descriptions and explanations in terms of the properties and dispositions of particulars are only legitimate if they can be reduced – at least in principle if not in actual practice – to descriptions and explanations in terms of their physical composition and structure, via theoretical identifications of phenomena at the reduced and reducing levels of theoretical description and explanation. In the case of psychological phenomena, this is held to be achieved by the identification of psychological states with states of the central and peripheral nervous system.

This is an enormously popular and influential doctrine in psychological science. Yet it confuses two distinct requirements or desiderata for theoretical explanation. The first is that a reductive physical account of any putative theoretical explanatory property or disposition is required in principle (even though it often cannot be detailed in practice), in order to establish the *physical possibility* of the explanatory property postulated on a 'higher' level of description and explanation, by documenting (often via illustrative examples rather than by exhaustive compositional listing) how these phenomena *can* be physically incarnated (on the neurophysiological, biological, chemical, atomic, or sub-atomic level). Thus many neurophysiological accounts of psychological phenomena explain how beliefs and emotions can be physically incarnated in the central and peripheral nervous system.

The second requirement or desideratum derives from the fact that science rarely reaches explanatory bedrock with explanations in terms of the properties and dispositions of particulars, but tries to integrate such explanations within a wider theoretical framework. However, it cannot be assumed, but unfortunately all too often is uncritically assumed, that this form of theoretical integration will necessarily be micro-reductive: in terms of internal composition and structure.

It is of course true that some forms of theoretical integration follow this pattern. It is paradigmatically true of theoretically integrative accounts of the properties and dispositions of chemical elements, for example, which are explicated in terms of the properties and dispositions of their common compositional components and structure. However, it is not true of all forms of theoretical integration. Mach's theory of mass provides an account of the mass of individual bodies in terms of the effects upon them of other bodies, and evolutionary theory looks to environmental history as well as to genetic mutations in its account of phenotypical differences (for further examples, see Schlesinger, 1961).

Science seeks explication and explanation of properties and dispositions at whatever level integrative and unifying patterns emerge, only requiring that such patterns be continuous with the rest of physical nature in the sense that a physical compositional account of all the phenomena at any explanatory level can be provided in principle. Whether theoretical integration best proceeds via micro-theoretical reduction is an entirely separate question. A compositional account of all the things that have the properties of acids is theoretically illuminating; a compositional account of all the things that can 'accelerate' (socks, snakes, Suzukis, stones, and so forth) is not (Blackburn, 1991). That is, there is no reason to suppose that theoretical explication and integration in psychological science must proceed micro-reductively. Thus it is an open question whether our best theories of identity and emotion will proceed in this fashion. In the following chapters I suggest that they may not.

For most of its recent history academic psychology – based upon traditional empiricism – has been committed to the principles of atomism and theoretical reduction. Practitioners have almost invariably conceived of psychological phenomena in terms of logically atomistic internal states, presuming that this was a condition of their scientific respectability, since it was held to be a precondition of their ultimate identification with isolable brain states – the assumed 'real' explainers of behavior. Thus British and German psychologists in the eighteenth and nineteenth centuries analytically decomposed thoughts into their atomic components, and suggested various identifications of these 'elements' with neural states: for example, the 'vibratiuncles' of Hartley and the 'punctiform excitations' of Lotze and Hering.[7]

This approach has had some notable successes in some branches of psychology, but its success is not guaranteed in all branches. For example, Freud originally worked within the reductive traditions of German physiological psychology, and only achieved his theoretical breakthrough when he came to recognize the bankruptcy of the micro-reductive approach with respect to the explanation of some hysterical disorders, notably 'conversion hysterias' involving forms of 'paralysis,' 'blindness,' and 'deafness' that have no physiological basis. Instead of looking to the underlying neurophysiology for theoretical illumination, he successfully explained these symptoms in terms of their common form of symbolic relationship to earlier traumas.

Other successful forms of theoretical illumination of psychological phenomena have turned out to be micro-reductive. We might contrast the above psychogenetic account of conversion hysterias with the contemporary theoretical explanation of some instances of depression in terms of neurochemical deficits (Wolman and Stricker, 1991). However, there is nothing inevitable about this, and the ability to achieve micro-reductive illumination *is no measure of the adequacy of theoretical explanations in psychology*. Nor is there any guarantee that successful micro-reductive explanations will be universal in their scope, or exclusive in their application. Thus some depressions may be best explained in terms of neurochemical deficits; other depressions may be best explained in terms of social location and personal history; and some depressions may require an explanatory reference to both micro-reductive and social relational factors.

In later chapters I sketch a social and relational theory of identity and emotion. The adequacy of this form of theoretical account is an open and empirical question. I have tried to illustrate in this chapter, and will attempt to demonstrate throughout this work, that there is nothing scientifically suspect about a theory of emotions, for example, interpreted in realist terms, whose theoretical descriptions are not operationally defined in terms of the empirical phenomena the theory is employed to explain; that recognizes that some emotions are social and relational in nature and require social forms of explanation; that holds that some emotions may not be, and that some are unlikely to be, invariant cross-culturally and transhistorically; that holds that explanations of behavior in terms of some emotions may not be, and that some are unlikely to be, universal in their scope; and that – unholy of unholies – is empirically based, at least in part, upon agents' accounts of their emotions. In doing so I hope to surmount some of the more insidious confusions and ambiguities that have dogged identity and emotion research for many years, and continue to plague much contemporary research.

First, however, we need to deal with the other meta-theoretical perspective that has contributed to contemporary confusions about these matters: namely, social constructionism.

Notes

1 This is not to say that any of these theoretical descriptions – or any other theoretical descriptions deployed as illustrative examples in this work – or the explanations in which they figure, are in fact true. I assume, for example, that, at least in their original form, the descriptions of Bohr's theory are in fact false.

2 This is not to endorse the principle of meaning empiricism, or at least not for all concepts – it may be seriously doubted that it holds for mathematical concepts, for example.

3 An implication acknowledged by Bridgeman (1927: 10), one of the originators of the doctrine of operational definition.

4 This is not to deny that some cognitive psychologists hold the view that images play a critical role in cognitive processing (e.g. Paivio, 1986). But very few, if any, would *identify* cognitions with images.

5 Although scientific realism does presuppose a correspondence theory of truth, it need not be committed to bivalance: the doctrine that theoretical descriptions must be determinately either true or false – that they must either completely correspond or completely fail to correspond to reality. A scientific realist can accept that some theoretical descriptions are approximately true, and that the truth-values of some others are indeterminate.

6 Bhaskar (1975: 249) claims that 'epistemological relativism . . . is the handmaiden of ontological realism' and a number of my colleagues have urged me to recognize this. However, by 'epistemological relativism' Bhaskar means only the thesis that all our knowledge is theoretically and linguistically mediated, the thesis that I have characterized as 'global relativism.' Bhaskar explicitly rejects the relativist doctrines drawn from philosophy of science that I have characterized as 'local' relativism, and although he does dismiss talk of truth as 'correspondence,' it is quite clear that his target is those theories which conceive of correspondence in terms of some form of resemblance or isomorphism – 'propositions cannot be compared with states of affairs' (p. 249) – and which play no role in the present account of scientific realism.

7 There are, however, some hopeful signs that things are changing. In contemporary 'connectionist' (or 'parallel distributed processing' (Rumelhart and McClelland, 1986)) theories of cognition, for example, basic representations are not identified with isolable neurons or aggregates of them, but rather with networks of connection weights between neurons. If connectionist theorists have come to expand their theoretical horizons fruitfully by considering how basic representational states can neurophysiologically emerge from 'great webs of structure' (Minsky, 1981), perhaps it is time for social psychological science to take seriously the suggestion that psychological states such as emotions and motives may emerge from great webs of socio-linguistic structure.

3

Social Constructionism

Social constructionism, at least in the form of the meta-theoretical position recently developed by Ken Gergen and his associates (Gergen, 1982, 1985; Gergen and Davis, 1985; Kitzinger, 1987; Potter and Wetherell, 1987; Shotter, 1984, 1987), involves a direct denial of both the linguistic and epistemic objectivity of theoretical descriptions, including theoretical psychological descriptions. According to Gergen (1985: 266), 'Social constructionism views discourse about the world not as a reflection or map of the world but as an artifact of communal exchange.' Gergen denies that putative 'discourse about the world' is really 'about' the world at all, in the sense that he denies that it has truth-values determined by independent features of the world. This is because the terms employed in theoretical discourse – including theoretical psychological discourse – are not held to be 'tied' to the world in any way: '. . . there seems good reason to view mental predicates as semantically free-floating. That is, the vocabulary of mind is not anchored in, defined by or ostensively grounded in real-world particulars in such a way that propositions about mental events are subject to correction through observation' (Gergen, 1989b: 71). Putative theoretical descriptions 'are in themselves uninformative about the nature of things' because 'descriptive languages are not derived from observation; rather such languages operate as the lenses or filters through which we determine what counts as an object' (Gergen, 1987a: 11).

Competing theoretical descriptions cannot be empirically adjudicated because empirical judgments based upon observations – and indeed observations themselves – presuppose or are informed by theories:

> . . . in order to count something as a fact or a datum one requires a forestructure of theoretical understanding – terms or concepts that are already sensible. These orienting terms are embedded within more elaborate theories, whether implicit or explicit. Thus, what counts as observation is determined by preexisting theoretical commitments, and these commitments do not themselves spring from the soil of observation.
>
> . . . once formulated, the theory will determine what counts as evidence, confirmation and disconfirmation. Competing theories, implying alternative ontologies, are thus incommensurable . . . . (Gergen, 1988: 2)

It follows that the acceptance or rejection of theories in natural and social and psychological science *cannot in principle* be explained by reference to the empirical evaluation of theoretical descriptions: 'the degree to which a given form of understanding prevails or is sustained across time is not directly dependent on the empirical validity of the perspective in question, but on the vicissitudes of social processes (e.g. communication, negotiation, conflict, rhetoric etc.) (Gergen, 1985: 268).

According to social constructionism, 'theoretical description and explanation' are 'constitutive elements of broader patterns of human exchange' that serve to 'coordinate' human actions and relationships (Gergen, 1988: 7) within social contexts:

> Descriptions and explanations of the world themselves constitute forms of social action . . . descriptions and explanations form integral parts of various social patterns. They thus serve to sustain and support certain patterns to the exclusion of others. To alter descriptions and explanations is thus to threaten certain actions and invite others. (Gergen, 1985: 268)

In consequence, and since traditional empirical criteria for theory evaluation cannot be employed, social constructionism 'reasserts the relevance of moral criteria for scientific practice. To the extent that psychological theory (and related practices) enter into the life of the culture, sustaining certain patterns of conduct and destroying others, such work must be evaluated in terms of good or ill' (Gergen, 1985: 273).

Social constructionists avow that many contemporary theories in psychological science (which inform our contemporary 'empirical evaluations') are grounded in ideological assumptions, where ideology is interpreted as 'the Weltanschauung and social beliefs of a community, developed with the purpose of justifying and promoting their economic and sociopolitical interests' (Prilleltensky, 1989: 796). Theoretical forms of discourse are held to 'operate as miniature ontologies' (Gergen, 1988: 2), which cannot be empirically evaluated, but which serve to promote certain forms of social practice and discourage others. Social constructionism thus directs attention to 'the social, moral, political, and economic institutions that sustain and are supported by current assumptions about human activity' (Gergen, 1988: 268). On this conception, the role of theory is not to produce potentially true descriptions of the natural, social or psychological world, but to 'challenge the guiding assumptions of the culture, to raise fundamental questions regarding contemporary social life, to foster reconsideration of that which is "taken for granted," and thereby to generate fresh alternatives for social action' (Gergen, 1982: 109).

On this account, identity and emotion are social constructions. Forms of theoretical discourse putatively 'about' identity and emotion are not linguistically objective descriptions of independent psychological phenomena. They are socially constructed theoretical forestructures that project diverse ontologies which are not empirically evaluable, since any putative 'empirical' data are themselves conditioned or informed by our theoretical projections. Such forms of theoretical discourse serve to promote certain social practices and discourage others. In consequence, with respect to discourse about identity and emotion, one is 'invited to look not for their referents, but for their consequences in social life' (Gergen, 1989b: 71).

A great number of theorists characterize themselves as social construc- tionists (such as Armon-Jones (1986), Averill (1980, 1985), Coulter (1979), Harré (1983a), and others), not all of whom – and perhaps few of whom – are committed to all the doctrines noted above, especially the more radical epistemic ones. However, in this chapter and the next I concentrate on Gergen's position (with occasional references to the work of others), for essentially two reasons. The first is quite simply that Gergen is the most articulate and eloquent spokesman for, and the leading exponent of, the meta-theoretical form of social constructionism that is generally discussed and referenced in social psychological science, and especially in social psychological discussions of identity and emotion. In the second place, Gergen deploys a whole battery of arguments drawn from a variety of disciplines, and it is important to distinguish these. Gergen's conclusions about identity and emotion, for example, are partly derived from considerations and arguments drawn from post-empiricist and relativist philosophy of science that are held to apply to atoms and acids as much as to identity and emotion. They are also partly derived from considerations and arguments derived from social psychological and anthropological research that would appear to apply only to psycho- logical phenomena such as identity and emotion. Many of those who call themselves social constructionists with respect to identity and emotion would accept only those considerations and arguments specific to psychological phenomena such as identity and emotion, and would reject some of the more extreme epistemic claims derived from relativist philosophy of science.

By distinguishing these various considerations and arguments, it becomes easier to theoretically locate the multivariety of species of social constructionist theorist, although I leave this academic exercise largely to the reader and avowed social constructionists themselves. I consider myself to be a social constructionist in the sense that I hold identity and emotion to be socially – and linguistically – created and constituted. I also hold this to be entirely consistent with a realist analysis of our theoretical psychological discourse about identity and emotion. The present work is essentially an attempt to demonstrate how these joint claims can be consistently maintained.

Linguistic Objectivity

The social constructionist critique of the notion of linguistic objectivity fails because it is based upon a number of false assumptions and non- exclusive contrasts which often essentially repeat many of the errors of traditional empiricist assumptions about linguistic objectivity.

Gergen claims that theoretical discourse is 'not a reflection or a map of the world' (1985: 266). Yet, as noted in the previous chapter, the notion that the truth or accuracy of theoretical descriptions depends upon their ability to 'picture,' 'copy' or 'mirror' reality is itself based upon an archaic conception of theoretical descriptions that derives from the classical empiricist account of concepts as 'images' derived from 'sense-impressions.' Such an account is not intrinsic to contemporary conceptions of linguistic objectivity, and plays no role in a realist account of the linguistic objectivity of theoretical descriptions. The realist does not maintain that theoretical descriptions are pictures or images of reality: that (true) theoretical descriptions are in some sense isomorphic with the 'contours' of reality. The realist does not postulate any mysterious relation of *resemblance* between (true) theoretical descriptions and the phenomena they purport to describe. The realist does not hold that Bohr's theoretical descriptions of the atom resemble the atom, or that empirical descriptions of tables resemble tables. Since the satisfaction of some form of resemblance relation is not a condition of linguistic objectivity according to realism, theoretical descriptions – or, for that matter, empirical descriptions – cannot be denied linguistic objectivity simply because of their failure to satisfy some form of resemblance relation.

The social constructionist in fact repeats the essential empiricist error by supposing that if theoretical descriptions are not tied to observations via ostensive or operational definitions, then they can be neither epistemically nor linguistically objective. As also noted in the previous chapter, neither of these conclusions follows from the fact – recognized by realism – that theoretical descriptions are not ostensively or operationally defined. Gergen is correct to claim that since theoretical psychological descriptions are neither ostensively nor operationally defined, they are in this respect 'semantically free-floating.' Yet this poses no threat to linguistic objectivity, because for the realist *all* theoretical descriptions are 'semantically free-floating' in this respect: they are neither ostensively nor operationally defined. It does not follow that they are semantically vacuous and therefore cannot function as linguistically objective theoretical descriptions, for according to the realist their semantics are autonomously determined via theoretical modeling.

This does, however, cause a problem for any social constructionist who denies the realist account of the semantics of theoretical descriptions (as most in fact do). In the absence of any *alternative* account of the semantics of theoretical descriptions, such descriptions, including theoretical psychological descriptions, are not merely 'semantically free-floating' – insofar as their semantics are not determined by ostensive or operational definitions – but are *semantically vacuous*: they are devoid of any meaningful content. This makes it hard to see how different theories can – or can be employed to – 'construct' or 'promote' or 'project' ontologies, as social constructionists maintain that they do, far less serve to coordinate social actions and relationships that promote or discourage certain forms of social practice. The ability of theories to perform these social functions requires some semantic content relating to some set of putative objects and properties.

I will stress this point throughout this chapter. As suggested in the previous chapter, there is nothing mysterious about the linguistic objectivity of theoretical or empirical descriptions. Rather, theoretical and empirical descriptions are linguistically objective by virtue of their *being descriptions*: by virtue of attributing properties or relations to postulated or observable entities. In consequence, to deny that theoretical or empirical descriptions are linguistically objective is to deny *that they are descriptions at all* – which is what much of the social constructionist argument concerning theoretical discourse comes down to. However, the general social constructionist position in fact *presupposes* the linguistic objectivity of theoretical descriptions, and its account of the 'social pragmatics' of theoretical discourse is parasitic upon the assumption of the descriptive function of theoretical discourse.

Meaning, Conventions, and Language-Games

It is of course true, as social constructionists insist, that 'words are not mimetic simulcures of an independent world, but derive their meaning (à la Wittgenstein) from their use' (Gergen, 1987b: 52). In claiming that meaning is based on conventions of use, Wittgenstein (1953) aimed to demonstrate that linguistic symbols do not derive their meaning via association with private mental images (via some form of private ostensive definition), as claimed by classical empiricist accounts of meaning. However, as noted earlier, these classical empiricist accounts play no role in a realist analysis of linguistic meaning: the realist can and does recognize that linguistic meaning is based upon conventions of usage.

According to the realist, the fact that linguistic symbols derive their meaning via conventions of linguistic usage is precisely what enables us to employ empirical descriptions like 'green,' 'tree,' and 'forest' to describe observable objects, even though descriptions like 'green' do not resemble green things, and are not necessarily associated with images of green. It also enables us to employ theoretical descriptions such as 'electron' and 'atom' – by developing conventions of theoretical meaning that exploit the semantics of empirical descriptions – to describe unobservable theoretical objects, even though descriptions like 'electron' do not – or are not assumed to – resemble electrons themselves, and are not necessarily associated with images of them. Indeed, according to the realist, this is precisely what enables descriptions to be linguistically objective, since it is precisely what enables them to have – conventionally defined – truth conditions which may be satisfied or fail to be satisfied.

We do need a richer account of descriptive meaning than that advanced by traditional empiricism. However, accounts such as Wittgenstein's that emphasize the social conventional dimensions of meaning do not deny or preclude the linguistic (or, for that matter, the epistemic) objectivity of empirical or theoretical descriptions. Wittgenstein justly opposed the *mystification* of linguistic objectivity. He objected to those theories that explicate the truth or accuracy of descriptions in terms of some form of resemblance or isomorphism between descriptions and the phenomena putatively described (such as his own earlier 'picture' theory of meaning (Wittgenstein, 1917)). Yet such theories form no part of a realist account of descriptive meaning.

However, social constructionists see such accounts of the conventional basis of linguistic meaning as having an entirely different implication. They see such accounts, and Wittgenstein's account in particular, as undermining the very notion of the linguistic objectivity of descriptions.[1] Social constructionists suppose that if descriptive meaning is governed by conventions, then judgments about the truth or falsity of descriptions must be made by reference to conventions, *rather than by reference to observable features of the world* (either directly in the case of empirical descriptions, or indirectly in the case of theoretical descriptions).

There is of course an unobjectionable sense in which judgments about the truth or falsity of descriptions must be made by reference to conventions: they must be made by reference to conventions about the meaning of descriptions. Thus, in determining whether the sentence 'the leaves are turning brown' is true or false, we need to take into account not only what we perceive, but also the conventional meaning of the descriptions 'leaves,' 'turning,' and 'brown.' However, given the conventional meaning of these descriptions, the sentence 'the leaves are turning brown' is true if and only if the objects referenced have the properties attributed to them by the descriptions employed in the sentence. The same holds for theoretical descriptions employed in sentences about atoms such as 'electrons orbit the atomic nucleus:' in judging the truth or falsity of such claims, we need to take into account not only the empirical evidence for such claims, but the conventional meaning (developed via theoretical modeling) of the descriptions 'electron,' 'orbit,' and 'atomic nucleus.' However, given the conventional meaning of these theoretical descriptions, the sentence 'electrons orbit the atomic nucleus' is true if and only if the objects putatively referenced have the properties attributed to them by the theoretical descriptions employed in the sentence.

However, this is not what social constructionists mean when they claim that judgments about truth or falsity are determined by conventions: they mean something more and something quite different. Social constructionists hold that descriptions are evaluated for their 'truth' or 'falsity' according to conventions *other* than conventions governing their descriptive meaning, such as those associated with or derived from a variety of ideologies:

> If statements and not things are true or false, then truth is necessarily linguistic: if truth is linguistic, then it is relative to language use (words, concepts, statements, discourses) at a given time and place; therefore, ideology,

interests, and power arrangements at a given time and place are implicated in the production of what counts as true. (Cherryholmes, 1988: 439)

Now it could be the case that some agents employ some descriptive terms according to conventions *other than* conventions governing their descriptive meaning. For example, I might understand what the description 'longer than' means, and may be able to demonstrate this in a wide variety of contexts if tested individually. However, I might also follow a convention that sanctions the employment of this description in the company of others only if it is employed by a majority of my peers (as in the case of Asch's (1951) original subjects), or only if it is employed by a majority of persons represented as members of my social class or collective (as appears to be the case among the Japanese (Frager, 1970)). Alternatively, I might very well understand what it means for someone to 'qualify for emergency welfare assistance,' and may demonstrate this in departmental tests, but might follow a convention according to which I, like others in my position, only employ this description with respect to persons of my own race or sex or religion. In these cases, conventions other than conventions of descriptive meaning would govern my employment of these descriptions.

Thus it might very well be that sometimes ideology, interests, power arrangements, and the like are implicated in the employment of theoretical or empirical descriptions: that is, that their employment is sometimes governed by conventions other than conventions of descriptive meaning. However, this is a substantive theoretical contention that is quite independent of the claim that meaning is governed by conventions of usage: it is not entailed or vouchsafed by the accepted fact that linguistic meaning is based upon conventions of usage.

This substantive theoretical contention would follow only from the claim that there are *no* conventions of linguistic meaning, at least as ordinarily understood. This is essentially what Gergen does claim, once again via an appeal to Wittgenstein, who observed that: 'There are countless . . . different kinds of use of what we call "symbols," "words," "sentences." And this multiplicity is not fixed; but new types of language, new language-games, as we may say, come into existence, and these become obsolete and long forgotten' (1953, no. 23). Gergen interprets this passage in the following fashion:

Essentially this would mean that any scientific term would derive its meaning from its context of usage, which context could also include ostensive means of securing word-object identities. The term 'rabbit' for example, may figure in many different linguistic, social, and environmental contexts. As a result it would be virtually impossible to determine the truth-value of propositions containing the term through observation. There simply is no stimulus event (or class of events), abstracted from context, to which the term is semantically wedded. (1987a: 4).

Now it is no doubt true, as Gergen claims, that the 'precise boundaries' of the conventions governing the use of the term 'rabbit' cannot be explicated: the 'open-ended' nature of all linguistic meaning is essential to the possibility of its development (Waismann, 1945). However, it does not follow from the fact that the term 'rabbit' may be employed or learned in different linguistic, social, or environmental contexts that 'it would be virtually impossible to determine the truth-value of propositions containing the term through observation.' This would only follow if there were *no* conventions of descriptive meaning, no conventions of usage linking symbols such as 'rabbit' and empirically discriminable features of the world. If this really were the case, then the term 'rabbit' would have *no intersubjective descriptive meaning*, and it would be impossible to employ the term to communicate to others, for example, states of affairs in the world that were not immediately perceived by others. I could not, for example, inform my daughter playing in the basement that there was a rabbit in the garden by employing the description 'rabbit,' if she and I had learned or regularly deployed the term in different linguistic, social, or environmental contexts: I by reference to those pesky destroyers of my cabbages, and she by reference to Beatrix Potter.

Nevertheless, Gergen is clearly committed to the claim that meaning is determined by individual vagaries of context of learning and employment, and *not* by social conventions of usage. According to Gergen, I mean something different by a term such as 'rabbit' or 'Argentina' if I learn or employ the term in a different context from another: 'What I mean by Argentina, for example, depends upon whether we are looking at a world atlas, reading a history book, requesting that it not cry for me, planning a visit, and so on' (1988: 3). If this really were the case, of course, it would be impossible for me to communicate to you where Argentina is by reference to the atlas, if you had learned about Argentina from a history book and were planning a visit. Meaning would be idiosyncratic to individuals depending upon vagaries of context of learning or application. This is *the very opposite of what Wittgenstein claimed*, and a direct denial of the notion that the meaning of symbols is based upon conventions of usage. It also undermines any claims about the 'social pragmatics' of theoretical discourse: for again it is hard to see how such forms of discourse could be employed to coordinate social actions and relationships and promote and discourage certain forms of social practice, if they are devoid of shared semantic content.

It is precisely this claim – that there are no conventions of empirical and theoretical meaning – that provides the putative justification of Gergen's remarkable and radical claim that 'any behavioral theory may, in principle, be applied to (used to describe and explain) virtually any action' (1987a: 5), since 'communities of scholars' are free to 'negotiate' how theoretical descriptions are employed – that is, are free to negotiate any conventions of usage they care to construct, in accord with their socio-moral-political predilections.

Gergen claims that there could not be conventions of descriptive meaning by which empirical and (indirectly) theoretical descriptions could be related to common empirically discriminable features, environments, contexts, and the like – there are 'principled impediments' (1987a: 4) that preclude this. He argues (Gergen, 1989a) that such conventions could be based upon neither learned nor innate empirical categories.

These arguments are not fully considered in this chapter, the primary aim of which is to demonstrate that the social constructionist account of the 'social pragmatics' of theoretical discourse presupposes, and is entirely parasitic upon, the assumption that theoretical discourse *is* based upon conventions of descriptive meaning, and is thus linguistically objective. In any case, if Gergen's – very doubtful – arguments were successful, they would establish too much. To deny that conventions of meaning can be related to commonly discriminable features, environments, contexts, and the like is not only to deny that there can be conventions of descriptive meaning (empirical or theoretical). It is to deny that there can be conventions *simpliciter* – including those that are supposedly negotiated for all sorts of socio-moral-political reasons. What enables us on occasions to follow alternative conventions for the employment of empirical or theoretical descriptions – as in the examples cited earlier – is precisely what enables us to form conventions of descriptive meaning in the first place: namely, our ability to relate such descriptions to common empirically discriminable features, environments, contexts, and the like.

In this context it is worth recalling Wittgenstein's claim about the variety of language-games, which Gergen interprets as denying the possibility of linguistically objective descriptions. Wittgenstein's point about the variety of language-games was not to deny that there are descriptive forms of language. His point was to distinguish descriptive forms of language – or descriptive language-games based upon conventions of descriptive meaning – from a variety of non-descriptive forms of language, such as ordering, insulting, promising, and the like.

Wittgenstein's (1953) analysis of the variety of language-games was a reaction to his earlier treatment of all legitimate linguistic forms as descriptions of atomic or molecular facts (or as degenerative formal sentences such as tautologies and contradictions), and dismissal of all non-descriptive forms of discourse as literal nonsense (Wittgenstein, 1917). His later emphasis on the variety of language-games did not involve any denial of descriptive uses of language, and he included many such forms in his list of the variety of language-games: he included 'describing the appearance of an object, or giving its measurements,' 'reporting an event,' and 'forming and testing a hypothesis,' as well as a variety of non-descriptive uses of language, such as 'giving orders, and obeying them,' 'making up a story, and reading it,' 'making a joke, and telling it,' and 'asking, thanking, cursing, greeting, praying' (1953, no. 24).

What Wittgenstein objected to was the *assimilation* of these diverse forms of language-games: in particular the assimilation of non-descriptive uses of language to descriptive uses. Social constructionists simply repeat this error in reverse: they assimilate descriptive uses of language to non-descriptive uses. They do so by claiming that theories in natural and social and psychological science – and everyday life – do not have a descriptive function: they serve social functions *other* than description, such as the coordination of social actions and relationships, and the promotion or discouragement of forms of social practice.

Constatives and Performatives

Social constructionist theorists regularly claim, for example, that theoretical attributions of psychological states to self and others are *performative* rather than descriptive (Gergen, 1989b; Harré, 1989; Potter and Wetherell, 1987; Shotter, 1989). According to social constructionists, theoretical discourse putatively 'about' emotions, for example, does not describe independent psychological states, but is rather employed to serve social performative functions such as warning, excusing, endorsing, and the like. According to this account, avowals of depression, for example, are employed to excuse one's behavior or elicit sympathy, rather than to describe one's psychological state. Thus Gergen, for example, claims that 'Mental talk is largely performative – that is, it does not mirror or map an independent reality but is a functioning element in the social process itself. In the case of mental predicates one is thus invited to look not for their referents but for their consequences in social life' (1989b: 71).

As Gergen acknowledges, this claim makes an appeal to J.L. Austin's (1962) distinction between *constative* and *performative* utterances, between utterances that are *sayings* such as descriptions, and utterances that are *doings* such as warnings and threats. Constative utterances such as 'The wine is chilled' or 'The train is late' are putative descriptions of independent states of affairs that are properly characterized as true or false. Performative utterances such as 'I promise to meet you tomorrow' and 'I apologise for being late' perform the social functions of promising and apologizing, and may be characterized as effective or ineffective, sincere or insincere, but are not appropriately characterized as true or false. Performative utterances cannot be characterized as true or false because they are not putative descriptions of natural, social, or psychological reality (past, present, or future). Gergen claims that theoretical attributions of emotion and other psychological states are performative rather than constative.

However, Austin himself quickly came to realize that the distinction between constatives and performatives is somewhat misleading, since in an important respect 'constative' and 'performative' are not mutually exclusive categories: constative utterances may be conceived as a special kind of performative utterance, namely those that perform the function of description. This is not to say that Austin assimilated the descriptive/ constative and non-descriptive/performative uses of language. Rather, he argued that his earlier distinction should be superseded by the recognition that different types of speech acts – describing, promising, warning, and the like – can serve a variety of social and communicative functions.

The significance of this for our present discussion is as follows. Austin noted that the same social or communicative function can be served by the employment of a traditional 'constative' description or a non-descriptive 'performative.' Thus I can perform the speech act of warning another by employing the non-descriptive 'performative' utterance 'Watch out for the bull!' or the 'constative' descriptive utterance 'There is a bull in the field.'

That is, speech acts can perform a variety of social functions – such as warning – while at the same time being descriptive. In consequence, the undoubted fact that theoretical attributions of emotions and other psychological states to oneself and others can be employed to perform all sorts of social functions, such as excusing one's behavior or eliciting sympathy, does not entail or even suggest that they cannot also (and at the same time) be employed to perform a descriptive function. The fact – assuming it is a fact – that avowals of depression can be employed to elicit sympathy does not prevent or preclude such avowals from also serving as descriptions of the person's distressing psychological state.

It might be objected that there are some locutions that serve social functions such as promising or excusing without performing any descriptive function: locutions such as 'I promise to repay you tomorrow' or 'Watch out for the bull!' The social constructionist might maintain that emotion ascriptions and other forms of psychological discourse are locutions of this sort: what may be called 'pure performatives' (Austin's original examples of 'performatives' that appear to serve no descriptive function). However, the social constructionist theorist provides no good reason for supposing that this is the case, and it seems very doubtful. One characteristic of 'pure performatives' is that they have fairly specific local – social and psychological – satisfaction conditions. I cannot promise or warn anyone about anything unless I am in some sort of social position to do so (and in the case of promising to repay someone I must have previously borrowed some money from them), and unless others have certain beliefs about my integrity, sincerity, and the like (remember Peter and the wolf). In contrast, as with other forms of theoretical description, I can meaningfully and truly describe myself or others as angry or ashamed at any place and time: that is, without the satisfaction of any local social or psychological conditions. The only social conditions that need to be satisfied in order for my descriptions to be meaningful are conventions of descriptive meaning; the only psychological conditions that need to be satisfied in order for my descriptions to be true are that I or others are in fact angry or ashamed.

It is true that emotion ascriptions, like any other form of social discourse, are governed by conventions of social propriety and justificatory warrant. The important point, however, is that such conventions are logically independent of the conventions governing the truth conditions of ascriptions. It may be socially inappropriate to utter 'all bodies fall with equal acceleration in a vacuum' at a cocktail party, and my idle – and offensive – speculation that my host's wife is bored and depressed may be wholly unwarranted. Despite the fact that such claims are inappropriate or unwarranted, I can nevertheless meaningfully assert them, and both claims would be objectively true – or false – if I were to assert them in such circumstances.

However, these points need not be laboured, for there is a far more serious objection to the social constructionist analysis of theoretical discourse as purely performative. It is not just the case that the ability of avowals of depression to excuse is entirely consistent with the assumption that they are also descriptive of the person's distressing psychological condition, or that the ability of statements of the theory of evolution to offend some Christians is entirely consistent with the assumption that such statements describe the hypothetical origin of species. It is also the case that a reference to the descriptive function of depression avowals provides the best explanation of the ability of such avowals to excuse behavior, and that a reference to the descriptive function of statements of the theory of evolution provides the best explanation of their ability to offend some Christians. It is in fact remarkably hard to excuse one's behavior *without* offering a description of one's debilitating or distressing psychological state, or of situational impediments or extenuating circumstances, in contrast to the relative ease with which we can apologize without offering any description: by just uttering 'I apologize' or 'I am sorry.' It is remarkably difficult to offend people without offering some description of their personal characteristics (or those of their relatives) or of some putative state of affairs that runs counter to their most cherished beliefs. The social constructionist does not – and cannot – provide any explanation of how avowals of depression can excuse behavior or how statements of the theory of evolution can offend some Christians, for these social powers appear to be firmly based upon the descriptive function of such locutions.

This objection runs considerably deeper, however, and blocks any attempt to treat such locutions as pure performatives. Those pure performatives that are undoubtedly employed in social life to coordinate social actions and relationships, such as promises, commands, requests, and warnings, would be impoverished and ineffective 'tools' – to employ a Wittgensteinian metaphor much favored by social constructionists – for coordinating social actions and relationships without descriptive forms of language. Although promises, commands, requests, warnings, and the like are not themselves descriptions, they generally serve their social functions by exploiting descriptive forms of language.

People do not generally promise *simpliciter*: they promise to repay the money they have borrowed today, they promise to meet you on the corner of 5th and 34th on Friday evening at 8 pm, they promise to arrange the flowers for the wedding, and to deliver the pizza within thirty minutes. People do not generally warn *simpliciter*: they warn others about the vote on redundancies at tomorrow's meeting, about the dangers of unprotected sex, and about the bull in the field. And so on for other 'pure performatives.' It is in fact usually impossible to perform the speech acts of promising, commanding, requesting, and warning without employing descriptive language: the utterances 'I promise,' 'Go,' 'Please,' and 'Watch out' *simpliciter* would frequently fail to function performatively as promises, commands, requests, or warnings (and as noted earlier, one can perform such speech acts without employing 'pure performatives' – the speech act of warning can be performed by simply reporting the presence of the bull in the field).

With respect to the coordination of scientific activities, Popper (1963) provides a nice example of how pure performative commands are ineffectual with respect to the social coordination of scientific activities. He describes how he used to demonstrate to a group of physics students in Vienna the absurdity of supposing that observations can be gathered inductively without reference to any theory, by:

> ... beginning a lecture with the following instructions: 'Take pen and paper; carefully observe, and write down what you have observed!' They asked, of course, *what* I wanted them to observe. Clearly the instruction 'Observe!' is absurd. It is not even idiomatic (unless the object of the transitive verb is taken to be understood). Observation is always selective. It needs a chosen object, a definite task, an [theoretical] interest, a point of view, a problem. And its description presupposes a descriptive language, with property words ... (1963: 46).

Social constructivists are correct to follow Wittgenstein in stressing that 'the speaking of language is part of an activity, or of a form of life' (1953, no. 23), and that it is imbedded in a set of purposive human actions and social activities. Language does not simply serve to describe these activities and other features of the world, but is a 'functioning element in the social process itself' (Gergen, 1989b: 71), serving to coordinate human actions and social activities, and no doubt – at least sometimes – serving to sustain or undermine certain social arrangements and power relations. This is entirely consistent with a realist account of theoretical and empirical discourse: it provides a plausible and potentially true description of ordinary language and the language of the various sciences. Both are imbedded within, and serve a variety of social functions within, human social practices.

The social constructionist fails to realize that most if not all of these social functions of language are parasitic upon its ability to serve descriptive functions. Without descriptive meaning – both empirical and theoretical – language simply could not serve the multitude of other

functions it does in fact serve. The upshot is this. The social constructionist account of theoretical discourse is entirely parasitic upon, and its
very intelligibility presumes, the linguistic objectivity of theoretical – and
empirical – descriptions: the fact that empirical descriptions are
meaningful and linguistically objective by virtue of conventions of usage
relating descriptions to empirically discriminable features of the world,
and that theoretical descriptions are meaningful and linguistically
objective by virtue of conventions of usage based upon theoretical
modeling that exploit the established semantics of empirical descriptions.
Without linguistic objectivity, theoretical discourse would not be merely
'semantically free-floating.' It would be semantically vacuous: devoid of
any content. It would be impotent as a social instrument, and the moral
evaluation of competing theories would be as redundant as their
empirical evaluation.

Linguistic and Epistemic Objectivity

These critical claims are not made in order to establish the semantic
vacuity of social constructionism, or the moral redundancy of its meta-
theoretical judgments. It seems plain that neither social constructionism
nor the theories that it holds to be social constructions are semantically
vacuous. It also seems plain that this is because social constructionism
presupposes – and is entirely parasitic upon – the fact that theoretical
and empirical descriptions in natural and social and psychological
science – and in everyday life – are meaningful and linguistically
objective.

At this point it is tempting to dismiss social constructionism out of
hand as just false. Yet social constructionism cannot be – and ought not
to be – so quickly dismissed. Although many social constructionists do
base their arguments upon denials of the linguistic objectivity of
theoretical descriptions, they *need not*. Most of the substantive claims of
social constructionism could in fact be preserved by accepting the
linguistic objectivity of theoretical descriptions, but by denying their
epistemic objectivity.

The social constructionist might accept that theoretical descriptions are
linguistically objective: that we can grasp their autonomous meaning
(based upon theoretical modeling) and thus know what would have to be
the case in order for such descriptions to be true. Yet the social
constructionist could maintain – and does in fact independently maintain
– that we can never have empirical grounds for accepting one set of
autonomously meaningful and linguistically objective theoretical
descriptions over another (or others). Since epistemic objectivity does
not follow from – and is not vouchsafed by – linguistic objectivity, the
social constructionist can employ – and does in fact employ – familiar
relativist arguments drawn from post-empiricist philosophy of science to
establish that competing theoretical descriptions cannot be empirically

adjudicated. If this conclusion can be established, then most of the standard and substantive social constructionist theses follow immediately. The adoption and rejection of theories can only be a matter of social pragmatics, and it is consequently right and proper to adjudicate theories in terms of our moral assessment of the consequences of adopting them. And so on and so forth.

There is a residual problem with this position, however, concerning the moral justification of the adoption of theories by reference to the consequences of adopting them. Social constructionists regularly make claims about the negative social consequences of adopting certain theories: for example, Gergen (1985: 269) cites 'the damaging effects on children of the prevailing constructions of the child's mind.' Yet this form of justification only has *moral force* – as opposed to merely social force – if different theories about the 'effects on children of the prevailing constructions of the child's mind' are empirically adjudicable. Otherwise these forms of putatively moral justification are as ungrounded as the theories they purport to justify.

In any case, in the following chapter I argue that the standard relativist arguments drawn from post-empiricist philosophy of science – based upon the so-called 'underdetermination' of theories by empirical data – do not establish the conclusion that competing theories are not – in principle – empirically adjudicable. Consequently, the general social constructionist position – minus the denial of the linguistic objectivity of theoretical descriptions – cannot be reestablished by reference to these relativist arguments.

Nevertheless, although I argue in the following chapter that there are no grounds in principle for denying epistemic objectivity, I also acknowledge that there may very well be grounds for denying that it can be achieved – or that it is achieved in actual practice – in particular cases of theoretical conflict. This is because, as I will also argue in the following chapter, there can be no a priori argument ensuring that competing theories can always be empirically adjudicated in practice: according to the analysis offered, whether this turns out to be the case with respect to any theoretical conflict is an entirely contingent matter. With respect to any theoretical conflict, it is an open – and ultimately empirical – question whether it can be empirically adjudicated.

In consequence, although the relativist arguments drawn from post-empiricist philosophy of science do not reestablish the general social constructionist position, they do indicate that it must be taken seriously with respect to any *particular* theoretical conflict in any science, including social psychological science. The social constructionist theses might hold – that is, might very well be true – not with respect to all theoretical conflicts, but with respect to particular instances of them. In particular cases of theoretical conflicts that cannot be empirically adjudicated, we can only appeal to moral judgments concerning the consequences of adopting either theory if we feel obliged to make a theoretical decision.

Moreover, in at least some of these cases, although the original theoretical disputes are not empirically adjudicable, theoretical disputes about the consequences of adopting the original conflicting theories might very well be: this might be the case in contemporary theoretical disputes about race and intelligence, for example. In the final analysis, this is why the social constructionist position deserves to be taken seriously, despite the inadequacy of the arguments generally advanced in its favor.

This restricted form of the social constructionist thesis is, however, entirely consistent with scientific realism, even when scientific realism is interpreted as maintaining a general commitment to the epistemic objectivity of theory evaluation, and does not entail or imply that identity or emotion is constituted – in any sense or to any degree – by our theoretical descriptions of identity and emotion.

Notes

1 Many social constructionists suppose that since conventions are constitutive of descriptive meaning, they must also be constitutive of the 'truth' and 'objectivity' of particular descriptions, and also suppose that Wittgenstein said something of this sort. He did not. In *Philosophical Investigations*, Wittgenstein provides the following exchange between his imaginary interlocutor and himself: '"So you are saying that human agreement decides what is true and what is false?" – It is what human beings *say* that is true or false; and they agree in the *language* they use. This is not agreement in opinions but in form of life' (1953, no. 142). Wittgenstein claimed that agreement in form of life is constitutive of the conventions of meaningful description. He did not claim that it is constitutive of the truth or objectivity of particular descriptions.

Wittgenstein also noted that the types of agreement in form of life that are constitutive of the meaning of descriptive discourse are not restricted to agreements about linguistic conventions. They also presuppose a certain degree of recognized empirical invariance. This is important for the following reason. Social constructionists often quote with approval Wittgenstein's claim that 'If language is to be a form of communication there must be agreement not only in definitions but also (queer as this may sound) in judgements' (1953, no. 242), suggesting that such agreements in judgment are socially negotiated (or determined) independently of any empirical grounding (Shotter, 1992). Yet Wittgenstein's point is almost precisely the opposite of this. It is only because of commonly discriminable empirical invariances that such agreement is possible. He goes on to say in the same passage: 'This seems to abolish logic but does not to so. – It is one thing to describe methods of measurement, and another to obtain and state results of measurement. But what we call "measuring" is partly determined by a certain constancy in results of measurement.' What kind of constancy is required? Consider *Philosophical Investigations* (1953), no. 142: 'The procedure of putting a lump of cheese on a balance and fixing the price by the turn of the scale would lose its point if it frequently happened for such lumps to suddenly grow or shrink for no obvious reason.'

Social constructionists often also quote with approval Wittgenstein, *On Certainty* (1969), no. 215: '. . . the idea of "agreement with reality" does not have any clear application.' Yet this is misleadingly quoted out of context. The sentence including this phrase is a response to the question at no. 214:

214 What prevents me from supposing that this table either vanishes or alters its shape and colour when no one is observing it, and when someone looks at it again changes back to its old condition? – 'But who is going to suppose such a thing!' – one would feel like saying.

215 Here we see that the phrase 'agreement with reality' does not have any clear application.

Wittgenstein's point is surely that *here*, in *this* context, the phrase 'agreement with reality' does not have any clear application. He does not deny that the phrase may have perfectly good uses in other contexts.

4

Relativism

I argued in the last chapter that social constructionist denials of the linguistic objectivity of theoretical descriptions are unfounded, and that in fact the general social constructionist position presupposes the linguistic objectivity of theoretical descriptions, including theoretical psychological descriptions. I also noted that the general social constructionist position – minus the denial of the linguistic objectivity of theoretical descriptions – might be reestablished by denying the epistemic objectivity of theoretical descriptions, including theoretical psychological descriptions. In fact many social constructionist arguments are directed towards the denial of the epistemic objectivity of such descriptions, based upon a number of recent relativist arguments drawn from post-empiricist philosophy of science. However, these arguments have considerably less force than has been generally supposed.

Epistemic Objectivity

It has been argued that scientists are never obliged to reject their theories in the face of falsified predictions (*contra* Popper, 1959). According to the so-called 'Quine–Duhem thesis' (Duhem, 1906; Quine, 1953), it is always possible for a scientist to accommodate recalcitrant experimental evidence by the modification or replacement of auxiliary theories and assumptions employed in the original derivation of the falsified prediction. If this is the case, there can be no such thing as 'crucial experiments' or 'critical observations,' for it is always open to a theorist to make such modifications to accommodate negative empirical results and preserve evidential parity with a competing theory. If this is the case, then epistemic objectivity cannot be achieved with respect to the empirical evaluation of scientific theories.

It is also often suggested that the epistemic objectivity of theory evaluation is threatened by recent claims about the 'theory-informity' (or 'theory-ladenness') of observations, which cast doubt upon the theoretical neutrality of observations employed in the evaluation of scientific theories. It is argued that what a scientist observes is dependent upon his or her prior theories and expectations, and that in consequence scientists committed to different theories will make different observations (Brown, 1979; Chalmers, 1976; Feyerabend, 1975; Hanson, 1958; Kuhn, 1970) when faced with the same stimulus situations. Just as one person may see a duck and another person may see a rabbit in the familiar gestalt duck–

rabbit figure, according to their interpretation of the figure, so too different scientists with different theories will observe different things when faced with the same evidence. Thus Brahe – a defender of the geocentric theory – facing east at dawn would see the sun rising against a fixed horizon, whereas Kepler – a defender of the heliocentric theory – would see the horizon rolling beneath a stationary sun (Hanson, 1958). What one sees is held to depend upon what one *sees it as*, and what one sees it as is held to depend upon one's prior theories.

It is argued that different scientists raised in and committed to different scientific traditions and theories make different observations – in the same stimulus situations – informed by different theories. According to Kuhn (1970), they may properly be said to inhabit 'different worlds.' In consequence there can be no 'crucial experiments' or 'critical observations,' since competing theorists are bound to interpret the same result differently according to their competing theories. In this essentially relativist account of theory evaluation, competing theories are said to be 'incompatible' but observationally 'incommensurable': consequently there can be no empirical adjudication of competing theories.

Gergen (1982, 1985) employs both the Quine–Duhem thesis and the doctrine of the 'theory-informity' of observations to support his claim that psychological theories are radically 'underdetermined' by observational data. These considerations lead him to advance the explicit relativist thesis that 'virtually any experiment used as support for a given theory may be used to support any alternative theory' (Gergen, 1982: 72). He also dismisses the possibility of a crucial experiment or critical observations by arguing that competing theories of 'cognitive dissonance' and 'self-perception' are incompatible but incommensurable, citing the differential interpretation of classic experiments on attitude-change as support (Greenwald, 1975).

Social Dimensions of Science

Considerations of this sort have encouraged the development of a number of sociological and social psychological accounts of the acceptance and rejection of scientific theories (including theories in social psychological science), many of which are explicitly social constructionist.

According to the proponents of the 'strong program' in the sociology of science, scientific theories are accepted, rejected, and adjudicated in accord with 'social interests' and 'collective needs,' rather than by reference to empirically discriminable features of the world (Barnes, 1982; Bloor, 1976). Proponents of the 'strong program' hold that such social explanations apply to *all* instances of 'the production of scientific knowledge' (including, reflexively, the accounts offered within the 'strong program' itself), 'scientific knowledge' itself being defined independently of and indifferently to the presence, absence, or degree of empirical support for scientific theories – in terms of whatever 'men take to be knowledge' or that which is 'collectively endorsed' (Bloor, 1976: 2–3).

Social studies of science based upon the 'discursive practices' of scientists are more explicitly social constructionist. According to 'new-wave' social studies of science (Collins, 1981, 1982, 1983; Knorr-Cetina, 1981; Knorr-Cetina and Mulkay, 1983; Latour, 1987; Latour and Woolgar, 1986; Pickering, 1984; Shapin and Schaffer, 1985), scientific theories are not putative descriptions of properties of postulated objects. Scientific theories – and the facts identified or objects putatively studied by science – are 'projections' or 'cultural objects' or 'social construc-tions': 'a scientist's activity is directed, not towards reality, but towards . . . operations on sentences' (Latour and Woolgar, 1986: 237).

Such denials of the linguistic objectivity of theoretical descriptions are utterly unfounded, and claims to the effect that social studies of science are studies of 'the construction of pulsars, brain peptides, N-rays' and the like (Potter, 1992: 168) – as opposed to the construction of *theories* of pulsars, brain peptides, N-rays, and the like – may be dismissed as rhetorical legerdemain. As in the case of Gergen's general social constructionist position, such accounts of the social construction and social adjudication of competing theoretical descriptions are entirely parasitic upon implicit assumptions about their linguistic objectivity. Like Gergen, such theorists also mistakenly presume that the denial of the epistemic objectivity of theoretical descriptions entails a denial of their linguistic objectivity.

Yet these errors need not concern us here. What concerns us here is the denial of epistemic objectivity, which is clear and unambiguous. According to these authors, theories are not empirically evaluated and competing theories are not empirically adjudicated: 'As we come to recognize the conventional and artifactual status of our forms of knowing, we put ourselves in the position to realize that it is ourselves and not reality that is responsible for what we know (Shapin and Shaffer, 1985: 344); '. . . the natural world has a small or nonexistent role in the construction of scientific knowledge' (Collins, 1981: 3). According to these authors, the selection of scientific theories is socio-linguistically negotiated in accord with all sorts of motivational, rhetorical, political, and moral considerations. As Latour (1983: 168) puts it, 'science is politics pursued by other means.' Feminist philosophers of science claim that the dominance of atomistic forms of scientific theory is a product, not of the empirical evidence in favor of atomistic theories, but of the androcentric assumptions of science that serve to perpetuate male dominance in society as well as in science (Harding, 1986; Keller, 1985).

Claims of this sort are regularly endorsed and advanced by social constructionist theorists in social psychological science, including those who engage in feminist or socio-political critiques of traditional social psychology, via attacks on its guiding, constraining, distorting – and socially damaging – ideology. Thus feminists regularly complain that traditional individualist – and hierarchical – theories in social psychology are a product of androcentric approaches to science that reflect male values and support social practices that sustain male dominance (Bleier, 1984; Scheman, 1983). Sampson (1977, 1981) has argued that the self-contained individualism of contemporary psychological theories is a product of, and serves the values of, capitalist economic systems, for example via the institutionalization of competition. Contemporary psychology in general is held to be a product of the socio-economic and political status quo, which it serves to sustain and maintain (Prilleltensky, 1989, 1990).

Now it is fair to say that both the theoretical and methodological adequacy of many of these social studies of science can be and have been seriously questioned (for a critical review, see Burge, 1991, 1992). It is hard, for example, to see the atomistic assumptions of science as a product of the androcentric nature of science. It would be difficult to find more *relational* theories than the theories of relativity and quantum mechanics, yet these twentieth-century theories were almost entirely a product of male-dominated science.

However, particular criticisms of particular studies need not be engaged or labored here. They would not themselves threaten the general legitimacy of the 'strong program' or 'new-wave' social studies of science. Such programs, like the general social constructionist program, are themselves *premised upon the denial of epistemic objectivity*: the denial that competing theories can be empirically adjudicated. If the relativist arguments against epistemic objectivity drawn from post-empirical philosophy of science are sound, there *has to be* a social – or social psychological – explanation of theory adjudication: that is, an explanation *other* than an explanation in terms of the established empirical superiority of one theory over another. Consequently, any errors with respect to particular social studies of science could only lie in the particular social – or social psychological – explanations advanced, and would not threaten the legitimacy of the general explanatory program.

These explanatory programs are themselves premised on the denial of epistemic objectivity of theory evaluation, for the denial of epistemic objectivity does not follow from the recognition of the social dimensions of scientific practice, as many social constructionists seem to suppose (just as, as noted in the previous chapter, denials of linguistic objectivity do not follow from the recognition of the social dimensions of the semantics of scientific theories).

Consequently, criticism of these programs designed to establish the irrelevance of social studies of science are misguided and misdirected, especially when it is argued that social explanations of science only hold in the case of the unscientific adoption of erroneous theories (Lakatos, 1970; Lauden, 1977). This type of criticism simply repeats the fundamental and original error of most social constructionist analyses of science: the error of supposing that a recognition of the social dimensions of science and theory evaluation somehow precludes acceptance of the epistemic objectivity of theory evaluation.

It does not. The mere fact that science is a social enterprise, with its conventions and values, located within broader social collectivities with their (often conflicting) needs and interests, and practiced by persons with diverse motives, emotions, and goals, who deploy rhetorical and other social strategies of self-advancement and self-presentation (and so on), does not itself entail that epistemic objectivity cannot be achieved via the empirical adjudication of competing theories.

According to at least one account of the social dimensions of science and the social psychology of scientists, the fundamental social convention and dominant social value of scientific work is a joint commitment by participants in scientific collectives to the empirical adjudication of theories: the social identity of scientists is determined in accord with their – almost moral – commitment to this convention or value. Consequently, there is a crucial ambiguity in the claim – advanced by Bloor (1976) and Barnes (1982), for example – that all instances of theory adjudication can be given a social explanation. Even if this were the case, it does not follow that they could all be given the *same type of social explanation*, for example, in terms of conformity with certain religious or political or economic principles. Some – or many – may be best explained in terms of decisions made in conformity with social conventions requiring the empirical adjudication of theories: a social form of explanation that treats theory construction and evaluation as 'the product of human actions' (Bloor, 1976: 3), but poses no threat to the epistemic objectivity of theory evaluation.

The degree to which this latter type of social explanation holds with respect to any actual historical instance of theory-adjudication is of course an open question. We know that it does not hold in some cases: namely, in those cases where theoretical decisions are made in the absence of, or well ahead of, any decisive empirical evidence in favor of one theory over another (or others). As Feyerabend (1975) notes, many scientists adopted the Copernican theory long before there was any decisive empirical evidence to favor it over the Ptolemeic theory (long before the telescope observations of the stellar parallax), which is why Feyerabend's account of the original acceptance of the Copernican theory in terms of Galileo's 'deception and trickery' is so convincing.

Unfortunately, many of the social studies of science advanced by those committed to the 'strong program' or some version of social construc-tionism do not enable us to assess how frequently theoretical decisions are made without reference to their empirical support. By refusing to consider the adequacy of the theories concerned – by reference to their empirical support at the time of their adoption – most researchers simply refuse to consider or take seriously the possibility that theoretical choices are sometimes – and perhaps often – made justifiably in accord with social conventions or values concerning the empirical adjudication of theories. Consequently, most of these studies are vitiated as contributions to the social epistemology of science – as empirically grounded theoretical accounts of how scientific theories are in fact socially adjudicated.

The 'Theory-Informity' of Observations

The claim that observations are 'theory-informed' may be denied. It has in fact been subject to sustained criticism, on both psychological and philosophical grounds (Clark and Paivio, 1989; Gilman, 1992; Shapere, 1964). It has been claimed that – in at least some cases – perception is not theoretically 'penetrable.' Thus the lines in the Müller-Lyer diagram still appear to be of a different length even after we learn that it is an illusion and the theoretical explanation of the illusion (Fodor, 1984). Nerve cells have appeared in pretty much the same way under microscopes to generations of lay and scientific observers, throughout historical changes in our theories of the nerve cell and our theories of the microscope (Hacking, 1983).

However, in this chapter I do not deny the claim that observations are theory-informed. Observations are regularly informed by theories – they presuppose, or are constructed in accord with, theories. But this does not pose any threat to the epistemic objectivity of theory evaluation: it does not somehow undermine our ability to adjudicate competing theories empirically. On the contrary, I will argue that the theory-informity of observations actually promotes epistemic objectivity: it frequently enables us to adjudicate empirically between competing theories.

It is important to dissociate the present defense of epistemic objectivity from a variety of common – and obviously frustrated – responses to relativist critiques of epistemic objectivity based upon the avowed theory-informity of observations. One is simply to insist that, although 'observation statements or other types of truth claims will be affected by theory,' nevertheless 'theory can eventually be corrected by comparison to the object itself which stands independently of thought' (Foster, 1987: 109). However, an appeal to this mythical form of theory evaluation plays no role in a realist defense of epistemic objectivity. Theoretical descriptions of atoms or emotions are not adjudicated via any sort of comparison between the theoretical descriptions and atoms and emotions themselves (since, according to the realist, the truth or accuracy of a theory is not determined by the satisfaction of any resemblance relation).

Yet another common response is simply to insist that there is a level of observation or observational description that is either so certain or so uncontaminated by theory that it cannot be denied (Craib, 1986; Eco, 1992): so-called 'death and furniture arguments' (Edwards et al., 1993). Again, this type of response forms no part of a realist defense of epistemic objectivity: the realist recognizes that there are no certain foundations of empirical – far less theoretical – knowledge. All observations and observation descriptions are informed by theories and are consequently revisable in principle (since any theory is revisable in principle); which is not to say that they are likely to be – or ought to be – revised in practice.

Another common response is to insist that scientists just usually are in agreement with respect to empirical judgments or observations, that although natural scientists and psychologists 'regularly disagree concerning which theory best explains a particular set of research results they are usually in agreement concerning descriptions of these data, especially where such descriptions are expressed in simple, commonsense observational terms' (Fletcher, 1993: 19). However, agreement alone is no guarantee of epistemic objectivity, since the relativist or social constructionist might reasonably complain that this may be a simple product of a common commitment to ideologically inspired theoretical constructions. Moreover, it may also be reasonably denied that 'disputes in psychology are hardly ever concerned with basic level descriptions of data' (Fletcher, 1993: 19). At least in social psychology, a great many disputes revolve precisely around the question of whether subjects in experimental studies were really aggressive, dishonest, cooperative, obedient, and the like (for reasons documented at the end of Chapter 1).

There is, however, more point to the last objection than first appears. It is important to recognize that scientists – even and especially *those holding competing theories* – regularly do agree in their theoretically informed empirical judgments, and to recognize the reasons for this.

The theory-informity of observations would only pose a threat to epistemic objectivity if the theories that do inform epistemically significant observations in science are identical to – or entail or presuppose – any of the competing theories that are the object of empirical adjudication. While this may occasionally be the case – the possibility cannot be excluded a priori – it is plainly not invariably or even regularly the case. The Watson–Crick theory of the double-helical structure of the DNA molecule was confirmed by the outcome of the X-ray diffraction studies produced by Rosalind Franklin. These observations were informed by the theory of X-ray diffraction, but *not* by Watson and Crick's theory of the double-helical structure of DNA. The theory of X-ray diffraction is not identical to – and does not entail or presuppose – Watson and Crick's theory of the double-helical structure of DNA, or any of the other theories about the structure of DNA advanced at the time (such as the theories advanced by Linus Pauling): it only states how different structures will appear under X-ray diffraction.

Analogously, experimental or field observations of humans attending or failing to attend to apparently suffering victims may be theoretically informed by the assumptions that such behaviors constitute instances of caring or apathy: in fact, they *have to be* if such experimental or field studies are to tell us anything about the conditions that promote or impede caring or apathy. However, such theoretically informed observations (or the theories that undoubtedly do inform them) do not entail or presuppose any theoretical causal explanation of the conditions that promote – or determine – 'bystander apathy.' They do not, for example, entail or presuppose that the probability of intervention will decrease as the number of other bystanders present increases (Latané and Darley, 1970). Whether the experiment or field study supports any particular explanation of bystander apathy depends upon whether the conditions cited by theories that purport to explain 'bystander apathy' are instantiated in the experiments or field studies, and this is not vouchsafed by characterizing behaviors as instances of apathy.

That is, the significant observations that enable scientists to adjudicate empirically between competing *explanatory* theories, based upon postulated structures, properties, or processes, are generally informed by quite different *exploratory* theories (to coin a convenient alternative description[1]): that is, theories that are not identical to, and are logically independent of, the competing explanatory theories that are the object of empirical evaluation.

Given the theory of X-ray diffraction, and given that theorists committed to different accounts of the structure of DNA accepted the theory of X-ray diffraction, the observations made by Rosalind Franklin established that DNA has a double-helical structure. The exploratory theory of X-ray diffraction – far less any of the competing explanatory theories of the structure of DNA – did not itself determine what would be observed by Rosalind Franklin, and eventually by Watson and Crick. The theory of X-ray diffraction only specifies how structures appear under X-ray diffraction: it specifies how DNA would appear if DNA has a double-helical structure, and how DNA would appear if it has a different structure. It is a contingent fact that DNA appeared the way it did under X-ray diffraction, as predicted by the theoretical description of its double-helical structure (in conjunction with the theory of X-ray diffraction), thus providing differential support for the double-helix theory over its rivals. *Nothing guaranteed that it would*: in particular it was not guaranteed by either the double-helical theory *or* the theory of X-ray diffraction. This explains, of course, why Watson and Crick went to such enormous lengths to get their hands on Rosalind Franklin's jealously guarded data (e.g. by one distracting her attention while the other searched her laboratory, by attempts to get her drunk over dinner and divulge her results, and so on (Watson, 1978)), which is hard to explain if one holds the view that any observations can be accommodated by interpretation in accord with any explanatory theory.

It is true that those who held an alternative theory of the structure of DNA could have refused to accept this evidence as supportive of the double-helix theory by denying the theory of X-ray diffraction. However, they could not have done so without cost: not only by denying a promising means of empirically adjudicating between the competing theories of the structure of DNA, but also by abandoning the empirical support for a whole range of other explanatory theories also based upon observations informed by the theory of X-ray diffraction.

Moreover, it cannot be assumed, yet all too regularly is assumed, that modifications of exploratory theories (or other assumptions or posits) can always be made that both accommodate results anomalous for an explanatory theory *and* preserve evidential parity with competing explanatory theories. This leads us to consideration of the so-called 'Quine–Duhem' thesis.

The Quine–Duhem Thesis

According to the Quine–Duhem thesis, it is always possible to accommodate a failed prediction by the modification or replacement of exploratory theories, causal posits, or auxiliary hypotheses employed in the derivation of the failed prediction. As a general logical principle, this is of course true. It is always logically possible to accommodate any particular result in this way. As Quine (1953: 43) puts it with respect to particular propositions: 'any proposition can be held true come what may, if we make drastic enough adjustments elsewhere in the system.' However, it does not follow with respect to any failed prediction derived from an explanatory theory that adjustments or modifications can always be made with respect to exploratory theories or auxiliary hypotheses that can both accommodate recalcitrant observations *and* preserve evidential parity with a competing explanatory theory (or theories). Whether this strategy is *epistemically viable* with respect to any explanatory theory in any particular case is an entirely different – and ultimately empirical – question. Some adjustments and modifications are simply too drastic: they undermine the prior empirical support for a theory (reducing its overall empirical support).

A theory may be said to be *epistemically viable* if it can originally accommodate a range of diverse empirical data, and can continue to accommodate any relevant empirical data while preserving its original empirical support[2] (which justified our adopting it in the first place). However, it is clear that many modifications of exploratory theories, causal posits, or auxiliary hypotheses to accommodate recalcitrant data will *not* preserve the epistemic viability of an explanatory theory. If certain exploratory theories or auxiliary hypotheses have been employed in the logical derivation of previous empirical results (in the successful prediction of these empirical results), then the modification or replacement of such exploratory theories or auxiliary hypotheses will result in the elimination or reduction of the original empirical support for the theory. The theory will no longer be able to accommodate the original empirical results: the original successful predictions will no longer be derivable. When competing explanatory theories that share the same empirical support license different predictions in a novel empirical domain, then it is rational to prefer the theory that makes the correct prediction, if modifications cannot be made that preserve the epistemic viability of the competing theory (or theories). In such circumstances, although we cannot talk about logically conclusive empirical results, we can talk about epistemically decisive ones, and can identify them in the history of science.

Consider the case of the observation of the deviant motion of Mercury's perihelion, which effectively falsified Newton's theory at the turn of the century.[3] How was this possible? Kuhn claims that this 'anomaly' generated a crisis for Newtonian theory. It certainly did, but it is hard to see how Kuhn can explain or justify this, since, as Gergen (1988: 10) rightly complains, 'it is difficult to see how such anomalies could emerge' if – as Kuhn maintains and Gergen insists – 'facts are themselves theoretically saturated': that is, if observations are theory-informed.

The reason why observations of the deviant orbit of Mercury's perihelion could be seen as anomalous for Newton's theory is simple enough. Although these observations were theory-informed, they were informed by *theories of telescopics*, not by Newton's gravitational theory. Now Newtonians did consider and try a number of strategies to accommodate the anomalous motion of Mercury's perihelion. In the late eighteenth century Leverrier had accommodated observations of the deviant or anomalous orbit of Uranus by modifying an auxiliary assumption about the number of planets. He postulated another planet beyond Uranus, and predicted where it had to be (and its mass and diameter) in order for it to account for the orbit of Uranus in accord with Newton's theory, and within a few days Neptune was detected in the required position. In the late nineteenth century Newtonians took the same tack by postulating an additional planet within the orbit of Mercury, and predicted where it had to be in order for it to account for the orbit of Mercury's perihelion in accord with Newton's theory. They even gave it a name – Vulcan. However, in this case the strategy failed – no planet could be detected in the predicted position.

Newtonians could not have accommodated the orbit of Mercury's perihelion by modifying or replacing the exploratory theory of telescopics that informed the observations that caused the 'crisis' for Newtonian gravitational theory. If they had, they would have abandoned all the prior empirical support for Newtonian gravitational theory based upon the original exploratory theory: that is, the bulk of the support for Newtonian gravitational theory. Given a different exploratory theory, the predictions of Mercury's perihelion could have come out right: but the predictions of the orbit of Uranus, Neptune, and just about everything else extra-terrestrial would have come out wrong. To adopt such a strategy in this case would not have been epistemically viable: it would have made a bad situation far worse.

That is, since exploratory theories that inform recalcitrant observations are also liable to inform a whole range of other observations that support an explanatory theory, then we may doubt that these exploratory theories (or other auxiliary hypotheses and the like) can always be modified or replaced to protect an explanatory theory from falsification, since it is doubtful if such modifications or replacements will always preserve the epistemic viability of the explanatory theory. In the nineteenth century some defenders of Prout's theory of the integral values of the atomic weights of elements suggested dismissing the deviant fractional weight of chlorine as due to inadequacies of separation and purification techniques. However, most scientists recognized that the adoption of this strategy would have cast equal doubt upon the approximately integral values of the measured weights of other elements that provided the original support for Prout's theory, and dropped Prout's theory for this very good reason. Analogously, it would be difficult for a genetic explanation of intelligence differences to accommodate recalcitrant data – that suggested a social or environmental explanation of these differences – by casting doubt upon the adequacy of standard tests used to measure intelligence and intelligence differences, for this would cast equal doubt upon any prior observations in favor of the genetic explanation that presupposed the adequacy of such tests.

Contrary to what is normally supposed, the fact that theoretical descriptions are linked to empirical predictions not directly (as noted in Chapter 2, they are semantically autonomous with respect to them), but by networks of auxiliary hypotheses and causal posits, and the fact that observations are themselves informed by exploratory theories (independent of the explanatory theories being empirically evaluated) *promotes* rather than undermines the epistemic objectivity of theory evaluation: for it is precisely what enables us to demonstrate – in many actual cases – that some theories are not epistemically viable.

It is important to distinguish the sorts of examples discussed above from quite different sorts of examples often deployed in support of the claim that the theory-informity of observations undermines epistemic objectivity. An example favored by relativists is Hanson's (1958) example of Brahe and Kepler – respectively supporters of the geocentric and heliocentric theories – facing east at dawn. Neither could appeal to what he observed to adjudicate between the geocentric and heliocentric theories. Brahe would have seen what transpired *as* an instance of the sun rising against a fixed horizon; Kepler would have seen it *as* an instance of the horizon rolling beneath a stationary sun. That is, their observations would have been informed by their respective *explanatory theories*. However, all this example shows is that the geocentric and heliocentric theories could not be empirically adjudicated by reference to this type of observation, which, like the so-called 'tower experiment' (as pointed out by Feyerabend (1975)) could be easily accommodated by both explanatory theories.

Yet one can *never* empirically adjudicate between competing explanatory theories by reference to empirical data that can be accommodated by the competing theories. Empirical adjudication can be achieved only by reference to empirical data that can be accommodated by only one explanatory theory but not the other (or others): by judgments about the epistemic viability of the competing theories in such circumstances. The geocentric and heliocentric theories were not in fact empirically adjudicable until the development of telescopics and the observation of the stellar parallax (the critical prediction of the heliocentric theory), which could not be accommodated by the geocentric theory.

To suggest that all forms of empirical evidence are of the same epistemic status as Brahe and Kepler observing the 'sunrise' is simply to beg the question in favor of the relativist account. It is to claim that no form of empirical evidence ever enables us to make judgments about the epistemic viability of competing explanatory theories. Yet as argued above, this is just false. Likewise, familiar relativist claims that observation in science is like the observation of the ambiguous figures of gestalt psychology – in which the line drawing can be seen as a rabbit or as a duck, for example – also simply beg the question. Such figures are specifically designed to be ambiguous – to generate two undecidable interpretative alternatives.[4]

We should also be careful to distinguish examples in which enthusiasm for a theory deludes researchers into claiming to discriminate what actually cannot be discriminated. In 1903, eight years after Röntgen discovered X-rays, the French physicist Blondlot announced his discovery of the existence and properties of a new type of radiation that he called N-rays. In the years up to 1905 there were a profusion of scientific reports of N-rays. In 1905 the American professor of optics and spectroscopy R.W. Woods visited Blondlot's laboratory. After being treated to an 'experimental demonstration' of the new phenomena, Woods denied that any rays were in fact polarized and refracted through quartz prisms, as Blondlot and his followers claimed: their 'observations' were simply a product of wishful thinking. After Woods published his account of his visit to Blondlot's laboratory, there were no further experimental reports of N-rays (although Blondlot never relinquished his belief in them). This type of theory-informity of observations – driven by *explanatory theories* – is quite different from the forms of exploratory-theory-informity discussed above and, when actualized, undermines rather than promotes epistemic objectivity. To claim that all examples of the theory-informity of observations in science are analogous to the theory-informed 'observations' of N-rays is again simply to beg the question. The X-ray diffraction data that enabled the empirical adjudication of competing structural theories of DNA were not theory-informed in this fashion, that is, by any of the *explanatory theories* of the structure of DNA; they were informed by the exploratory theory of X-ray diffraction.

Realism and Epistemic Viability

I do not claim a priori that it is never possible to make adjustments or modifications that can accommodate both a failed prediction and the original support for an explanatory theory, or that it is never possible to do this to preserve evidential parity with a competing explanatory theory. The point is rather that it is a *contingent matter* whether epistemic viability can be preserved in this way in any particular case.

I recognize that this strategy can sometimes be successfully employed, as in the case of Newton's theory and the orbit of Uranus. Yet it was a *contingent matter* whether this strategy could be employed in this case – it could not be in the case of Newton's theory and the orbit of Mercury's perihelion. The preservation of the epistemic viability of explanatory theories via modifications or adjustments of exploratory theories or auxiliary hypotheses is simply not guaranteed a priori by any philo-sophical – or social or psychological – argument, contrary to what most relativists and social constructionists suppose.

There are also no doubt cases where two (or more) competing theories will both (or all) remain epistemically viable in the face of the 'total evidence.' This is sometimes argued with respect to competing theories of space (van Fraassen, 1980), and may be the case with respect to competing theories of 'cognitive units' (Anderson, 1981) and counter-attitudinal behavior (Greenwald, 1975). If this is a fact about these competing explanatory theories, it has to be faced. Yet no argument advanced by relativists or social constructionists establishes that this is regularly – far less invariably – the case.

It is also true that sometimes theories that are rejected for good empirical reasons can make a comeback – may become epistemically viable – at a later date. By adopting a modified version of Prout's hypothesis to include isotopes, it became possible to accommodate both the average fractional weight of chlorine and the original integral weights of elements, as well as accounting for a range of novel empirical data predicted in accord with the isotope assumption. Again whether this turns out to be the case is a contingent matter. The phlogiston theory was abandoned because it was no longer epistemically viable, but it never made a comeback: it never became epistemically viable again.

The present argument does demonstrate that, contrary to common relativist and social constructionist accounts, the fact that theoretical structures form a 'web of belief' (Quine and Ullian, 1970) – an interrelated structure of theoretical descriptions, causal hypotheses, and auxiliary assumptions, supported by a range of empirical data informed by exploratory theories – *decreases* rather than increases the room for intellectual maneuver when scientists are faced with failed predictions or 'anomalies.' Moreover, as theoretical sciences become more advanced and accommodate an increasingly wide range of empirical data, it becomes increasingly difficult to modify or change parts of the structure to accommodate failed predictions, because assumptions used to generate the failed prediction are so closely tied to the prior empirical support for the theory. This explains why, at least in the case of advanced theoretical sciences, rather than there being a host of epistemically viable theories that can all provide a theoretical accommodation of a varied range of empirical data at any point in time, at any point in time working scientists consider themselves very fortunate if they can come up with *one* epistemically viable theory. Oftentimes they cannot – often enough none of a number of competing explanatory theories are epistemically viable.

Now this account of epistemic objectivity will not satisfy those empiricists or social constructionists who insist that our empirical evaluation of scientific theories can only be epistemically objective if there is some way of comparing our theoretical descriptions with theoretical reality, or testing them via observations that are not themselves theory-informed, or that can be known with certainty. These requirements can never be satisfied, but they were misguided in the first place. The certainty requirement in particular derives from misguided attempts to assimilate natural, social, and psychological sciences to mathematics (with its self-evidently true axioms) or to the dictates of religious authority. Yet theoretical science has no certain foundations: its warrant and whatever intellectual authority it has derive from its commitment to the empirical evaluation and adjudication of theories.

Nevertheless, the present account does satisfy the general requirements of a realist analysis of epistemic objectivity. This account does enable us to characterize our acceptance and rejection and adjudication of explanatory theories, based upon our exploratory-theory-informed observations, as governed and constrained by the nature of reality, and *not* by our ideological predilections. It is ultimately the nature of the natural, social, and psychological world that determines the epistemic viability of our explanatory and exploratory theories.

This is not to beg the question about how our theoretical judgments are in fact determined. As noted above, the argument only demonstrates that theoretical decisions can be justifiably based upon judgments about the epistemic viability of theories. It does not guarantee that theoretical conflicts can be empirically adjudicated in any particular case: according to the present account, it is a contingent matter whether they can be in any particular case. (It is also a contingent matter whether theoretical conflicts were in fact empirically adjudicated – rather than morally or ideologically adjudicated – in historical situations where they could have been.)

However, since it is a contingent matter whether accommodations of recalcitrant data can be made to preserve the epistemic viability of explanatory theories, we are entitled to the realist presumption that our theoretical judgments can be, and often enough are – based upon the examples cited earlier and others that could be readily deployed – grounded in the nature of the natural, social, and psychological world, rather than being based upon our ideological predilections: namely, precisely when we can provide a potential or actual account of the theoretical decisions of scientists in terms of judgments about epistemic viability – in terms of decisions made in accord with social conventions concerning the empirical adjudication of theories.

To claim that it is ultimately the nature of natural, social, and psychological reality that determines the epistemic viability of our explanatory and exploratory theories is not to beg the question in favor of realism either. In particular, it is not to maintain that such a claim is grounded in some form of extra-theoretical or extra-linguistic access to reality: our access to natural, social, and psychological reality is only via our exploratory-theory-informed empirical evaluations of explanatory theories. It is simply to recognize that there are limits to what can be accommodated by our explanatory and exploratory theories, and that these limits are imposed by the phenomena to which our theoretical endeavours are directed – whatever their ultimate nature. Realism does not of course assume that we can ever determine their ultimate nature, far less determine it a priori. All the realist maintains is that it is their ultimate nature that constrains our attempts at theoretical accommodation at the explanatory and exploratory level: that this is what ensures the contingency of the question whether particular explanatory theories are epistemically viable.

Contrary to what most relativists and social constructionists claim, it is simply not always epistemically open to us to make accommodations of empirical data to suit our favored explanatory theories when faced with anomalous empirical results. Moreover, this external constraint applies all the way down to the level of basic exploratory theories and empirical descriptions. It is simply not the case that any exploratory theory can accommodate any range of empirical data. The heroic – or bloody-minded – theorist who holds an alternative theory of the structure of DNA and who refuses to accept the evidence provided by X-ray diffraction studies, informed by the original exploratory theory of X-ray diffraction, might introduce a new exploratory theory to accommodate the X-ray diffraction data, even though this requires the abandonment or falsification of other explanatory theories supported by empirical data informed by the original exploratory theory of X-ray diffraction. Yet there is simply no guarantee that this new exploratory theory will be able to accommodate any other range of X-ray diffraction data that ought to fit with her theory of the structure of DNA, or any other favored explanatory theories for which X-ray diffraction data are relevant. The same is true even on the most basic level of empirical descriptions: there are empirical limits to the types of descriptions that can be employed, based upon what is commonly discriminable by humans.

These constraints also reach all the way up to rationality itself: to the basic rules or norms of logic. This is not to claim that rationality – or logic – is extra-linguistic or absolute, or to deny that in some sense it is a socio-linguistic construction. The basic rules or norms of logic are modifiable in principle: logicians and scientists have considered modifying the law of excluded middle to accommodate some of the anomalous indeterminacies of quantum mechanical theory. Yet it remains a contingent question whether such modifications are epistemically viable in any particular case, including the case of quantum mechanics, and it cannot be assumed that there is – or are – any epistemically viable general alternative – or alternatives. Certainly there are none to be found on the contemporary intellectual horizon.[5]

None of this is to deny that scientific communities, or individual scientists, may sometimes – and perhaps often – make theoretical decisions on ideological grounds irrespective of the available evidence, or refuse to face the epistemic implications of their empirical research. There seems little doubt that the adoption of biological theories suggesting the intellectual – and moral – superiority of Caucasian races in the early twentieth century were driven by ideological assumptions and not by the available – and ambiguous – empirical data (Gould, 1981; Leahey, 1992). Blondlot never abandoned his belief in N-rays, and Morley never abandoned his belief in the ether (despite the fact that his attempt to measure 'ether drift' – the Michelson–Morley experiment – clearly suggested the absence of any 'ether'). All that has been maintained is that no argument or evidence demonstrates that this is regularly – far less invariably – the case.

Theory Evaluation in Social Psychological Science

All the points and arguments discussed in the previous sections apply with equal force in the domain of social psychological science. At the very least, the social psychological scientist is epistemically no worse off than any other scientist when it comes to the empirical adjudication of explanatory theories, and indeed – as Vico suggested in the seventeenth century – may enjoy unique and considerable epistemic advantages.

Social constructionists advance a number of arguments suggesting that there are special reasons for doubting the epistemic objectivity of theory evaluation in social psychological science. However, none of these have any real merit, and they often merely reiterate standard – and misguided – empiricist doubts about epistemic objectivity.

Gergen (1982: 62), for example, claims that the identification and explanation of any action is 'subject to infinite revision.' It is not empirically grounded – any action can be accommodated by a variety of different (and competing) interpretations. Thus (to cite Gergen's fictional example) Ross's reaching out to touch Laura's hair at a social gathering could be treated as a 'signal of affection' or as a 'mark of derision.' According to Gergen, the expansion of our analysis of the context (to include what he calls the 'retrospective' and 'emergent' contexts) only *multiplies* the number of plausible identificatory and explanatory interpretations.

It is true that a number of different and competing identifications and explanations are epistemically viable when actions are considered in isolation, but more often than not attention to details of the context (and past history and the like) does not preserve the epistemic viability of the original interpretations, far less increase the number of epistemically viable interpretations. On the contrary, it usually becomes increasingly difficult to accommodate theoretically all the details of behavior and context, to the point where only one interpretation remains epistemically viable.

A good example of this is the research project conducted – over three years – by the Belgian psychiatrist J.P. De Waele (1971) to produce a detailed psychobiography of imprisoned murderers (as a means of judging whether they are likely to murder again if released). This type of research project employs a team of researchers, comprising about a dozen sociologists, psychologists, and psychiatrists, and including the murderer as a voluntary and active member of the research team. After extensive interviews with the murderer, colleagues, family members, and others associated with the murderer, record checks, and batteries of psychological tests, the project culminates in a jointly produced and agreed psychobiography of the murderer. The research project generates a mass of data, and although researchers begin with a variety of competing accounts and analyses, they almost invariably find that by the end of the three years only one remains epistemically viable – only one theoretical explanatory account can provide an accommodation of the range of theory-informed data (De Waele, 1992).

Of course researchers rarely have the time or resources to engage in this type of intensive inquiry, and I do not claim that they should – or need to – in order to achieve epistemic objectivity. Rather I employ this well documented example to illustrate the instantiation of a principle within social psychological science, which regularly holds with respect to the empirical adjudication of theories in natural science: that an increase in the (theoretically informed) empirical data base tends to *reduce* – rather than increase – the number of epistemically viable explanatory theories. There is no reason to suppose that this general principle does not hold in social psychological science – or in everyday life, for that matter.

Gergen (1982: 70–1) also claims that virtually any form of behavior treated as a measure of one postulated psychological state can be treated as a measure of any other psychological state, and that consequently theoretical claims about psychological states cannot be empirically adjudicated by reference to behavior. For example, the action of going out of one's way to help another in trouble could be construed in some circumstances as a measure of 'need for social approval,' and in other circumstances as a measure of 'hostility.'

This is only true in the sense that it is always logically possible to explain any isolated behavior by reference to any theoretical psychological state, given a sufficiently elaborate story citing – perhaps rather special and peculiar – circumstances. The epistemic viability of such a theoretical account is of course a different question, especially when we look to the details of the actual circumstances. Thus, for example, the epistemic viability of an explanation of an agent's going out of her way to help another in trouble in terms of 'need for social approval' is seriously threatened if the agent in question goes to great lengths to maintain anonymity, and if we establish that she has also done this in the past (assuming that in the present case she is unaware of any psychologists observing her). It is simply not true that in specified social circumstances, governed by conventions and grounded in forms of folk knowledge that are available to any socially competent person, a wide variety of competing theoretical psychological explanations of a particular behavior are epistemically viable: in a great many everyday social contexts, an explanation of helping in terms of hostility is not.

Gergen (1988: 10) claims that, because of these supposed problems, the meaning or intention of an action is never 'transparent.' Yet in actual fact, given details of the context, and knowledge of the conventions of the forms of life in which we are socially competent participants, it often is. Ironically, despite his regular rhetorical references to social context and conventions, Gergen fails to grasp Wittgenstein's point that the meaning or intention of an action often *is* transparent precisely because of its 'imbeddedness' in the social context: 'We tell a man who has driven his car over a curb, up a steep hill, thus running down the man who was blackmailing him, that his car was not out of control. Such cases lead us very readily to think of intentions as "imbedded in human customs and situations" (Wittgenstein, *Investigations*, para 337)' (Louch, 1967: 112).

Gergen claims that since action descriptions reference intentions, they cannot be descriptions of spatiotemporally locatable behaviors, and consequently cannot be subject to empirical evaluation: 'When we speak of a person being aggressive, obedient, conforming, and the like, we are speaking not of the overt movements of the body but of his or her psychic dispositions' (1988: 9). It was of course precisely for reasons of this sort that empiricist psychologists felt obliged to conclude that psychology should restrict itself to the description and explanation of behavior *simpliciter*. This enabled them to avoid – but not resolve – this supposed problem concerning action identification.

However, Gergen's argument in support of this claim is fallacious. It is true that actions cannot be identified with behaviors per se, and that they cannot be identified with classes of behaviors individuated according to their common physical dimensions. There are very many behavioral ways in which persons can be aggressive, dishonest, and the like, and to attribute such actions to a person is to ascribe the appropriate intention. However, it does not follow that actions are not spatiotemporally locatable behaviors. On the contrary, most human actions just are – are to be identified with – purposive or directed behaviors: aggressive actions, for example, are just those multifarious behaviors directed towards the injury of another; acts of succor – or helping – are just those multifarious behaviors directed towards relieving the distress of another, and so on. As noted above, there is no special problem concerning the identification of those intentional behaviors that are human actions, given our access to context and conventions – except in artificial experimental situations, where the context and conventions are far from clear (Greenwood, 1989).

It is also important to recall (from Chapter 2) that although descriptions of certain behaviors as acts of aggression or dishonesty or succor do presuppose that the behavior was directed or intentional in the appropriate way – in this respect such empirical descriptions are informed by these exploratory theories – such descriptions do not entail or presuppose any of a possible variety of competing theoretical psychological explanations of these forms of action. For example, the description or identification of a behavior as an aggressive action leaves it quite open whether the aggressive action is best explained in terms of motives of revenge, exposure to 'violent stimuli' (Berkowitz and LePage, 1967), or abnormal excitations of the lateral hypothalamus. None of these explanations are vouchsafed by the correct description or identification of a behavior as an aggressive action. Thus, *contra* Gergen (1987b: 122), such theoretical explanations of aggressive actions are not trivial or circular conceptual truths.

Gergen (1982) also follows the standard empiricist line in denying that agent accounts of their actions and psychological states can provide us with any empirical grounds for their identification. In Chapter 10 I will argue that the generally reliable ability of human agents to provide accounts of their intentions, emotions, and motives constitutes one of the most powerful exploratory resources of social psychological science (albeit one that is presently underexploited and systematically misunderstood): in this respect social psychological scientists have very considerable epistemic advantages over natural scientists.

Nevertheless, in the present historical moment, the arguments of this chapter only establish that there are no impediments in principle to epistemic objectivity in social psychological science. It remains an open question whether contemporary social psychological science is epistemically objective.

There are good reasons to doubt that it is. Often enough it does appear that the same empirical data can be accommodated by a number of different explanatory theories, which explains why social constructionism does often enough provide a plausible interpretation of the *current state* of social psychological science. The critical question, of course, is why this is the case. According to the present account, it is precisely because of the anemic nature of contemporary social psychological theory and the impoverished and artificial nature of many empirical studies, especially experimental studies: both more or less direct consequences of the abiding commitment to traditional empiricism, which restricts the contents of theories to operational definitions, and the subject matter of social psychological science to observable behavior.

It may also be doubted if there has been any significant theoretical progress in social psychological science to date (Gergen, 1973, 1982), for the same sort of reasons.[6] Yet it remains an open – and ultimately empirical – question whether epistemic objectivity can be achieved in social psychological science, and whether significant theoretical progress can be made in the future. A realist can remain optimistic about this. A richer body of theoretical descriptions (whose contents are based on theoretical modeling), in conjunction with a mature body of theory-informed empirical data derived from a variety of sources, including agent accounts, might very well enable social psychological science to become epistemically objective, by making it possible to assess the epistemic viability of competing explanatory theories. At present, however, we are nowhere near it. Indeed what is primarily required is a richer body of theory-informed empirical descriptions of behavior with which to begin the enterprise (Moscovici, 1989).

There is, of course, no guarantee that epistemic objectivity will be achieved, or that it will be achieved with respect to all theories. In some areas of theoretical conflict there may be cases where two or more theories are – and remain – epistemically viable (and one reason for this may be moral constraints on the type of empirical studies that can be conducted). As noted in the previous chapter, in these circumstances – but only in these circumstances - a restricted form of social constructionism might be true and applicable.

However, since no arguments or evidence presently suggest that theoretical descriptions cannot be empirically adjudicated, social psychological scientists have no reason to accept or adopt moral criteria for theory selection (Gergen, 1985), or those derived from literary theory, rhetoric, democratic politics, or whatever. To adopt these criteria would be to abandon social psychological science. This is not to deny the legitimacy of other intellectual disciplines. But we ought not to labor under any illusions. If there are no disciplines whose theoretical explanations can be empirically adjudicated, then there are no sciences as traditionally conceived. None of the relativist arguments discussed in this chapter establish this doubtful conclusion.

Theories and the Social Dimension

Gergen (1982) does not object to the employment of theories, but extols their social virtues, recommending 'theoretical audacity' in social psychological science. This is consistent with his relativist position: it makes a virtue out of a purported necessity. However, the purported necessity is no necessity at all.

Others object to the employment of theories, and see this as the source of the basic problems in social psychological science. For example, Linda Nicolson (1991) complains of the 'arrogance of theory' (although it turns out that she complains – with some justification – of the arrogance of many theorists). John Shotter (1985, 1987, 1992) also sees the problem as deriving from the employment of theories in social psychological science: according to Shotter, this obscures and leads to the neglect of certain important features of social life. In Shotter's terms, the employment of such theories renders certain aspects of social life 'rationally invisible': 'The *formative* nature of rhetorical language is such that the very stating of a theory works rhetorically to influence our perceptions selectively: to render aspects of our own activities "rationally invisible" to us' (1987: 283).

This complaint is partly based upon a misconception, insofar as it is expressed as a complaint about the realist analysis of theory: 'why study such [social] conditions and activities only in terms of models and analogs of them? Why not formulate accounts of the *real* politico-moral transactions people conduct between themselves, rather than analogs of them?' (Shotter, 1992: 179). However, the realist does not restrict the content of theory in *any* way: the appeal to theoretical models merely explains how meaning can be extended and developed in theoretical descriptions. According to the realist, there is no reason why theoretical descriptions in social psychological science cannot be putative descriptions of the '*real* politico-moral transactions people conduct among themselves,' nor does the realist deny that the accounts offered by participants in such 'politico-moral transactions' *might* be superior to those offered by professional social psychologists: according to the realist, this is an open and empirical question.

Nonetheless, one always ought to be at least mildly suspicious of anyone who wishes to dispense with theories: as in the case of the anti-theoretical stance of radical behaviorists, such claims are usually employed to privilege a preferred theory or set of theories. It is quite clear that Shotter thinks that the accounts offered by participants in social action are superior to those offered by professional social psychologists, who tend to neglect the social dimensions of human action, identity, emotion, and the like.

These claims take us to the heart of the matter. Shotter maintains that there are important social phenomena that are ignored by traditional theories in social psychology and that deserve serious study. It is true that traditional empiricist forms of social psychology have neglected the social dimension, as I will argue in the following chapter. Yet, at the end of the day – somewhat ironically – a similar charge may be advanced against social constructionism.

The point may be made in the following fashion. Those of a realist or objectivist inclination might be sympathetic to many of the arguments already advanced in this work. Yet they might remain reluctant to accept the conclusions as applied to social psychological science. They might – as a great many do – hold that there is a far more intimate and constitutive connection between theories and phenomena in the case of social psychological phenomena than there is between theories and phenomena in the case of natural phenomena. They might hold that, although atoms and antelopes may be said to exist independently of our theories about them, human actions and social relations, and in particular psychological phenomena such as identity and emotion, are – at least partially – constituted by our lay and scientific theories about them.

Thus it may be objected that although a realist account works well for natural sciences, it is necessarily limited as an account of social psychological science, because in social psychological science the phenomena are not suitably – or sufficiently – *independent* of our theoretical conceptions of them:

> However, the realist emphasis has its limitations when applied to the human realm, where we are not so much concerned with natural objects and the dynamic processes that govern these objects as we are with human meaning and its elaboration into complex systems: linguistic, political, legal, familial, and so forth. It is here that we see that the realm of inquiry is not so much *given*, in the realist sense, as it is *constructed* through human action into artifacts (e.g. culture, language, societies, texts, works of art, technologies, etc.). (Salner, 1988: 69)

This objection reveals the major error of social constructionism and all positions mildly sympathetic to it: that the social dimensions of identity, emotion, action, self-knowledge, and the like are a constitutive product of our *theories about them*. Yet socially constructed phenomena such as identity and emotion *are* given to us in the realist's sense: they are given to us as socially constructed phenomena that exist independently of our socially constructed theories about them.

By restricting the social dimensions of identity and emotion, for example, to the social dimensions of our socially constructed theories of them, social constructionists end up with an *impoverished* account of the social dimensions of identity and emotion. They cannot – and do not – provide any account of the social dimensions of identity and emotion themselves. The social dimensions of identity and emotion are rendered 'rationally invisible' by the social constructionist account.

The great virtue of a realist account of theoretical descriptions in social psychological science is that it enables us to recognize that identity and emotion can and do have social dimensions *independently* of the social dimensions of our theories about them. To this issue we now turn. First, however, we need some working account of the social.

Notes

1 The term is also designed to suggest the utility of such theories that regularly do inform significant observations in science. Of course the distinction between explanatory and

exploratory theories is relative, not absolute: an explanatory theory may sometimes be employed as an exploratory theory, and any exploratory theory can be explanatory. This does not affect the main point that the theories informing observations employed in the empirical adjudication of competing theories are rarely to be identified with any of the competing theories (and in fact the rare cases in which they can be identified cause no special epistemic problems – see Greenwood (1990)).

2 These two conditions are held to be necessary conditions of epistemic viability. It follows that judgments of the epistemic viability of theories can only be made after theories have been given some time to develop. But that seems right.

3 However, Newton's theory was not abandoned until there was something better to replace it with – namely, Einstein's theory.

4 Collins (1983: 90) remarks with respect to the duck–rabbit figure: 'The nicest feature of this example is that we can see how foolish it is to ask which of these it *really* is.' This just demonstrates the question-begging nature of the example. A clearer example to illustrate social constructionist claims would be the situation where one was face to face with an animal in broad daylight: the social constructionist claims that competing theories about what kind of animal it is cannot be empirically adjudicated, and that it is foolish to ask whether it is really a duck or a rabbit (or some other animal). According to the present account, this is just false.

5 To make this claim is not of course to claim that we, or scientists, or the Azande, or psychologists, or cult members, or logicians, are perfectly rational, or regularly exercise our rationality (Nisbett and Ross, 1980).

6 However, it should also be noted that diachronic changes in theories in psychological science are not necessarily indicative of lack of theoretical development or progress, since they might be indicative of diachronic changes in social psychological phenomena themselves, if – as maintained in this work – such phenomena may vary transhistorically (as well as cross-culturally).

5

The Mark of the Social

Before moving directly to provide some answer to the question of the sense (or senses) in which identity and emotion may be said to be social in nature, I shall attempt to address the more basic question, surprisingly neglected by those who advance claims about the social dimensions of this, that and the next thing: namely, what property or set of properties (or relations) do we attribute when we characterize groups, collectives, actions, agents, development, language, identity, emotion, and the like as *social* in nature?[1] This question is of considerable interest in itself, and the provisional answer to it advanced in this chapter will have significant bearing on the consequent discussion of the social dimensions of identity and emotion (and particularly with reference to social theories of identity).

In this chapter I approach the question by considering the contributions of Durkheim and Weber, the founding fathers of academic sociology, both of whom were concerned to delineate distinctly social phenomena: those phenomena which they held to constitute the appropriate subject matter of sociology.[2] This is for essentially two reasons. In the first place their accounts illustrate two very common errors in conceiving of social phenomena that have vitiated most consequent conceptions of the social, particularly in Anglo-American social psychological science: namely, the treatment of social phenomena as supra-individuals, as entities on a higher ontological stratum than human individuals; and the mistaken identification of the social and the interpersonal. In the second place, despite these shortcomings, the accounts offered by Durkheim and Weber contain the germ of a relatively simple and straightforward but potentially fertile answer to the critical question concerning the demarcation of social phenomena, enabling us to get some real intellectual grip upon a variety of muddled disputes about social phenomena, and to provide some substance to theoretical claims about the social dimensions of identity and emotion.

Durkheim and Social Facts
In the *Rules of Sociological Method* (1895: 50), Durkheim made an attempt to identify the 'distinct characteristics' of social phenomena or 'social facts.' Unfortunately, although he did provide an intuitively acceptable list of social phenomena such as family obligations, legal codes, religious practices, languages, financial instruments, and the like

(1895: 50–1), he failed to provide an account of the 'distinct characteristics' of social phenomena that mark them off from purely
psychological or biological phenomena, for example. He cited two
properties that he held to be common to all the phenomena he
characterized as social facts: they are independent of an individual's
consciousness and will, and constrain his or her behavior. Social facts –
the subject-matter of the scientific discipline of sociology – were thus
characterized by Durkheim as: 'manners of acting, thinking and feeling
external to the individual, which are invested with a coercive power by
virtue of which they exercise control over him' (1895: 52).

However, these two properties of social facts – externality and
constraint – are not properties by virtue of which certain facts are *social*
in nature, as opposed to psychological or biological in nature, for
example. That is, in offering this characterization of social phenomena,
Durkheim was more concerned to characterize those properties of social
phenomena by virtue of which they are appropriate objects of scientific
study – namely, those constitutive of their 'reality' or 'thinghood' – than
to characterize those properties by virtue of which they are social. For
the properties he cited – externality and constraint – are of course
properties shared by the other sorts of objects or 'things' studied by the
various natural sciences, including non-social phenomena such as trees,
tarantulas, and tornadoes.

The source of this error was Durkheim's concern to establish the
objectivity of sociology by demonstrating that social phenomena are as
real as material objects: 'we do not say that social facts are material
things, but that they are things just as are material things' (1901: 35). In
doing so, however, he tended to ignore the critical differences between
social phenomena and material objects. Social phenomena such as
customs and conventions, like material phenomena such as cells and
molecules, exist independently of the consciousness or will of any
particular individual. However, social phenomena such as customs or
conventions, unlike material phenomena such as cells and molecules, do
not exist independently of the consciousness and will of *all* individuals.
On the contrary, they would appear to exist only insofar as they are
instantiated in the psychologies of all those individuals who are party to
the custom or convention. To note such a difference is, however, to deny
neither the – linguistic – objectivity of our descriptions of customs and
conventions, nor the reality of customs and conventions themselves.

Durkheim's emphasis on the reality or 'thing-like' nature of social
phenomena also led him to advance a number of extreme ontological
claims about social phenomena. Although Durkheim recognized that
many social phenomena are generally diffused among individuals, he
nevertheless insisted that every social phenomenon – such as a custom,
practice, or set of obligations – has 'an existence of its own, independent
of its individual manifestations' (1895: 59). Although many social
phenomena – such as collective representations of laws or customs – are

generally diffused among individuals, Durkheim held such individual instantiations to be manifestations of a distinct entity that is the 'collective consciousness': 'The states of the collective consciousness are of a different nature from the states of the individual consciousness; they are representations of another type. The mentality of groups is not that of individuals; it has its own laws' (1901: 40). It is hard to see how social representations could exist independently of their individual instantiations, in the sense of existing independently of all individual instantiations (although they can and do exist independently of any particular individual instantiation). It is, of course, precisely this sort of extreme ontological claim about a mysteriously distinct and independent entity that has led many – and particularly those of an empiricist and individualist persuasion – to dismiss Durkheim's 'holistic' account of social phenomena.

Durkheim seems to have supposed that social phenomena are real – and that there are distinctive forms of social explanation – *only if* social phenomena exist as supra-individuals with distinctive properties and causal powers, as entities of a higher ontological order than the human individuals that compose them:

> ... society is not the mere sum of individuals, but the system formed by their association represents a specific reality which has its own characteristics ... it is in the nature of that individuality and not in that of its component elements that we must search for the proximate and determining causes of the facts produced by it. (1895: 129).

He clearly conceived of the relation between social phenomena and human individuals as formally identical to the relation between cells and the molecules that compose them. According to Durkheim, social facts: 'lie outside the consciousness of individuals as such, in the same way as the distinctive features of life lie outside the chemical substances that make up a living organism' (1901: 40). In both cases we have an entity of a higher ontological stratum whose properties and causal powers are different from the properties and causal powers of the elements out of which it is composed: 'the whole does not equal the sum of its parts: it is something different, whose properties differ from those displayed by the parts from which it is formed' (1895: 128).

I argue that Durkheim was fundamentally wrong in supposing that we must conceive of social phenomena as supra-individuals in order to recognize the reality of social phenomena and the distinctive nature of social explanation. He was nevertheless on the right track in recognizing a number of distinctions critical to the demarcation of social phenomena. For example, he was correct to insist that collective or social representations – of rules, customs, conventions, and the like – are not merely representations shared by – or common to – the members of some population of individuals. There is, for example, an important distinction between those representations that we happen to share because of our common genetic endowment or perceptual experience – such as our representations of the 'deep structure' of grammar or our representations of distance – and those social representations that we share by virtue of our being parties to a set of arrangements or conventions – such as our representations of moral prescriptions and financial practices. These are sufficient grounds to anticipate that there may very well be different and distinctive types of explanation of – and by reference to – social representations and merely shared individual representations – although they are no grounds at all for supposing that social representations exist independently of individual representations.

Moreover, this sort of distinction plays an important role in Durkheim's attempt to articulate the critical distinction between what may be termed genuine *social collectives* that have some form of 'internal structure,' in the sense that they are composed of individuals who are parties to sets of arrangements, conventions, and agreements, and what may be termed *aggregate groups* of individuals that do not have any form of 'internal structure,' characterized by Durkheim as those populations that constitute 'only contingent and provisional aggregates' (1895: 108).

Unfortunately, Durkheim thought that this critical distinction was grounded in the emergent causal powers of supra-individuals, which led him to focus on external causality rather than structure per se in his explication of the distinction. Consequently, he employed the worst sort of example as an example of a genuinely social phenomenon, namely a crowd emotion. A crowd emotion appears to be a paradigm example of a 'contingent and provisional aggregate.' It can often be readily explicated and explained in terms of individual psychology. Statements like 'the crowd was angry,' for example, do seem to reduce analytically to statements like 'all or most of the members of the crowd were angry.' Explanations of the generation of anger in a crowd may be explained by all or most of its members being individually angered by the same state of affairs (the president's speech or the price of bread in the market-place), or by the anger of some being transmitted to most of the others via behavioral cues and signals, in the manner that originally unperturbed individuals may become afraid when they enter the dentist's waiting room and perceive the fear of others (Wrightsman, 1960). The emotional behaviour of individuals in a crowd exemplifies potent interpersonal actions and reactions among members of a certain form of aggregate group. It does not exemplify a social practice manifested by members of a social collective.

That is, aggregate groups such as crowds are quite different from the structured social collectives – such as financial or religious communities – that Durkheim aimed to demarcate as distinctly social phenomena. This is perhaps best illustrated by noting the different transtemporal identity conditions for aggregate groups such as crowds, on the one hand, and structured social collectives, such as City College and the Roman Catholic Church, on the other.

We treat the group of individuals on the street corner or at the ball park on Saturday night as the same crowd on the street corner or at the ball park on Friday night if and only if it is composed of all or most of the same individuals. The transtemporal identity of crowds is determined by identity of composition. In contrast, social collectives such as City College and the Roman Catholic Church maintain their identity over considerable periods of time, despite perhaps total changes in their membership. The transtemporal identity of such social collectives is determined by their maintenance of internal structure – in the form of jointly accepted arrangements, conventions, and agreements.

However, even this way of making the distinction is seriously misleading, and it is easy to see how Durkheim was misled into thinking that it amounts to a distinction between those populations of individuals that constitute supra-individuals – social collectives – and those that do not – aggregate groups.

The distinction between social collectives and aggregate groups is not grounded in any differences with respect to emergent properties. Both social collectives and aggregate groups have emergent properties: that is, properties – including causal properties – that cannot be identified with the properties of their components. Thus the Roman Catholic Church is rich although most of its members are poor, and crowds can fill a town hall but individual members cannot.

Rather, social collectives are different from aggregate groups by virtue of the fact that the former are structured and the latter are not. This is correct, but yet again is potentially very misleading. It suggests that the difference between social collectives and aggregate groups is formally identical to the difference between complex structured entities such as cells and complex non-structured or aggregate entities such as gases. The emergent properties of gases are an aggregate function of the properties of the individual molecules that compose them (and their interactions), whereas the emergent properties of cells are at least partially a function of their structure. Analogously, the emergent properties of crowds may be treated as a function of the properties of the individuals that compose them (and their interactions), whereas the properties of social collectives may be treated as – at least partially – a function of their structure.

As noted earlier, this is precisely how Durkheim did conceive of social structure, as formally identical to the physical structure of cells or organisms. Unfortunately, because of his focus on external causality rather than structure per se, he overlooked the salient difference.

It is true that just as the behavior of the molecular components of a cell is – at least partially – explained by reference to the structure of the cell, so too the behavior of individuals in a social collective is – at least partially – explained by reference to the structure of the collective: by reference to its members being parties to sets of arrangements, conventions, and agreements. Yet here the similarity ends. The structure of a cell is external to and in this respect distinct from the components of the cell, which enables us to attribute to the structure of the cell a form of causality extraneous to any and all of its components. In contrast, the structure of a social collective – the arrangements, conventions, and agreements to which its members are parties – is *not* external to or distinct from the psychological commitments, acceptances, and acquiescences of its members. Consequently, no form of causality can be attributed to the social structure of a collective that is extraneous to all of its component individuals (although a form of causality can be attributed that is extraneous to any of them individually, in the form of sanctions or consequences that maintain the commitment, acceptance or acquiescence of particular individuals). Social structure – in the form of arrangements, conventions, and agreements[3] – is *immanent* in the psychology of the individuals who comprise the collective.[4]

It was precisely because Durkheim mistakenly conceived of social phenomena as supra-individuals with distinctive causal powers that he held that social phenomena must be explained in terms of social causes at the supra-individual level, and not in terms of individual psychology: 'every time a social phenomenon is directly explained by a psychological phenomenon, we may be sure the explanation is false' (1895: 129). However, this is pure dogma. There is no reason at all why 'social facts' such as differential suicide rates between different social groups (Durkheim, 1897),[5] for example, might not turn out to have a psychological explanation. Differential rates of suicide in different groups might be best explained in terms of differential rates of depression caused by different degrees of exposure to sunlight due to different geographical location, or by differences in biochemistry (as in the case of different gender groups, for example).

Weber and Social Action

Like Durkheim, Weber sought to provide a characterization of social phenomena by reference to the supposed subject-matter of sociology, which he took to be *social action*. Weber (1922: 4) defined *action* as including any human behavior to which 'the acting individual attaches a subjective meaning,' by which he seems to have meant any form of directed or intentional behavior or non-behavior, since an action may be 'overt or covert,' involving 'omission or acquiescence.' Weber defined *social* action as any action whose 'subjective meaning takes into account the behavior of others and is thereby oriented in its course' (1922: 4).

The main trouble with this definition of social action is that it characterizes social actions in terms of the objects towards which the actions are intentionally directed, namely persons, as opposed to animals, artifacts or inanimate objects, for example. Thus intentional behaviors oriented towards inanimate objects were classified by Weber as non-social actions, as were actions such as solitary prayer (1922: 22).

In consequence, Weber's definition of social action is both too broad and too narrow. Certain intuitively non-social interpersonal actions, such as many acts of aggression and sexual advances, turn out to be social actions according to Weber's definition, and certain intuitively social phenomena, such as convention-bound forms of genuflection before a cross and solitary prayer, turn out to be non-social.

Weber's essential error was to identify social action with *interpersonal* action: that is, action directed towards and taking into account the behavior of another person or persons. Weber also tried to provide an 'individualist' explication of social collectives in terms of networks of social actions: 'When reference is made in a sociological context to a state, a nation, a corporation, a family, an army corps or to similar collectivities, what is meant is . . . *only* a certain kind of development of actual or possible social actions by individual persons (1922: 14). Unfortunately, sequences of actual or possible social actions by individual persons do not seem sufficient to constitute a social collective. As Gilbert (1989: 36–41) notes, a population of individuals who lived alone in different parts of a forest where they all picked mushrooms for sustenance, and took steps to avoid other individuals if they came across them in the forest, would not intuitively constitute a social collective, even though there is the manifestation of a sequence of actions that are oriented towards others (a sequence of social actions according to Weber's definition). They would merely constitute a population of individuals engaged in interpersonal actions such as avoidance, and sequences of interpersonal actions are intuitively insufficient to constitute a social collective.

To be fair to Weber, however, an alternative interpretation of social action can be gleaned from his various comments on the nature of social action, an interpretation that does not equate social action and interpersonal action by characterizing social actions in terms of the type of objects – namely persons – to which they are intentionally directed.

Thus, for example, Weber noted that the other persons towards whom social actions must be oriented need not be *specific individuals*:

> The 'others' may be individual persons, and may be known to the actor as such, or may constitute an indefinite plurality and be entirely unknown as individuals. Thus money is a means of exchange which the actor accepts in payment because he orients his action to the expectation that a large but unknown number of individuals he is personally unacquainted with will be ready to accept it in exchange on some future occasion. (1922: 22).

According to this interpretation of social action, social action is not oriented towards other persons in the sense of being directed towards particular persons, but is rather oriented towards other persons in the sense of being based upon certain expectations about the behavior of other persons. A social action may be oriented towards other persons in this latter sense even if it is *not* directed towards particular other persons. On this interpretation, the interpersonal action of presenting a check to a cashier for payment, and the impersonal action of depositing cash at a teller machine, both count as instances of social action. On this interpretation, convention-bound forms of genuflection before a cross or solitary prayer count as social actions, and many interpersonal acts of aggression or sexual advances do not.

Furthermore, as Weber rightly recognized, not any old form of behavior based upon an expectation about the behavior of others counts as a social action. Actions based upon expectations only insofar as they imitate the regular behavior of others (such as following others in the direction in which the crowd is moving), or which are grounded in useful facts learned by observing the regular behavior of others (such as the most efficient way to gut fish), do not count as social actions (1922: 23–4). Actions based upon imitation, for example, only count as social actions according to Weber when 'the action of others is imitated because it is fashionable or traditional or exemplary' (1922: 24), when the form of expectation involved is 'a justified expectation on the part of members of a group that a customary rule will be adhered to.'

That is, Weber clearly recognized that many forms of social action, such as speaking a language, cashing checks, voting, getting married, and the like, are based upon 'a mutual declaration to the effect that a certain kind of action will be undertaken or is to be expected' (1913: 1376). This suggests that Weber had a concept of social action as action oriented towards others only in the sense that it is in accord with a recognized set of arrangements, conventions, or agreements, independently of whether or not it is directed towards any particular person or group of persons.

This characterization of social action has a number of significant virtues. For example, it suggests a promising means of defining social collectives, in terms of parties to recognized arrangements, conventions, and agreements, and one which enables us to distinguish genuine social collectives from aggregate groups, whose members merely share a common property or set of properties (such as crowds or the populations comprised of females or deaf persons). Thus, for example, if Gilbert's (1989) population of solitary mushroom pickers came to some arrangement or agreement to pool their resources and distribute the tasks of picking, separating, and preserving the mushrooms for future individual use, then intuitively this population would count as a genuine social collective.

Nevertheless, Weber strenuously resisted any account of social collectivity in terms of such a 'consensual order' (1913: 1377) in his meta-theoretical and methodological writings. His reluctance to accept such an account seems to have derived from his metaphysical concern about the *reification* of social collectivity[6] – in contrast to Durkheim's positive enthusiasm for it. Weber seems to have held that to grant the reality of social collectives would be to posit some mysterious entity 'over and above' individuals and their actions: a supra-individual with properties and powers that are analogous to, but distinct from, those of ordinary individuals. This appears to be why he constantly stressed that theoretical 'references' to social collectives are merely an intellectual or instrumental convenience, and should not be treated as descriptions of anything other than descriptions of – actual or possible – individual actions:

> It may be ... convenient or even indispensable to treat social collectivities, such as states, associations, business corporations, foundations, as if they were individual persons. Thus they may be treated as the subjects of rights and duties or as the performers of legally significant actions. But for the subjective interpretation of action in sociological work these collectivities must be treated as *solely* the resultants and modes of organization of the particular acts of individual persons, since these alone can be treated as agents in a course of subjectively understandable action. ... for sociological purposes there is no such thing as a collective personality which 'acts'. (1922: 14–15)

That is, Weber appeared to have equated questions about the reality of social collectives – and legitimacy of social explanations by reference to social collectivity – with questions about the supra-individuality of social collectives. Despite their different views about the desirability of reification, Weber appeared to share with Durkheim the assumption that questions about the reality of social collectives and the distinctive nature of social explanation by reference to social collectivity can be answered in the affirmative only if social collectives exist at a higher order of ontological statification than human individuals: that is, only if they are supra-individuals. Durkheim held that there are distinctively social explanations referencing real social collectives because he believed that social collectives are supra-individuals. Weber held that there are no distinctively social explanations referencing real social collectives because he did not believe that social collectives are supra-individuals.

This common assumption is profoundly mistaken. As I will try to demonstrate in the following sections, an account can be provided of the reality of social collectives and the distinctive nature of social explanations by reference to social collectivity that does not require any commitment to the ontological thesis that social collectives are supra-individuals.

Social Actions and Social Collectives

In the last two sections I suggested that the essential dimension of social phenomena might be the sets of arrangements, conventions, and agreements recognized and jointly accepted by populations of individuals. This sort of account is implicit in the writings of both Durkheim and Weber, and provides a fair characterization of the dimension common to all the intuitively plausible examples of social phenomena they cited, such as financial and religious practices, marriages, forms of language, states, institutions, and the like. In this section, I attempt to characterize social phenomena by reference to arrangements, conventions, and agreements,[7] while at the same time avoiding the historical errors of Durkheim and

Weber: the errors of equating social collectivity and supra-individuality, and of equating the social and the interpersonal.

In what follows the term *intrinsically social* is employed to delineate those phenomena that are social in nature, or have social dimensions. The term *derivatively social* is employed to delineate those phenomena that are not social in nature, or do not have social dimensions, but which are legitimately characterized as 'social' by virtue of some relation they bear, or some relation borne to them, by intrinsically social phenomena.

I suggest that what may be termed *intrinsically social actions* are intentional (directed) behaviors that are enacted in accord with a set of recognized arrangements, conventions, or agreements between individuals. This recognition may only be tacit, but it at least involves the recognition that other individuals are parties to such arrangements, conventions, or agreements. Examples of intrinsically social actions would include cashing a check, driving on the right-hand side of the road, paying wages, speaking Russian, genuflecting in front of a cross, declaring war. Intrinsically social actions are oriented towards others only in the sense that they are based upon certain assumptions about the behavior of other persons in similar sorts of situations. They are not, however, necessarily directed towards any particular person or set of persons.

The recognition of this point enables us to distinguish between intrinsically social actions and interpersonal actions. *Interpersonal actions* may be defined as actions that are directed towards particular other persons. Examples of interpersonal actions that are not intrinsically social would include some sexual advances and some acts of aggression, and the action of circumventing another person who is blocking a doorway.

Of course the categories of intrinsically social action and interpersonal action are not mutually exclusive, and a great many intrinsically social actions are also interpersonal actions, and vice versa. Thus intrinsically social actions such as cashing a check or paying wages are regularly also interpersonal actions that are directed towards other persons, such as bank tellers and employees. However, not all instances of intrinsically social actions are also instances of interpersonal actions, or vice versa. Some intrinsically social actions, such as solitary prayer or depositing money in a bank teller machine, are not interpersonal actions, and some interpersonal actions, such as some acts of aggression and avoidance, are not intrinsically social actions.

I further suggest that what may be termed *intrinsically social groups* – or *social collectives* – are those populations whose members are parties to a set of arrangements, conventions, or agreements governing their behavior. Examples of intrinsically social groups or social collectives would include the populations of bankers, married persons, professional psychologists, Russian speakers, the Azande, Hell's Angels, Act-Up, the Roman Catholic Church, City College, the Danish state and the British Commonwealth.

Such intrinsically social groups or social collectives must be carefully distinguished from non-social *aggregate groups*: populations whose members merely share a common property or set of properties, such as the populations comprising persons born in 1952, or who have a mole on their lower left arm. *Contra* Durkheim, many crowds are non-social aggregate groups because the only property shared by their members is a general spatiotemporal location,[8] such as the crowd that happens to fill Bryant Park in New York at 3.25 p.m. on Wednesday, 4 August 1993. These aggregate groups are non-social groups because their members are not party to any set of arrangements, conventions, or agreements that constitute them as intrinsically social collectives.

Intrinsically social groups or collectives must also be carefully distinguished from what may be termed *derivatively social groups*: those aggregate groups comprising populations whose members share a common property (or properties) that is (or are) socially significant according to some convention or agreement. Examples of such derivatively social groups would include aggregate groups such as the populations of men, women, blacks, senior citizens, and persons who are deaf, have AIDS, are unemployed, have an income within a certain specified range, are engaged in manual labor, or who were in the lobby of the Washington Hilton the day Reagan was shot.

Many (if not most) intrinsically social groups or collectives are also derivatively social groups, since groups constituted as collectives by their members being parties to sets of arrangements, conventions or agreements are also usually represented as comprised of members sharing socially significant properties, if only (although in fact rarely only) by their members. The population of Catholics, for example, forms both a social collective (whose members are party to a set of arrangements, conventions and agreements) and a derivatively social group (since the property of being Catholic has social significance according to certain conventions and agreements, and for individuals other than Catholics). However, not all derivatively social groups are social collectives. Derivatively social groups such as the populations of deaf people, the unemployed, and the homeless are not social collectives, because their members are not parties to any set of arrangements, conventions, or agreements that constitute these aggregate groups as social collectives.

Perhaps the best way to illustrate this point, while at the same time demonstrating the derivatively social nature of such aggregate groups, is to note that the properties that members of such aggregate groups share only have social significance according to some convention or agreement, and that the parties to the convention or agreement that gives a certain property its social significance *cannot be generally identified with the members of the population who share the property that has social significance according to the convention or agreement.* Thus, for example, the parties to conventions or agreements about the social significance of being a black person, a woman, or a person with AIDS, cannot be identified with the persons who are black, who are women, and who have AIDS (although some persons who are black, are women, or who have AIDS may accept the prevalent or dominant convention or agreement about the social significance of being black, being a woman, or having AIDS). In the case of women and black people, for example, it is often recognized that the parties to the prevalent or dominant conventions and agreements about the social significance of being a woman or a black person are not restricted to women and black persons. On the contrary, they tend to be predominantly male and white.

Given these distinctions, we can also characterize intrinsically social agents (individuals who are party to a set of arrangements, conventions, or agreements: that is, members of an intrinsically social group or social collective) and derivatively social agents (individuals with a property that has social significance: that is, members of a derivatively social group), and derivatively social actions (those interpersonal actions that are directed towards intrinsically or derivatively social agents or groups, or which have social significance for observers but not actors). However, the details of such analyses need not be documented here, for they have minimal relevance to the ensuing discussion.

As the above analysis suggests, this account can also be readily extended to characterize a great many properties and relations as derivatively social, since virtually any property or relation may be derivatively social according to some convention or agreement. In the following sections, I focus upon the question of whether certain forms of relations, structures, and explanations are intrinsically social in nature, recognizing that those relations, structures, and explanations that are characterized as non-social in nature – as not intrinsically social in nature – may of course be derivatively social.

Social Relations and Social Structure

In accord with the above analysis, we may recognize that the term 'social relations' is systematically ambiguous. It may be employed to characterize those relations between intrinsically social agents and groups that are *themselves intrinsically social in nature*, or those relations between intrinsically or derivatively social agents and groups that are *not themselves intrinsically social in nature*.

Relations of marriage and debt between social agents are intrinsically social relations because they are constituted as relations of marriage and debt by actions in conformity with constitutive arrangements and conventions, and social relations of employment between employers and employees are intrinsically social relations because they are constituted as relations of employment by sets of arrangements and agreements between employers and employees. In contrast, relations of economic inequality between female and male teachers or between husbands and wives, asymmetric power relations between capitalists and the proletariat or between mothers and children, and differential suicide, divorce, or unemployment rates between different intrinsically or derivatively social groups are not intrinsically social relations, because such relations are not constituted by – although they may be causal consequences of – any set of arrangements, conventions, or agreements. Both types of social relations – intrinsically social relations between intrinsically social agents and groups, and non-social relations between intrinsically or derivatively social agents and groups – can, and regularly do, figure as both explananda and explanantia in social science.

A precisely analogous ambiguity attaches to references to social structure. The term 'social structure' may be employed to characterize relations between intrinsically social agents or groups that are themselves intrinsically social in nature, or it may be employed to characterize relations between intrinsically or derivatively social agents or groups that are not themselves intrinsically social in nature. Consequently, so-called structural explanations that reference relational conditions that enable, promote, or constrain certain forms of actions, interactions, and other social relations, may reference intrinsically social relations between intrinsically social agents or groups, such as marriage, employment, or treaties, or non-social relations between intrinsically or derivatively social agents or groups such as asymmetric power relations, economic inequality, or geographical distance.[9]

Thus, many of the social structural explanations advanced in social science are not themselves *social* explanations, in the sense that they are not intrinsically social explanations referencing sets of arrangements, conventions, or agreements. Many social structural explanations in terms of economic differences, power relations, and geographical location are non-social in nature, since they reference certain non-social relations between intrinsically or derivatively social agents or groups.

It might be objected that explanations in terms of economic inequalities are forms of intrinsically social explanation, since forms of financial practice would appear to be paradigm cases of intrinsically social phenomena constituted by sets of arrangements, conventions, and agreements. However, all this shows is that certain forms of non-social structural explanation presuppose – or are parasitic upon – certain intrinsically social facts, not that the relations referenced by such explanations are themselves constituted by such intrinsically social facts.

Most economic equalities, for example, are not constituted by the sets of arrangements, conventions, and agreements that are constitutive of economic practices – such as banking, capital investment, stock markets, and the like – although they may very well be a causal consequence of them, and are certainly parasitic upon them. The capitalist system is constituted by the sets of arrangements, conventions, and agreements accepted or acquiesced to by individuals, but the economic inequalities that undergird the power of owners of the means of production to exploit the providers of industrial labor are not constituted by such sets of arrangements, conventions, and agreements, but are rather – at least according to Marx – a causal consequence of them.

Of course, some economic relations may be constituted by the acceptance of, or acquiescence in, certain sets of arrangements, conventions, and agreements, such as the lower average wages of women and minorities in the teaching profession. Analogously, some asymmetric power relations between husbands and wives may be grounded in intrinsically social relations in the form of jointly accepted arrangements, conventions, and agreements about differential rights and responsibilities, whereas in other cases – where marriage partners do not jointly accept such arrangements, conventions, and agreements – they may be grounded in economic inequalities that are a causal consequence of the acceptance by others of certain sets of arrangements, conventions, and agreements (governing employment opportunities, for example). These are properly empirical matters to be determined by social scientific research – they cannot be prejudged by any conceptual analysis of intrinsically social relations or structure.

Realism and Social Explanation

Most debates about the reality of social phenomena and the distinctive nature of social explanations are vitiated because it is regularly assumed that the reality of social phenomena and the distinctive nature of social explanations can only be maintained if social phenomena constitute supra-individuals. This erroneous assumption underlies most of the confusion in traditional debates between so-called realists and instrumentalists, and between holists and individualists (for reviews of these debates, see Lukes, 1973 and Rosenberg, 1988).

Being a holist – or better, *collectivist* – and realist about social collectives does not entail any commitment to the supra-individuality of social collectives: it does not involve any commitment to the view that social collectives exist on a 'higher' ontological stratum than individuals. Social collectives are real – they are ontologically distinct from aggregate groups – and theoretical references to them entirely legitimate – and not convenient fictions – if there is a genuine difference between social collectives such as the communities of professional psychologists, practicing Christians, armies, and states, and aggregate groups such as crowds and the populations of persons born in 1952, black persons, females, and persons with AIDS. According to the present account there is a genuine difference: social collectives are composed of individuals who are parties to sets of arrangements, conventions, and agreements, whereas aggregate groups are not, and this genuine difference has significant explanatory implications. Thus one can be a holist – or collectivist – and realist about social collectives insofar as one holds that some populations are constituted as social collectives by their members being party to sets of arrangements, conventions, and agreements, and that others are not, without committing oneself to any dubious ontological claims about the supra-individuality of social collectives.

Nor is there any special difficulty about maintaining the distinctive nature of intrinsically social explanations, as distinct from individual psychological explanations. It likewise does not entail any commitment to the supra-individuality of social phenomena. Intrinsically social explanations are explanations that make reference to recognized arrangements, conventions, and agreements. Of course intrinsically social explanations cannot be independent of psychological explanations, because, as Rosenberg reasonably protests (1988: 121), any form of causally efficacious social factor must 'pass through people' – it must exploit the psychology of persons to generate actions putatively explained by such factors; and because, as noted earlier, the arrangements, conventions, and agreements that are constitutive of intrinsically social phenomena are instantiated – are immanent – in the psychology of persons. Yet there need be nothing mysterious about this. All that is required is the recognition that some explanations – namely intrinsically social explanations – can be *psychological without being individual*. All that is required is that we distinguish between intrinsically social psychological explanations and individual psychological explanations.

Intrinsically social psychological explanations may be defined as explanations by reference to sets of arrangements, conventions, or agreements, recognized and accepted by persons who are party to them. *Individual psychological explanations* may be defined as explanations by reference to psychological states or attitudes that do not involve any recognition or acceptance of sets of arrangements, conventions, or agreements – such as desires to harm another person, relieve one's pain, avoid depression, and egoistic or altruistic motives that are products of evolutionary selection and inheritance. Thus, although intrinsically social explanations are a form of psychological explanation, they can be distinguished from individual psychological explanations.

On this account, the explanation of differential rates of aggression, dishonesty, or suicide in terms of different sets of arrangements, conventions, or agreements governing these forms of action in social collectives such as street gangs, professional psychologists, married persons, Catholics, and primitive tribes, are intrinsically social – psychological – explanations. Explanations of human altruism in terms of biologically inherited 'evolutionary stable strategies' (Dawkins, 1976), and explanations of differential suicide rates among men and women due to differential depression rates (due to the different biochemistry of men and women) are – aggregative – individual psychological explanations.

Of course, whether any of these phenomena require an intrinsically social or individual psychological explanation (or some distribution or combination) is an open and empirical question. It is an open and empirical question whether acts of aggression, inflation, differential suicide and divorce rates between different social groups, economic domination, and the like, will turn out to have intrinsically social psychological explanations or aggregative individual psychological explanations.

This applies equally to those illustrative examples of explanations favored by 'holists' and 'individualists' respectively. It is no accident that 'holists' regularly employ illustrative examples drawn from anthropology and sociology, where explanations in terms of arrangements, conventions, and agreements tend to abound, and that 'individualists' regularly employ illustrative examples drawn from economics, where aggregative explanations based upon individual self-interest tend to abound (notably in 'rational-choice' theories). However, it might very well turn out, for example, that certain phenomena such as incest avoidance are not best explained in terms of conformity with the 'incest taboo' (Lévi-Strauss, 1960), but are best explained in terms of biologically inherited disinclinations to mate with blood relations, with moral prescriptions such as the 'incest taboo' merely functioning as 'labelling devices for things that would happen anyway' (Fox, 1977: 134). It might also turn out that certain economic phenomena are not best explained in terms of the aggregation of self-interested actions (as in 'rational-choice' theories), but are best explained in terms of actions in conformity with conventions of economic rationality and other social commitments (Sen, 1982).

It is thus also an open question whether the types of psychological phenomena that will be referenced in our best explanations in any branch of psychology will turn out to be social or individual. There is no intrinsic reason for supposing, for example, that our best explanations in cognitive psychology will reference individual psychological states, although in fact virtually all our present explanations in cognitive psychology do – they might very well reference intrinsically social psychological states of the sort described by Vygotsky (1962). Nor is there any reason for supposing that our best explanations in social psychology will reference intrinsically social psychological states. They might very well reference individual psychological states, as many – if not most – of our present explanations in social psychology in fact do – for a variety of reasons.

The Social Constitution of Social Reality

One virtue of the present account is that it can be easily extended to provide an account of what we are committed to when we claim that language, development, and the like are – intrinsically – social in nature. Language may be said to be social insofar as it is based upon certain conventions or agreements about linguistic meaning. Development may be said to be social insofar as it involves the learning of conventions and agreements (and acceptance of, commitment to, or acquiescence in them), including those underpinning language and other forms of social practices (that is, practices governed by arrangements, conventions, and agreements). And so on and so forth.

It also enables us to articulate the sense in which identity and emotion may be said to be intrinsically social in nature, as argued in the following chapters: identity and emotion are social psychological phenomena that are grounded in commitments to sets of arrangements, conventions, and agreements. They are constituted by and individuated by reference to commitments to recognized arrangements, conventions, and agreements. In accord with scientific realism, I claim that this is a contingent and autonomous fact about identity and emotion. It is not vouchsafed or constituted by the intrinsically social nature of our theoretical descriptions of identity or emotion.

Now this general analysis of intrinsically social phenomena – in terms of arrangements, conventions, and agreements – has a number of rather immediate and significant implications. The first is that *all intrinsically social phenomena are social constructions*, in the following respect. All intrinsically social phenomena are the constitutive product of arrangements, conventions, and agreements. All intrinsically social phenomena are constituted by or constructed out of – and maintained and sustained by renewed and fresh commitments to – arrangements, conventions, and agreements: they are *socially constituted*. It is in this respect that identity and emotion may be said to be socially constructed or socially constituted. Throughout this work I prefer to use the latter term when characterizing identity and emotion as intrinsically social in nature, to avoid confusion with the meta-theoretical form of social constructionism advocated by theorists such as Gergen and his associates.

The second implication is that theoretical descriptions – including those employed in natural and social psychological science and by ordinary folk – are intrinsically social phenomena. Like all other intrinsically social phenomena, they are socially constructed or constituted in the respect noted above: they are a constitutive product of arrangements, conventions, and agreements. Yet nothing in the analysis suggests – far less entails – that the intrinsically social dimensions of identity and emotion, or of language, cognition, development, or whatever, are a constitutive product of the intrinsically social dimensions of our linguistic theories about them. On the contrary, it suggests, as I will argue in the following chapters, that identity and emotion are intrinsically social – and socially constructed or constituted – quite independently of our intrinsically social – and socially constructed or constituted – theories about them.

That is, according to the present account, intrinsically social phenomena such as theoretical descriptions (and other forms of description or language) form but a sub-class of the domain of intrinsically social phenomena: they are just one form of intrinsically social phenomena among many. This makes it easy to clarify the earlier charges that social constructionism renders most intrinsically social phenomena 'rationally invisible'; that it has an impoverished conception of the social; and that it denies the reality of the social dimensions of identity, emotion, and most other social phenomena. Social constructionism restricts the intrinsically social to the *linguistic*: according to social constructionism, there are no other intrinsically social phenomena that exist independently of the intrinsically social dimensions of our theories of them. To the degree that phenomena such as identity and emotion may be said to have social dimensions, these dimensions are *derivatively social*: they are constituted by the intrinsically social dimensions of our putative descriptions of them. In consequence, the social constructionist is no champion of the social dimension against the empiricist and naturalist: as much as the empiricist and the naturalist, the social constructionist essentially denies the intrinsically social nature of identity, emotion, action, development and the like.

To claim that identity and emotion are intrinsically social in nature does not itself entail that identity and emotion have linguistic dimensions, since intrinsically social phenomena cannot be identified with linguistic phenomena. Linguistic phenomena form a sub-class – albeit a very important sub-class – of intrinsically social phenomena. Nevertheless, I will argue in later chapters that most forms of identity and emotion are socio-linguistic constructions, or are socio-linguistically constituted, again, quite independently of our socially constructed or constituted theories about them.

It is an important consequence of this analysis that intrinsically social phenomena – such as identity and emotion – are identified as *relational* in nature: they are constituted and individuated by reference to the fact that agents – to whom identities and emotions are attributed – are parties to sets of arrangements, conventions, and agreements. In the absence of joint commitments to these arrangements, conventions, or agreements, there would be no identities and no emotions.

However, the converse does not hold: not all relational phenomena are social in nature. Magnetic fields are obviously not, but neither, according to the present account, are many relations of economic domination. I stress this because a good many social constructionists (Gergen, 1989b), and many feminists who think of themselves as closely affiliated with social constructionists (Farganis, 1986; M. Gergen, 1990; Scheman, 1983), mistakenly suppose that relational phenomena can be identified with intrinsically social phenomena.

What Happened to the 'Social' in Social Psychology?

According to the present account, intrinsically social explanations are those that reference intrinsically social psychological phenomena – such as identity and emotion – that are grounded in commitments to sets of arrangements, conventions, and agreements. I noted that it is rare to find theoretical references to intrinsically social psychological phenomena in contemporary social psychology. This requires some explanation.

Anglo-American 'social' psychology – which has long dominated the field – has never really been a *social* psychology. It has consistently neglected the social dimension throughout most of its history, and continues to neglect it. For example, despite the recent avowed interest in 'social cognition,' there is precious little of the social to be found in contemporary Anglo-American studies of social cognition. Unlike European studies of 'social representations' (Farr and Moscovici, 1984; Moscovici, 1976), where attention is focused upon the *social dimensions of* cognition (the epithet 'social' qualifies cognition in these studies), in contemporary Anglo-American studies of social cognition – such as those reviewed in Fiske and Taylor (1991), for example – attention is focused upon the cognition *of social phenomena* (the epithet 'social' here qualifies the objects of cognition), social phenomena themselves being generally conceived in terms of other persons and social situations. There is virtually no consideration of the possibility that cognition itself has social dimensions – is intrinsically social – and it is simply assumed that the same individual psychological explanations that apply to our cognition of non-social objects will apply in the social domain.

This individualist assumption in social psychology has a long pedigree. It can be found, for example, in J.P. Dashiel's chapter on experimental social psychology in the 1935 *Handbook of Social Psychology*, edited by C. Murchison: 'Particularly it is to be borne in mind that in this objective stimulus–response relationship to his fellows we have to deal with no radically new concepts, no principles essentially different to those applying to non-social situations' (Dashiel, 1935: 1097). Why did social psychology, which after all was cognitive long before other branches of psychology (studying attitudes, for example, from the early 1920s onwards) abjure the social dimension? What happened to the 'social' in social psychology?

The social dimension was not always neglected. Wundt's *Völker-psychologie* (1920) advocated an intrinsically social and relational psychology in the tradition of Kant, Herder, and Vico: the study of psychological phenomena such as emotion and motivation through their social products, such as language, myth, and custom (Wundt, 1897: 23). However, although this form of social or folk psychology impressed G. Stanley Hall, it did not appeal to the bulk of Wundt's American students, and it never really caught on in American psychology (although it was developed in anthropology through the work of Franz Boas, Margaret Mead, Ruth Benedict, and others). W. McDougall originally tried to explain group processes by reference to the 'group mind,' in a work entitled *The Group Mind*, and maintained: 'the group mind exists only in the minds of its members. But it nevertheless exists' (1920: 5). However, McDougall vigorously denied this in the 1928 edition of the same work (although the original title was retained).

Social constructionists have their own explanations for the rampant individualism of contemporary social psychology: it promotes and sustains male dominance, the capitalist system, and the like. Although there may be some truth in this, we ought to beware of the weakness of functionalist explanations of this sort. Even if individual psychological explanations do promote and sustain male dominance and the capitalist system, these may simply be fortuitous consequences for men and capitalists that follow because psychologists are committed to individual psychological explanations for entirely different reasons – not *because* they promote male dominance or capitalism. Moreover, there would appear to be different reasons, clearly articulated in the historical literature, for their continued – and continuing – commitment to individual psychological theories.

Two of these are simply reflections of the Weberian errors documented earlier in this chapter. The first is the mistaken equation of the social and the interpersonal, which treats the study of crowd or mass behavior (at political rallies, for example) as the paradigm of the social. For example, a great deal of experimental social psychology – and particularly the study of small group processes – amounts to little more than the study of interpersonal behavior, not behavior in accord with arrangements, conventions, and agreements (although many of the actual studies no doubt ought to be explained in these intrinsically social terms).

The second and closely related reason concerns Weberian fears about the reification of social phenomena – the erroneous fear that a commitment to the reality of social phenomena entails a commitment to mysterious supra-individuals. In *Institutional Behavior* (1933), Floyd Allport advanced explanations of the dynamics of institutions purely in terms of interpersonal behaviors held to be the product of individual attitudes, motives, and habits. His justification for doing this and ignoring the social dimension was clearly the product of a Weberian fear of 'personification' or 'reification': like Weber, he insisted that social groups or collectives are mere 'fictions.' Indeed much of the following passage – taken from a later response to a 1926 review of his *Social Psychology* (1924) by the sociologist L.L. Bernard – could easily have been written by Weber himself:

> Bernard's remark that sociologists have applied individual terminology to 'uniformities of behavior in groups as wholes' seems not inappropriate here. To say that the 'team' runs down the field, though useful, does, however, imply a personification and a specious singularity.
>
> Suppose now that forward pass occurs . . . we say the team 'executes a forward pass.'
>
> Since we are unable to describe the forward pass episode as an act of an individual, suppose that we call it an act of the group. The 'team' carries out the play. Here, at the social level, we have again invented through the term *team* a useful singularity. . . . The 'corporate fiction' is something without which our economic, political and organizational life in general could hardly go on. But the trouble here, from the standpoint of objective science, is that

the term for the agency which is said to 'execute the forward pass' is devoid of any unambiguously denotable referent. When we try to touch or speak to the 'team,' we are addressing only individuals. The corporate fiction, though a useful orienting device for perceiving and handling a situation in a certain way, is still a fiction. (F. Allport, 1961: 195).

Floyd's brother, Gordon Allport, was even more rigorous in his denial of the reality of the social, and was particularly vehement in his rejection of any theoretical references to social dimensions of psychological phenomena. With respect to the concept of 'collective representations,' he lamented that 'it is regrettable that the concept was ever used by anyone' (1985: 32). Quite remarkably – for a social psychologist – he recommended that the word 'shared' be avoided when describing attitudes, ideas, norms, and values.

However, Allport's rejection of the reality of the social was not merely motivated by fears about reification. He had other reasons for rejecting any commitment to the reality of the social. He rightly associated such a commitment with the type of social psychology exemplified by Wundt's *Völkerpsychologie*, but wrongly associated this with forms of political totalitarianism – as part of a tradition originating in Hegel and culminating in Nazism (and Stalinism):

> Hitler, as well as Marx, was among the spiritual children of Hegel. Like Hegel, they equated personal freedom with obedience to the group, morality with discipline, personal growth with the prosperity of the party, class, or state. *Du bist nichts: dein Volk ist alles* was the Nazi rallying cry.
>
> It is hardly necessary to point out that the psychological apologists for racism and nationalism tend no less than Hegel to apotheosize the group mind, as represented by the state, race, folk, or *Kultur*. (G. Allport, 1985: 27)

As Brock (1992) has argued, this does Wundt – and *Völkerpsychologie* – a gross historical injustice. In fact it stands the actual history on its head. The 'intellectual apologists' for Nazism, such as von Eickstedt (1936), did not cite Wundt – or Hegel, for that matter – in support of their 'racism and nationalism': on the contrary, they explicitly maintained that their new 'racial psychology' was directly opposed to the older form of psychology – such as Wundt's – that sought to define 'Volk' in terms of culture and social institutions. The works that they did cite included McDougall's *Is America Safe for Democracy?* (1921), and the works of other psychologists and eugenicists who advocated programs of applied eugenics, such as Grant (1916), Stoddard (1920), and Garth (1931). Those who opposed the Nazis – and the eugenics programs – were primarily the anthropological inheritors of the mantle of Wundt's *Völkerpsychologie*, such as Franz Boas (who was introduced to Wundt by G. Stanley Hall, and later brought by Hall to Clark University to set up the first Department of Anthropology in the United States).

The charge that commitment to the reality of the social is conceptually tied to totalitarianism and racism is thus completely unfounded. Nevertheless, the charge seems to have stuck, and continues to exert its debilitating influence.[10] Conjoined with the factors noted above, it seems sufficient to explain the neglect of the intrinsically social in 'social' psychology, and the continuing commitment to individual forms of psychological explanation.

It might be objected that not all forms of Anglo-American social psychology maintain such an individual commitment. It might be objected that much of mainstream social psychology, particularly in the Lewinian tradition – as represented by theorists such as Schachter, Festinger, Cartwright, Milgram, and others – does not, being based upon 'holistic' gestalt psychology.

In one sense this is true: this form of social psychology is anti-individual insofar as it is explicitly *relational*. Yet, as noted in the previous section, this does not ensure that it is intrinsically social in nature, since the relational cannot be identified with the social. It is also true that much of the work in this tradition draws its inspiration from gestalt theories of perception. However, that is precisely the problem, for such theories are themselves relational but not social.

Gestalt theories of perception – unlike many classical theories of perception based upon atomist Newtonian models – are based upon twentieth-century physical field theories (Kohler, 1924). The dynamics of the perceptual field in classical gestalt theories of perception is held to be governed by forms of equilibrium and disequilibrium of electrical (or electro-magnetic) fields in the brain. The model of fields in dynamic tension is simply carried over into social psychology by Lewinian theorists, who characterize social and psychological 'fields' as 'tension systems' (Lewin, 1951), and advance explanations of behavior by reference to the distribution of promoting and impeding forces. Perhaps the best example of this is to be found in Milgram's (1974) analysis of his famous experiments on 'destructive obedience.' As the experimenter becomes more physically proximate to (or distant from) the subject/teacher, the force promoting destructive obedience increases (or decreases) and leads to an increase (or decrease) in destructive obedience; as the subject/teacher becomes more physically proximate to (or distant from) the learner/stooge, the impeding force increases (or decreases) and leads to a reduction (or increase) in destructive obedience.

Such 'field' theories – with their talk of promoting and impeding 'forces' – may have some real substance and application (Greenwood, 1993a). However, they are of necessity limited, since they make no reference to and pay no attention to intrinsically social phenomena (despite the fact that there is little doubt that certain forms of arrangements, conventions, or agreements underlie the forms of behavior purportedly explained in terms of such field theories, such as Milgram's experiments, for example (Mixon, 1972)).

Theories in this tradition maintain that social psychological phenomena are 'out there' – in the 'social situation' – rather than immanent in the psychology of persons. Thus even more enlightened Lewinian social psychologists such as Ross and Nisbett, who in their most recent work (1991) call for a broader conception of social psychology that includes a theoretical rapprochement with sociology and cultural anthropology, still conceive of phenomena such as social expectations and commitments as 'situational factors' or 'situational variables' exerting external promoting and constraining forces. In consequence, they can scarcely conceive of the possibility of theories of the intrinsically social nature of identity and emotion, in which the social dimensions of identity and emotion are located within the psychology of persons: the sort of theories that will now be considered.

In the following chapters I develop a theory – or at least the form of a theory – of the intrinsically social nature of identity and emotion, one that is entirely consistent with a realist interpretation of the linguistic – and epistemic – objectivity of our theoretical descriptions of identity and emotion. However, this theory does not follow from, nor is it vouchsafed by, a realist account of the semantics of theoretical descriptions, which is also entirely consistent with a whole range of individualist theories of identity and emotion.

I stress this because the adequacy of the realist account of the semantics of theoretical descriptions – and of their empirical adjudication – does not depend upon the accuracy of the following theories of the intrinsically social nature of identity and emotion: it would not be threatened by the demonstration of their inaccuracy. Although I personally believe that the following theories are fairly close to the truth, the primary point of the present analysis is to demonstrate that the recognition of the intrinsically social nature of identity and emotion poses no threat to the linguistic – or epistemic – objectivity of our theoretical descriptions of identity and emotion. In recognizing the intrinsically social nature of identity and emotion, we are not obliged to accept – in any form or to any degree – the central social constructionist thesis that identity and emotion are constituted by our socially constructed theories of identity and emotion.

Partly for this reason, I make no attempt in the following chapters to associate the theory of identity and emotion offered to those offered by other theorists; the other reason is that, although many theories of the social dimensions of identity and relation do bear some relation – and in some cases a fairly close relation – to the theory I offer, most remain ambiguous on the issue – critical to the present work – of the constitutive role of our theoretical discourse about identity and emotion.

Notes

1 It cannot of course be presumed a priori that social phenomena do in fact have a common property or set of properties, just because we apply the term 'social' to them all. Our use of this term may be tied to sets of 'family resemblances' (Wittgenstein, 1953; Rosch, 1975) between those things we call 'social.' Alternatively it may be the case, as argued in this chapter, that some phenomena are intrinsically social by virtue of a common property or set

of properties they share, and that other phenomena are derivatively social by virtue of the relations they bear to, or relations borne to them by, intrinsically social phenomena.

2 The fact that they conceived of this question in terms of the subject-matter of sociology – as opposed to social psychology, psychology, or anthropology, for example – is neither here nor there. There is no good reason to suppose that social scientific disciplines are individuated by their subject matters, or that any have social phenomena exclusively as their subject-matter. Most of the disciplinary divisions in social science are historical and artificial – they are not grounded in any form of ontological stratification (as may be held to be the case with respect to physics, chemistry, and biology, for example). See Greenwood (1991a).

3 Later in this chapter I note that there are other forms of social structure: that is, that the concept of 'social structure' is systematically ambiguous.

4 Durkheim denied this (1895: 54–5), for very bad reasons:

> Collective custom does not exist only in a state of immanence in the successive actions which it determines, but, by a privilege without example in the biological kingdom, expresses itself once and for all in a formula repeated by word of mouth, transmitted by education and even enshrined in the written word. Such are the origins and nature of legal and moral rules, aphorisms and popular sayings, articles of faith in which religious and political sects epitomise their beliefs, and standards of taste drawn up by literary schools, etc. None of these modes of acting and thinking are to be found wholly in the application made of them by individuals, since they can even exist without being applied at the time.

However, it is not the external written transcription of sets of customs and conventions that gives social facts their reality. A 'custom' or 'convention' that is externally transcribed but is not accepted or followed by any set of persons is not a custom or convention for that set of persons, has no causal force with respect to their behavior, and cannot constitute that set of persons as a social collective.

5 As is well known, Durkheim also tried to characterize 'social facts' in terms of *statistical facts* about social groups, such as statistical facts about differential rates of suicide between different age, gender, and religious groups (1895, 1897). However, this characterization of social facts fares no better than his earlier characterization in terms of 'externality' and 'constraint,' for it also fails to delineate the 'distinct characteristics' of social phenomena. Social facts do not appear to be social by virtue of their statistical nature. There would appear to be plenty of statistical facts about populations that are not themselves social facts: such as differential death rates for populations of slim persons as opposed to obese persons, or differential rates of depression for populations defined in terms of diet or geographical elevation. This suggests that statistical facts about certain populations are only derivatively social facts by virtue of their being statistical facts about those populations that constitute *social groups*. That is, Durkheim's characterization of social facts as statistical facts does not explicate the *social nature* of such facts. Rather it presupposes – but does not provide – some prior account of the social nature of some populations that enables us to characterize certain statistical facts about certain populations as facts about *social* groups or collectives.

Durkheim's related characterization of distinctive social explanations (of such statistical social facts) in terms of the different forms of 'association' or 'integration' of groups is not much help either, for it ignores his own critical distinction between genuine social collectives and aggregate groups. In this chapter I argue that distinctive social explanations are explanations that reference genuine social collectives, but not – derivatively social – aggregate groups.

6 Thus Weber claimed, for example:

> Even in cases of such forms of social organization as a state, church, association, or marriage, the social relationship consists exclusively in the fact that there has existed, exists, or will exist, a probability of action in some definite way appropriate to this

meaning. It is necessary to emphasize this *in order to avoid the 'reification' of those concepts.* (1922: 27; my emphasis)

7 The terms 'arrangement, convention, and agreement' are employed to mark increasing degrees of explicit recognition by parties to such forms of association, and to allow for the possibility that non-linguistic animals can engage in forms of social action and constitute social collectives. I do not hold these forms of association to be exhaustive, but offer no analysis of the differences between these and other forms of association in this work.

8 This is not to deny that crowds sometimes constitute social collectives – even if only temporary ones – for example, when people agree to meet at a certain time and place to protest the latest tax increase, military intervention, or supreme court ruling.

9 Failure to distinguish between these different forms of social structure and structural explanation has been a source of much confusion in contemporary social science, particularly concerning the question of whether social structure is 'cultural' or 'material': whether it is instantiated in the 'rules' or 'norms' shared by social agents and groups (Giddens, 1981), or in the material resources of, and relations between, social agents and groups (Isaac, 1987; Porpora, 1989). As the present analysis suggests, social structure can be instantiated in either form. It is always an open and empirical question whether a social phenomenon – e.g. poverty – is best explained in terms of non-social 'material' relations or intrinsically social 'cultural' relations.

10 Possibly because the association of 'holism' or 'collectivism' and totalitarianism is also maintained by Popper (1945) and Hayek (1954).

6

The Social Constitution of Identity

Personal identity remains a central concern of modern philosophers (Kolak and Martin, 1990; Parfit, 1984; Perry, 1975; Rorty, 1975), and is one of the few philosophical issues that remains of perennial interest to laypersons, perhaps because it is tied so closely to everyday moral and legal concerns about personal responsibility, abortion, euthanasia, and the like. Interest in personal identity has also returned to center stage in mainstream psychology, particularly in recent personality theory and social psychology (Breakwell, 1983b; Mischel, 1977a; Shotter and Gergen, 1989; Wegner and Vallacher, 1980; Yardley and Honess, 1987). Unfortunately, despite this joint interest, philosophers and psychologists appear to have remarkably little of value to say to each other, for even a cursory glance at the respective literatures shows them to be concerned with quite different sets of concepts and issues. About the only thing that contemporary philosophical and psychological theories of identity have in common is a commitment to atomism and individualism. This is also true, as I will suggest in the following chapter, of most avowedly 'social' theories of identity.

A detailed discussion of the philosophical issues concerning personal identity is beyond the scope of this work. However, in this chapter I present an outline of a philosophical theory of personal identity, the primary virtue of which is its ability to incorporate an intrinsically social and relational conception of identity which can serve as the basis of a social psychological theory of identity.

Philosophical Theories of Personal Identity

Most philosophical accounts of personal identity are logically atomistic in nature, and variants of one of two basic positions. The standard 'Cartesian' or 'traditional' view is that personal identity over time is determined by a continuous entity that persists through time – such as the 'soul,' the 'ego,' or the 'self.' 'Reductionist' accounts of personal identity deny that personal identity is determined by any continuous entity. Theorists from Locke (1690) to Parfit (1984) have claimed that personal identity is rather determined by psychological connections – notably memory connections – between psychological states and other discrete events in the lives of persons.

Reductionist accounts of personal identity are far and away the most popular amongst philosophers, although there remain a few defenders of the Cartesian view (e.g. Swinburne, 1986). The Cartesian view is itself often identified as the account that would be offered by most laypersons, at least by those of some form of religious persuasion. This is, however, doubtful. It seems certainly false to identify this with the traditional Christian account, although it is frequently attributed to Christians. The doctrine of the 'immortal soul' has precious little support from the Bible and traditional theology. If anything, the traditional theological view of persons, Christ, and God is thoroughly social and relational in nature (Thatcher, 1987).

Be that as it may, most laypersons would be naturally inclined to deny reductionist accounts, since they are committed to the notion that *something* does remain relatively constant throughout the lives of many persons. I will argue that this lay intuition is entirely justified, but that there is no need to identify the continuant that determines personal identity with any mysterious 'soul,' 'ego,' or the like.

Reductionist Theories of Personal Identity

Reductionist theorists deny that the normal spatiotemporal continuity requirement for transtemporal numerical identity, which holds in the case of ordinary physical particulars such as tables, trees, and tarantulas, holds in the case of persons. The transtemporal numerical identity of ordinary physical particulars is determined by the maintenance of the intrinsic properties of the kinds of things they are: thus tables, trees, and tarantulas remain numerically identical to themselves throughout time so long as they remain spatiotemporally continuous with themselves and maintain the intrinsic properties of tablehood, treehood, and tarantula-hood. Reductionist theorists deny that this is the case with respect to transtemporal personal identity: this enables them to countenance as possible the preservation of personal identity under conditions that violate the normal spatiotemporal continuity requirement, such as body or brain transfer, molecular duplication, reincarnation in a different body, and the like (Parfit, 1984).

Locke and later reductionist theorists do not, however, establish that the normal spatiotemporal continuity requirement for the numerical identity of particulars does not hold in the case of transtemporal personal identity. They merely note that strict continuity of physical composition – in the sense of the maintenance of all the original components of a physical particular – is not necessary for the transtemporal numerical identity of persons. Thus, for example, although most of the cells of a person's body are extinguished and replaced during that person's lifetime, the person can remain one and the same person throughout his or her lifetime.

Yet this does not demonstrate that there is no spatiotemporal continuity requirement in the case of the transtemporal numerical identity of persons. Precisely the same is true of ordinary particulars, such as vegetables and animals: they do not retain all their original components throughout their existence as vegetables and animals. Yet as Locke, for example, clearly recognized, the transtemporal numerical identity of particular vegetables and animals is nevertheless determined by a continuant, namely a form of 'organization' sufficient to maintain vegetable or animal life (1690: 209): that is, to maintain the intrinsic properties of particular vegetables or animals.

Locke essentially demonstrated only that strict continuity of physical composition is not required for the *spatiotemporal continuity* of physical particulars: all that is required is that any compositional changes be gradual and partial. This form of spatiotemporal continuity is sufficient to enable particulars to *continuously realize* the intrinsic properties of vegetables and animals.

This form of spatiotemporal continuity is, however, absolutely necessary for the transtemporal numerical identity of particular vegetables and animals, for this is the only means by which the intrinsic properties of particular vegetables and animals can be continuously realized. Precisely the same is true with respect to the transtemporal numerical identity of persons. The spatiotemporal continuity of the physical particulars that realize the intrinsic properties of personhood – such as intentionality, rationality, consciousness, and the like (Dennett, 1975; Wilkes, 1988) – is the only means by which such particulars can continuously realize the intrinsic properties of personhood, in other words, the only means by which such particulars can remain persons through time.[1]

That is, reductionist theorists provide no grounds for denying the normal spatiotemporal requirement in the case of personal identity. Nevertheless, Locke and later reductionist theorists are correct to maintain that transtemporal personal identity is in an important respect *disanalogous* to the transtemporal numerical identity of ordinary particulars, such as tables, trees, and tarantulas. In the case of ordinary particulars such as tables, trees, and tarantulas, the maintenance of intrinsic properties by a spatiotemporally continuous particular is both necessary and sufficient for transtemporal numerical identity. In the case of persons, however, the maintenance of the intrinsic properties of personhood – intentionality, rationality, consciousness, and the like – by a spatiotemporally continuous particular is necessary, as argued above, but *not sufficient* for transtemporal personal identity. Transtemporal personal identity is determined not only by the maintenance of the intrinsic properties of personhood – by the maintenance of the general form of the psychologies of persons – but by the maintenance of *particularities of our psychologies.*

In this respect transtemporal personal identity is more closely analogous to the transtemporal numerical identity of paintings than to the transtemporal numerical identity of ordinary particulars such as tables, trees, and tarantulas. Although there is an important sense in which the painting on my wall remains the same painting on my wall so long as it remains a painting of some scene (so long as it maintains the intrinsic properties of paintings), there is also an important sense in which it becomes a different painting if a new scene is painted upon it: a river scene of Paris rather than a street scene of Vienna, for example. The painting remains *a* painting but becomes a different painting: with a new content, as it were. Analogously, a person can remain the same person, in the sense that he or she remains *a* person (so long as he or she maintains the intrinsic properties of personhood), but can become a different person, if the particularities of his or her psychology change.

Psychological Atomism

Where Locke and later reductionist theorists err, however, is with respect to their interpretation of the particularities of the psychology of persons that determine personal identity, in terms of memory (or 'quasi-memory'[2] (Parfit, 1984)) and other psychological connections. Moreover, their reductionist interpretation of the particularities of our psychologies that determine our personal identities is not accidental: it is a natural consequence of their essentially *atomistic* conception of psychological states. Such theorists invariably conceive of psychological phenomena as transient phenomena: as logically independent events in the lives of persons.[3] This conception simply precludes any account of transtemporal personal identity in terms of a *psychological continuant*, since on this conception psychological states are not continuants.

This conception is itself a product of the very narrow range of psychological phenomena that form the favored objects of analysis of philosophers of mind and psychology: namely, sensations such as pain and occurrent thoughts and memories. Pains and occurrent thoughts are transient phenomena. The pain I feel today when I hit my finger with the hammer is quantitatively different from the pain I felt yesterday when I also hit my finger with the hammer, although they may be qualitatively similar or identical. The thought occurring to me today (again) that it is time to take my books back to the library is quantitatively different from the qualitatively similar or identical thought that I had yesterday.

Yet not all psychological phenomena are of this transient nature. Many, notably most beliefs, principles, commitments, and the like – unlike most sensations, episodic memories, occurrent thoughts, and the like – are essentially dispositional. We maintain these beliefs, principles, commitments, and the like so long as we retain the dispositions that are constitutive of them. Beliefs, principles, and commitments are the kinds of things that we can and do continue to have, even though they do not continuously occur to us, and even though we are not continuously conscious of them. My present belief in my wife's fidelity is the same belief – quantitatively as well as qualitatively – that I had yesterday and ten years ago. The responsibilities to my colleagues that I accept today are the same responsibilities – quantitatively as well as qualitatively – that I have accepted for most of my mature years. My commitment to freedom of speech is the same commitment – quantitatively as well as qualitatively – that I had when I first began my public defense of it.

Beliefs, principles, and commitments – unlike most sensations, episodic memories, occurrent thoughts, and the like – are the kinds of thing that persons can and do continue to have. This enables such phenomena to ground a superior account of transtemporal personal identity in terms of a psychological continuant.

A Sense of Identity

Since beliefs, principles, and commitments are the kinds of thing that persons can continue to have, I suggest that transtemporal personal identity is determined by the maintenance of sets of fundamental beliefs, principles, and commitments by spatiotemporally continuous particulars that retain the intrinsic properties of personhood.

Most philosophical accounts of personal identity seem to lack any reference to a person's *sense of identity*: not a mysterious inner feeling unique to persons, but a set of concerns about reputation, honor, dignity, and self-worth that are arguably unique to persons. Now these concerns are best explicated in terms of the set of fundamental beliefs, principles, and commitments by which persons aim to govern their lives. These fundamental beliefs, principles, and commitments play a central role in the psychological explanation of the intentional behavior of persons, because they provide the evaluative matrix for a great many contentful psychological states such as emotions and motives that are unique to persons, and that play an important role in the psychological explanation of the intentional behavior of persons. These fundamental beliefs, principles, and commitments determine the things we care about in our everyday lives. They determine the types of action that we are proud of, offended at, ashamed of, that we hope to achieve, seek revenge for, try to compensate for, and so forth.

The types of emotion and motive that we uniquely attribute to persons, such as anger, shame, jealousy, envy, pride, ambition, revenge, and the like, presuppose such a set of fundamental beliefs, principles, and commitments concerning matters of reputation, honor, dignity, self-worth, and the like, and a local moral order of recognized rights and obligations. To be angry is to see another's action as offensive, as an unjust violation of one's rights and honor. To be ashamed is to represent one's action (or failure to act) as degrading and humiliating, as reflecting negatively upon oneself. To harbor a motive of revenge is to represent one's contemplated action as a justified retribution for a prior personal injury or offense. To care about these things at all is to care about one's identity – to have a sense of one's identity.

This analysis essentially provides an account of personhood by reference to the applicability of certain forms of psychological explanation of intentional behavior in terms of certain emotions and motives (such as shame and revenge), which presuppose a background of fundamental beliefs, principles, and commitments. According to this analysis, transtemporal personal identity is determined by the maintenance of sets of fundamental beliefs, principles, and commitments by spatiotemporally continuous particulars that retain the intrinsic properties of personhood. According to this analysis, not all persons remain personally identical through their lifetimes. If they change their fundamental beliefs, principles, and commitments, they become *different* persons: the principles of their psychology change.

Now this analysis of personal identity has two main virtues that are lacking in reductionist accounts in terms of memory and other psychological connections. The first is that it is *theoretically grounded*. It is based upon a theoretical account of persons that purports to describe dimensions that are causal explanatory with respect to their intentional behavior. Much of the intentional behavior of persons requires a psychological explanation in terms of their fundamental beliefs, principles, and commitments, or in terms of emotions and motives that presuppose them.

The primary justification for explicating transtemporal personal identity in terms of the maintenance of fundamental beliefs, principles, and commitments is the role that such psychological phenomena play in the explanation of the intentional behavior of persons. Persons who maintain the same fundamental beliefs, principles, and commitments continue to behave in much the same way, and their earlier and later forms of behavior are explained by reference to these same basic psychological principles. Persons who change their fundamental beliefs, principles, and commitments behave in different ways, and differences in their earlier and later forms of behavior are explained by reference to differences in these basic psychological principles.

The second virtue of this account is that it is *phenomenologically grounded*. It generally accords with the accounts that persons provide of their own identity. Thus a person who has maintained the same fundamental beliefs, principles, and commitments over ten years will normally consider himself or herself to be the same person that he or she was ten years ago. A person who has abandoned his or her fundamental beliefs, principles, and commitments of ten years ago and replaced them with new fundamental beliefs, principles and commitments will normally consider himself or herself to be a different person from the one he or she was ten years ago.

However, this is a subsidiary consideration, for phenomenological accounts will only generally but not invariably accord with theoretical accounts. They are based upon memory, which can be inadequate, inaccurate, or deceptive. Persons may not be able to remember what they believed or were committed to ten years ago, or may delude themselves that they have remained the same person or have changed: that they still hold or have changed their fundamental beliefs, principles, and commitments.

Another advantage of this account of transtemporal personal identity – or diachronic singular personhood – is that it naturally extends to cover cases of contemporaneous personal identity – or synchronic singular personhood. We attribute synchronic singular personhood to most persons because their intentional behavior can be explained by reference to an integrated set of fundamental beliefs, principles, and commitments, and because they regularly affirm their singular personhood. We attribute synchronic multiple personhood to persons precisely when the explanation of their behavior requires a reference to more than one integrated set of fundamental beliefs, principles, and commitments, as in those cases documented in the 'multiple personality' literature.

For example, our motivation for ascribing (at least) dual personhood to 'Christine Beauchamp' is precisely analogous to our motivation for attributing transtemporal changes in personal identity. The explanation of the different forms of behavior at different times of the two persons that Morton Prince (1905) designated as 'Sally' and 'B1' requires a reference to two distinct sets of fundamental beliefs, principles, and commitments. Thus, for example, Sally spent extravagantly the money that B1 cautiously saved, because she had a quite different conception of the value and utility of money than B1. Sally despised and quit the jobs that B1 valued and strived to make a success of, and so on and so forth. This theoretical motivation for ascribing dual personhood, as in most cases of transtemporal personal identity, is also phenomenologically grounded. Both Sally and B1 steadfastly denied that they were personally identical, despite the fact that Sally had complete cognitive access to the thoughts, perceptions, and memories of B1.

Identity and Identity Projects

The philosophical account of personal identity sketched above is of course individualist in the following respect: it treats persons as spatiotemporally identifiable and discriminable physical particulars with the constitutive psychological properties of persons. Transtemporal personal identity requires both spatiotemporal continuity and the maintenance of fundamental beliefs, principles, and commitments – both are necessary conditions of personal identity. Thus different persons are distinguishable by their different spatial locations: Tom and his brother Al and his friend Jerry are different persons because they are different physical particulars occupying different regions of space, however similar they may be in psychological make-up. Different persons are also distinguishable by reference to their psychological make-up: Tom today is a different person from Tom ten years ago if he has changed his fundamental beliefs, principles, and commitments, even though the physical particular that is Tom today is spatiotemporally continuous with the physical particular that was Tom ten years ago. This philosophical account is opposed to reductionist accounts based upon an atomistic conception of psychological phenomena as transient states. In contrast, it maintains that personal identity is grounded in the maintenance of enduring psychological states such as fundamental beliefs, principles, and commitments by spatiotemporally continuous physical particulars. It does, however, maintain that persons are distinct individuals, and that it is to these distinct individuals that psychological states such as emotions and motives, as well as identities, are attributed.

However, although the present philosophical account maintains that persons are distinct individuals – distinct physical particulars with psychological properties – it says nothing of the nature of these properties that determine personhood and singular personhood. It thus leaves entirely open the question of whether these properties, and consequently individual persons, *are themselves social or individual in nature*. One of the great virtues of the present philosophical account of personal identity – unlike traditional reductionist accounts – is that it can incorporate *psychological theories* of identity, since it ties the notion of personal identity to the fundamental beliefs, principles, and commitments referenced in psychological explanations of the intentional behavior of persons. Consequently, it has no difficulty incorporating the form of social psychological theory of personal identity that I will now sketch, in which identity is conceived as an *intrinsically social* phenomenon.

As suggested in the previous section, a person's sense of identity is not a mysterious inner feeling, but a set of relatively enduring and integrated fundamental beliefs, principles, and commitments, references to which can provide an integrated explanation of much of their intentional behavior. It may be further suggested that the distinguishing feature of persons – and this may be taken as true of all persons in all cultures in all historical periods – is that their psychological lives are organized around what may be termed their *identity projects*[4] (Harré, 1983b). This is the unique feature that decisively distinguishes persons from all other animals, infants, and computers (and other more dubious candidates for personhood).

These projects, uniquely attributable to persons, are their forms of psychological engagement in the social world, encompassing their representations of the persons they are and aim to continue to be. They are the social psychological means by which persons attempt to determine their reputation and self-worth in the myriad social ways that are available to them in any culture or historical period. Identity projects are perhaps best explicated in terms of sets of *moral careers* (Goffman, 1961), defined as the culturally available routes for the creation and mainten-ance (and destruction) of personal reputation and self-worth, via the success (or failure) with which a person meets the social hazards and threats to reputation and self-worth that arise within the course of such a career.[5]

It should be plain even from this simple description that identity projects and the moral careers[6] they encompass are intrinsically social and (thus) relational in nature. The very possibility of a moral career presupposes the existence of a social collective of which the agent is a member (or apprentice member or candidate for membership), constituted by sets of arrangements, conventions, and agreements governing rites of passage and defining success and failure within the moral career, that members of the collective are parties to. Our identity projects can no longer encompass the moral careers of feudal barons or samurai, nor can anyone in the West pursue the moral career of a witch-doctor or harem-master. In this respect our personal identity may be said to be *socially constituted*: it is determined by our commitments to socially located identity projects and the moral careers they encompass.

Consider a fictional person Jake, who is engaged in an identity project that encompasses the forms of moral career open to many men in the Western world today. His engagement in *an* identity project is constitutive of his identity as *a* person. His particular identity project includes the moral careers of his profession, his family, and his religion. He is a professional psychologist, a devoted husband and father, and a committed Christian. He works hard to make a success of this project. This is what constitutes his identity as this individual person in this particular time and place, and what remains constant so long as he remains this individual person. If he changes his identity project, if he abandons one set of moral careers in favor of another, he becomes a different person, both from the point of view of a philosophical account of personal identity and social psychological theory of identity. He will behave in different ways, and the differences between his earlier and later forms of behavior will require an explanatory reference to sets of quite different fundamental beliefs, principles, and commitments.[7]

The great virtue and promise of this social psychological theory of identity is that it enables us to provide a theoretically integrative account of explanations of human behavior in terms of characteristically human emotions and motives of shame, pride, achievement, jealousy, disappointment, anger, revenge, and the like. For the represented dimensions of honor, dignity, desert, offense, status, respect, responsibility, entitlement, and the like that provide the evaluative matrix for such emotions and motives are also the essential representational dimensions of moral careers within social collectives. Consequently a theoretical reference to identity projects can provide an explanation of integrated forms of behavior in terms of integrated sets of emotions and motives. The integrated forms of behavior of persons who share the same identity projects are explained by reference to similar sets of integrated emotions and motives; the integrated forms of behavior of persons with different identity projects (including persons who have changed their identity projects) are explained by reference to different sets of integrated emotions and motives.

If this is correct, one might be tempted to equate identity with personality. There are some grounds for this: since the forms of behavior of persons who change their identity projects will be different and require different forms of psychological explanation, we will often be inclined to say that their personalities have changed. However, this temptation ought to be resisted. There may be some aspects of personality – such as certain (perhaps innate) traits, or clusters of traits, such as cleanliness, punctuality, excitability, introversion, and the like – that are common to persons committed to quite different moral careers, including persons who change their commitments to different moral careers. Alternatively it might prove to be the case that such traits are all tied to specific forms of moral career, as many 'presentational' theories of personality suggest (Harré et al., 1985). Or it may be the case that some are and some are not. The point is that it is an open and empirical question whether identity – interpreted in terms of identity projects – can be equated with personality. At present, any such identification would be theoretically premature.

To claim that persons and their identities are socially constituted by their commitment to socially located identity projects is to claim that persons and their identities are intrinsically social and (thus) relational in nature. The present account consequently denies personhood and identity to logically solitary human beings: human beings who live their lives without contact with or reference to other persons.

This claim and its implication might appear too strong. It might be objected that it would be counter-intuitive to deny personhood and identity to hermits or recluses, or to shipwrecked travellers on desert islands. However, it is doubtful if the hermit and recluse do in fact live their lives without reference to others. On the contrary, the whole point of being a hermit or recluse is precisely to avoid others. Being a hermit or recluse would appear to be a socially recognized form of identity project: there are conventionally recognized ways of succeeding and failing in such a project. In contrast, the behavior of feral children and other severely deprived children (maternally or socially) seems a clear reflection of their lack of personhood and personal identity – their lack of identity projects and associated emotions. They seem, for example, to be totally devoid of shame.

The maintenance of an identity project requires the existence of other members of the social collectives within which moral careers are pursued – the other parties to the conventions of moral careers within collectives – although not necessarily their physical proximity. Thus shipwrecked travellers can retain their personhood and identity so long as they retain some semblance of commitment to their former identity projects, and ability to satisfy conventions of success and failure. This may be possible to a greater or lesser degree for poets, priests, and carpenters, who can pursue their projects with minimal resources (they can continue to write poetry, be devout, and craft furniture), but virtually impossible for rock stars, professional thieves, and lawyers, who cannot.

This attenuated and parasitic form of personhood and identity is not precluded by a social psychological theory of identity in terms of identity projects. What is precluded is the theoretical possibility of a person who has never had any contact with other persons, or who lives his or her life without reference to other persons. The reason for this is very basic. According to the present account, the attributability of emotional states such as pride, shame, anger, guilt, envy, disappointment, and the like is a condition of personhood: the essential representational dimensions that form the evaluative matrix of characteristically human emotions are essential representational dimensions of moral careers within social collectives. These emotional states involve acceptance of and commitment to the conventions of social collectives governing matters of reputation, honor, obligation, and the like, that involve the representation of one's own position in relation to others. Persons are intrinsically social and relational in nature because many of their constitutive psychological states – such as emotions – are intrinsically social and relational in nature: they presuppose the existence of other members of social collectives – the other parties to the conventions of emotional life.

Identity Projects and Psychological Theory

According to the form of social psychological theory of identity presented in this chapter, the identity of a person is determined by the identity project he or she is engaged in. Theoretical descriptions of identity projects are theoretical descriptions employed in the explanation of intentional human behavior, or human actions. According to this form of social psychological theory of identity, a theoretical reference to intrinsically social identity projects – and their associated emotions and motives – provides the *best* explanation of many human actions, and of the similarities and differences in actions to be found between different persons, and the same person at different times and places. Thus for example similarities and differences in the preparation and performance of high school and college students may be explained in terms of differential levels of commitment to the moral career of academia. The disruptive activities of some high school students may be best explained in terms of their commitment to alternative moral careers, such as those provided by teenage gangs (Marsh et al., 1978).

As theoretical descriptions, references to identity projects are inter- preted in accord with a realist account of theoretical meaning. They are semantically autonomous with respect to the forms of behavior they are employed to explain, and purport to describe the socially located forms of moral career that persons are committed to: the arrangements, conventions, and agreements of different forms of moral career within different social collectives. They are not mere abstractions from behavioral regularities or tendencies that may be described in terms of clusters of traits.

As theoretical descriptions, references to identity projects are defined in terms of the contents of moral careers that are socially available to members of social collectives, quite independently of any behavioral regularities and tendencies that they may be employed to explain. In order for anyone – either layperson or professional psychologist – to understand theoretical descriptions of identity projects, they must comprehend the content of moral careers that comprise identity projects, not the content of any operational definition in terms of behavioral regularities or tendencies: they must comprehend the arrangements, conventions, and agreements of moral careers within social collectives. Theoretical descriptions of identity projects are descriptions of the sets of moral careers to which persons are committed. These theoretical descriptions are linguistically objective: they are true or accurate if and only if persons are committed to the sets of moral careers attributed to them by such theoretical descriptions.

This has the following significant consequence, which distinguishes the present account from many other theoretical psychological accounts of identity. Social psychologists have traditionally distinguished between a person's *sense of identity*, which needs to be explained, and a person's *actual identity*, conceived as an explanatory theoretical construct:

> Theorists see identity simultaneously in two ways. Firstly, identity is something to be explained – the fact that individuals have an identity must be explained. Psychologically and socially, identity is a phenomenon and theories can be constructed to account for its development and changes over time. Second, identity is something which can be used to explain why other things occur. Used in this way, identity becomes a theoretical construct which can be used to explain why an individual behaves in a particular fashion. For instance, a person's actions may be said to be the result of a need to act in accordance with his or her self concept.
>
> Confusion of these two aspects is frequent and needs to be avoided: identity as a psychological phenomenon cannot be equated with identity as a theoretical abstraction. (Breakwell, 1983a: 4–5)

(Compare Harré, 1983b; Rosenberg and Gara, 1985).

According to a realist interpretation of the form of social psychological theory of identity in terms of identity projects, there is no confusion involved. It is of course true that identity as a psychological phenomenon cannot be equated with identity conceived as a theoretical *abstraction*. The social psychological theory of identity in terms of identity projects is not defined in terms of, or abstracted from, descriptions of behavioral regularities and tendencies (which it may nevertheless be employed to explain). The social psychological theory of identity in terms of identity projects is defined in terms of the contents of identity projects, and what it references is precisely identity conceived as an – intrinsically social – psychological phenomenon. The theoretical descriptions of the social psychological theory of identity in terms of identity projects make reference to a person's *sense of identity*: not a transient inner feeling, but an enduring commitment to a set of socially located moral careers. No doubt our sense of identity – in the form of enduring commitments to identity projects – itself requires a theoretical explanation, and most likely in social developmental terms. However, this does not preclude a theoretical reference to this psychological phenomenon from serving as a primary explanatory construct with respect to human action.

One of the reasons for the acknowledged failure to link personality or self-concept with behavior (Argyle, 1976; Mischel, 1977b; Wylie, 1979) may be that many actions are motivated by situational demands that are best understood in terms of the long-term commitments of a moral career. Much of the research on 'situated identities' (Alexander and Knight, 1971; Alexander and Scriven, 1977; Wiley and Alexander, 1987), for example, may be best conceived in terms of the conventional demands of local moral orders. Our actions may very well often be not a function of how we currently represent ourselves, but rather a function of what we currently hope to become or achieve. This would seem to be particularly true of the immense efforts we expend, and deprivations that we endure, that bring us little immediate gratification or success, which are wholly intelligible in terms of our continuous commitment to long-term identity projects encompassing professional career and family. As Nuttin (1984) has demonstrated, only a very small proportion of a person's goals can be located within a time perspective of a week or a month. Many if not most of our everyday actions are regulated by goals related not to our current representation of our actual selves, but to our projected future 'possible selves' (Markus and Nurius, 1986).

Furthermore, the primacy of identity projects as explanatory constructs is not simply a consequence of the distant future orientation of many of our goals and aspirations. Rather, it derives from the fact that our complex human emotions and motives relating to present actions, and referenced by our theoretical psychological explanations of actions, are themselves constituted as emotions and motives by being encompassed within identity projects. Emotions and motives such as envy, pride, shame, guilt, jealousy, anger, disappointment, obligation, and the like, all presuppose that the person to whom they are attributed has grasped and accepted the conventions of the moral orders of social collectives. Certain actions (and failures to act) are matters of concern to persons in relation to their identity projects: the outcome of such actions is held by persons to reflect positively or negatively upon their identity in terms of the success or failure of their identity projects.

Thus a person can only be ascribed shame for failure to support a comrade at arms, or for cheating in an exam, if these activities are conventionally represented within the moral order of a social collective as degrading negative reflections upon the person's reputation and self-worth, and if the person accepts such evaluations. Contrastingly, someone committed to the different moral order of a different social collective might treat successful cheating as an admirable achievement that is a proper source of personal pride and public reputation – within some high school sub-cultures, for example. Envy and jealousy (whatever their differences), like pride, presuppose a background of conventionally recognized achievements within some accepted moral career. I may, for example, be envious of a colleague's promotion if I am committed to the moral career of a professional psychologist, but I am hardly likely to be envious of his status in the local Republican Party if I am a committed Democrat or indifferent to politics.

Such characteristically human emotions and motives do not simply occur in splendid atomistic isolation and regularly cause particular behaviors (in terms of which some suppose they might be operationally defined). Such phenomena are intrinsically social and relational in nature: their contents are determined by a person's evaluation of her own and others' actions in relation to her socially located sense of identity in the form of an identity project. If this is correct, then no-one without at least a minimal sense of identity – in the form of a commitment to an identity project – could be ascribed such characteristically human emotions and motives, for anyone who did not care about their present and future reputation and self-worth could not be supposed to care in the appropriate ways about their own and others' actions.

For this reason the theoretical concept of an identity project references perhaps one of the few plausible candidates for a universal dimension of human social psychological life. It is hard to imagine any person in any form of social life – however historically or culturally distant – whose actions could be wholly explained without any reference to an identity project: for this would be to imagine a person devoid of characteristic human emotions and motives.

For this very reason the notion of an identity project perhaps deserves to function as one of the primary explanatory constructs of social psychology. It enables us to provide a systematic and illuminative integration of diverse explanations of a person's actions in terms of their emotions and motives, by demonstrating their common imbeddedness within a person's identity project. It also enables us to make illuminating cross-cultural and transhistorical comparisons of emotions and motives in terms of similarities and differences in the contents of identity projects, and the moral careers they encompass. For although identity projects may be universal, the contents of the moral careers that comprise them may be as diverse as the diverse forms of social collectivity to be discovered cross-culturally and transhistorically.

Although, according to the social psychological theory of identity in terms of identity projects, persons are continuously committed to identity projects, the theory does not suggest that commitment to such projects is necessarily a product of conscious choice, or that persons are in general reflexively conscious of their commitment to identity projects. Of course, sometimes this is the case: for a wide variety of reasons and causes, some persons may in a consciously considered way decide to become doctors or missionaries. Other persons, some perhaps grudgingly and others with stoic resignation, may find themselves developmentally imbedded in certain moral careers. They may simply follow their fathers into a banking career or their mothers into a life of domestic drudgery. Their identities are fixed by such moral careers only if they make such moral careers part of their identity project, if they become committed to making a (conventionally defined) success of such endeavors, and become concerned to avoid (conventionally defined) failures. Analogously some schoolchildren may never consciously decide to pursue or reject an academic moral career, but their commitment or non-commitment to an identity project that includes this is reflected in their concern or lack of concern with their scholastic performance.

Few persons could spontaneously articulate a fully detailed descriptive account of the contents and conventions of the diverse moral careers that comprise their identity projects – and certainly few would employ theoretical descriptions such as 'identity project' and 'moral career' in doing so. However, they do not need to in order to pursue identity projects within social collectives: all that is required is that they grasp and accept the sets of conventions that socially constitute moral careers within social collectives.

Identity and Individualism

The philosophical theory of personal identity advanced in the earlier sections of this chapter treated persons – to whom psychological states and identities are attributable – as distinct and discriminable individuals. This philosophical claim does not entail that the psychological states of persons, or the identities of persons, are themselves individual. It is entirely consistent with the recognition that psychological phenomena such as sense of identity and emotion, and indeed persons themselves, are intrinsically social, as in fact has been suggested by the form of social psychological theory of identity in terms of identity projects advanced in subsequent sections. Intrinsically social forms of identity in terms of identity projects are nevertheless attributable and attributed to distinct individual – albeit intrinsically social – persons: that is, precisely those distinct individual persons discriminated by the philosophical account of personal identity.

This might appear contradictory, but it is not. The fact that something is intrinsically social does not preclude it from being a distinct individual, far less a discriminable one. It only rules out the possibility that its identity as an individual is individualistic – that its constitutive properties are not grounded in any form of arrangement, convention, or agreement. Jurors that make up a jury in a trial by jury are individual jurors: each juror is distinct from every other juror (and qua juror, not merely qua person), and each juror can be discriminated as an individual juror from other individual jurors. Nonetheless, the property of being a juror is intrinsically social – and relational – in nature, in this case doubly so: it is grounded in the sets of conventions and agreements governing the selection and function of juries that jurors are parties to, and the particular arrangements involved in the formation of particular juries.

The basic point may be made in the following fashion. Although individual persons (and jurors) are distinct from each other, individual persons (and jurors) and their properties are not *independent* of each other, if they, and their properties, are intrinsically social and (thus) relational in nature: if they are grounded in joint commitments to arrangements, conventions, and agreements.

Questions about the causal autonomy of persons are quite separate questions.[8] Persons are distinct individuals who are intrinsically social in nature: it is an open theoretical question whether their actions are causally autonomous with respect to other persons. Again the example of jurors may illuminate this point. Jurors are distinct individuals that are intrinsically social in nature: it is an open theoretical question whether the judgments of individual jurors – concerning the guilt of the defendant, for example – are causally autonomous with respect to the judgments of other individual jurors, or causally influenced by them (and some may be causally autonomous and others causally influenced).

However, although, according to the theory of identity in terms of identity projects, such intrinsically social identity projects are attributable and attributed to distinct individual persons, it does not follow that these projects must be conceived, by – distinct individual – persons themselves, in *individual* terms.

The Western conception of the person or self as a distinct and independent and autonomous individual probably emerged toward the end of the Middle Ages (Lyons, 1978; Morris, 1972). Although the identity projects of Western folk are socially located within the moral orders of social collectives – as are the identity projects of all persons in all places and times – Westerners paradigmatically treat the individual as the locus of achievement and failure with respect to such projects. Although the intrinsically social contents and objects of emotions such as pride and shame, for example, are appropriated from the conventions of the social collective, emotions themselves are characteristically only ascribed to, and only experienced by, the individual who has succeeded or failed.

However, this is a characteristic feature of the content of the identity projects of individual persons in the post-medieval Western world. It is not an intrinsic feature of identity projects pursued by individual persons per se. There is no reason why the actions of an individual person could not be regulated by an identity project conceived in *collective* terms. The actor and observer may represent the actions of the actor as reflecting positively or negatively upon the identity of the collective, and pride and shame may be attributed and experienced collectively.

Something like this appears to have been true in the West during and prior to the Middle Ages. According to Williams (1961), throughout most of the Middle Ages the term 'individual' meant 'inseparable' or 'member of a group.' Certainly one does not have to look far in the anthropological record to identify social collectives whose members seem to make precisely this form of identification of individual and collective identity projects. Thus Inuit society seems to lack a moral order relating to autonomous actions (or has only a very attenuated form of this): theft and honesty among individuals are not treated as important vices and virtues (Harré, 1981). Rather those actions that are the object of moral concern are those that directly affect the social collective, or at least the extended family group, and the emotions associated with triumphs or failures are experienced by all members. Analogously Best (1924) reported of Maori culture that: 'It is well to ever bear in mind that a native so thoroughly identifies with his tribe that he is ever employing the first person pronoun [when referring to his tribe]' (1924: 397). (Compare Johansen, 1954: 35–9.) In the Maori custom of *muru*, a man can be punished – by institutionalized plunder – for accidental damage to himself. By damaging himself he damages the social collective – given the identification – and the members of the social collective are thus entitled to reparations (Smith, 1981).

It would of course be wrong to suggest that cultures fall neatly into the categories of individualist versus collectivist conceptions of identity projects. Rather they occupy different positions along a continuum differentially emphasizing individualism and collectivism. Thus Inuit society appears very close to the collectivist extreme, but Maori society does retain elements of individuality (since those assigned high status within the collective also have to earn and maintain the respect of other members of the collective to maintain these positions, and Maori myths also extol the individual virtues – bravery, oratory, leadership, and the like – of individual heroes (Smith, 1981)). Conversely, although the West may tend towards the extremity of individualism, one can discriminate analogous forms of collective identification within interdependent groups, such as combat units or athletic teams.

Furthermore, there is a respect in which a version of collectivism is prevalent in Western culture. While it may be rare for Westerners to conceive of their identity projects in generally collectivist terms, nevertheless something like this would appear to be the case with respect to intimate relations, such as love and friendship. If one were to try to characterize the essential features of Western love that distinguished it from mere physical or personal attraction (and approval, friendship, and the like), it may be suggested that it has to involve the desire to make the other person's identity a part of one's own. This is not the desire to absorb the other's identity as one's own, or be absorbed by the identity of the other (although this latter does appear to be an element in the Japanese emotion of *amae* (Morsbach and Tyler, 1976)), but the desire to instigate and institute what might be termed a *joint identity project* – to create a new or extended and richer identity out of (ideally) the best elements of both. The institutions and conventions of marriage and married life in many cultures provide the enabling conditions for one kind of joint moral career. Something similar would appear to be true of friendship between persons, which seems to minimally involve at least some real concern (and willingness to aid or advise) with the development of the identity project of the other person. This perhaps explains the point of criticizing certain actions as posing threats to 'our marriage' or 'our friendship.'

This distinction between individualist and collectivist conceptions of identity projects should not be confused with a traditional distinction made by social psychologists between *personal identity* and *social identity* (Brewer, 1991; Hogg and Abrams, 1988). According to the present account identity projects – whether individualistically or collectivistically conceived – are intrinsically social projects pursued by individual persons within social collectives. That is, according to the present account, personal identity is to be identified with social identity: it comprises nothing more or less than the – more or less successful – attempt to establish a social identity through moral careers within social collectives.[9]

Identity and Moral Psychology

Now some might agree that identity is intimately connected to the moral orders of social collectives. They might, however, object that identity is fixed essentially or ultimately by moral character, by the moral actions and decisions of individual persons, and that this is a universal feature that is largely independent of particular moral careers such as professions and family, and largely independent of possibly diverse forms of social life.

It is of course true that many Western philosophers and psychologists have largely conceived of moral matters in these terms. Accordingly matters of morality are conceived in terms of autonomous rational decision making, and the strength of will to act in accord with such decisions. It is however very doubtful if such analyses accurately characterize the moral psychology of persons in many cultures. According to Benedict (1967) and Morris (1975), for example, the moral universe of the Japanese is regulated by very clearly defined systems of – usually asymmetrical – responsibilities and obligations to specific others in specific collectives (family, work, state, and the like). There are no abstract rules that must be rationally applied to the diverse situations of work and family: Japanese morality is based upon the very specific obligations and responsibilities of local moral orders. Indeed there are perhaps few cultures that share the Western conception of – and concern with – the rational autonomy of the moral agent. Most cultures are rather more concerned to ensure that most persons are enabled to fulfill their local responsibilities and obligations: via education, coercion, ritual practices, and the like.

Western philosophers and psychologists may bemoan this moral psychological fact about other cultures. However, there are grounds for suspecting that it is also largely true of Western cultures. Without denying that there are some real moral dilemmas, most of our own moral lives seem to be governed by local matters of honor: by very specific obligations and responsibilities to colleagues, students, children, friends, fellow gang members, priests, and the like. We may characterize the moral dilemma of Sartre's (1948) student who was faced with the choice of staying to support his invalid mother or going off to fight for the Free French as a paradigmatic example of radical or autonomous choice. Yet it may be doubted if this is a regular feature of real moral life, even in the West – and even in France. At the outbreak of the First World War, droves of Scottish Highlanders essentially deserted their impoverished farms and families to fight for King and country on the fields of Flanders, without a second thought about the consequences, and their actions were not questioned by their friends and families. No doubt the same was true of many French farmers who went off to fight for the Free French.

Notoriously, traditional moral philosophical theories have enormous difficulty in providing moral recommendations about the right thing to do in cases involving strangers and intimates. In artificially constructed scenarios where an agent has the hypothetical choice to save the life of a stranger, or a friend or family member (where the scenario is constructed so that the agent can only save the life of one), moral philosophical theories seem to provide no rational or plausible grounds for preferring one decision over another. However, few persons in few cultures would have much difficulty in deciding such a question if it arose in a real-life situation.

Moreover, according to some traditional moral theories, there will be possible situations where on utilitarian grounds one ought to save the life of a stranger rather than a family member or friend. Whatever the avowed consequentialist rationale for such a recommended decision, many cultures would consider and abhor the very contemplation of such an alternative as the epitome of moral corruption (cf. Flanagan and Adler, 1983).

These reflections may throw some light on recent criticisms of Kohlberg's (1981a, 1981b) stage theory of moral development. Empirical studies of moral development based upon Kohlberg's theory have suggested that most women, and persons in Africa and other underdeveloped countries, do not achieve Kohlberg's highest stage of moral development, the post-conventional 'principled' stage of universal abstract duties and rights (in the formal philosophical tradition of Kant,

Hare, and Rawls), but generally manifest forms of moral thought that remain at the conventional stage of moral development, grounded in concrete obligations and responsibilities to one's family or tribe.

Gilligan (1982) has criticized Kohlberg's account for being dominated by adherence to male-generated moral philosophies, and has objected to the implicit moral judgment that the highest stage identified by male philosophers and achieved by many men[10] is somehow morally superior to the moral thought of women. She has claimed that there are two distinct – but interlocking – moral orders: the moral order of women, based upon responsibilities grounded in and restricted to local social relations; and the moral order of men, based upon universal rights and the equitable distribution of goods. She argues that the moral order of women is just different from the moral order of men, and not deficient in relation to it. Analogously, other feminist theorists have argued that traditional African moralities are just different, not deficient, and many have pointed to the similarities between female moral orders and the moral orders of traditional African societies (Harding, 1987).

There may well be some truth in this, perhaps more truth than is usually supposed. Although educated males – like educated women (Gilligan, 1986) – can produce accounts in terms of abstract and universal moral principles when required, it may be seriously doubted if most men determine their everyday actions in accord with such principles. The actions of most men, even in modern Western society, would appear to be governed by local obligations to wives, children, colleagues, friends, clients, students, parishioners, and the like. That is, the moral thought of most men would also appear to be locatable at Kohlberg's conventional level: the level of local moral orders of moral careers within specific social collectives.

Moreover, it seems doubtful if there are distinct male or female – or African – moral orders per se, as opposed to the particular moral orders of the moral careers within specific social collectives that tend to be the focus of engagement by men or women – or Africans – in any particular historical time or cultural place. That is, it is very doubtful if there is any universal moral order over and above the particular moral orders of particular social collectives – such as family, profession, gang, religion, and tribe; or that there are moral orders specific to men, women, or Africans by virtue of their being men, women, or Africans.

In some societies it may be the case that all persons form a social collective in which all persons are committed to rights and obligations that are held to apply universally to all persons in that society, and in such societies it may be the case that persons can make a moral career out of being a 'moral agent.' It may be doubted, however, whether there are societies that themselves form a moral collective with a moral order in addition to, and distinct from, the moral orders of the variety of social collectives in which moral careers are normally pursued; just as it may be doubted that 'society' itself forms a social collective in addition to, and distinct from, the various interlocking social collectives that might more naturally be held to comprise it.

These claims are not advanced as a general critique of traditional or contemporary moral philosophy. Nevertheless, one might suspect that at least some of the problems of traditional and contemporary moral philosophy derive from their abstraction from the powerful conventions of local moral orders. One indication of this is the standard moral philosophical treatment of human emotions as an unfortunate form of bias and impediment to rational moral judgment (Rachels, 1986; Regan, 1986). This sort of analysis presupposes some form of the traditional distinction and opposition between reason and passion, according to which emotional phenomena are treated as intrinsically irrational.

However, according to the account of complex human emotions to be developed later in this work, the contents of our emotions are rationally evaluable. The objects of our shame and the contents of our anger may be considered to be socially inappropriate or unjustified, and we may be persuaded out of our shame and anger when we are persuaded of this. Conversely we may be persuaded (or taught) to be ashamed in socially appropriate situations. What we are persuaded of in such situations is the adoption of a certain evaluative attitude to our own and others' actions in relation to our identity projects. These evaluative attitudes that comprise the contents of emotions such as concern, sympathy, shame, guilt, anger, and the like seem to be at the heart of our moral lives as well as our identities. It would be hard to ascribe moral judgments to agents who did not represent their own and others' actions in terms of the evaluative dimensions of such emotions.

This is not to devalue the cherished conception of the moral agent as an autonomous and rational agent. It is merely to stress that this is simply one possible way of fixing one's identity in one particular – albeit very familiar if perhaps only hypothetical – social collective. The existential reflector is a sort of moral hero for some of us. For many Eastern cultures he would be the epitome of moral weakness and failure.

To make these claims is not to advocate or endorse any form of moral relativism. If what I have said about the universality of identity projects and their imbeddedness in the moral orders of social collectives is correct, then concern for matters of obligation and responsibility based upon the recognition of the dignity and worth of persons would be common to all persons pursuing identity projects within social collectives. It appears to be true, for example, of all the cultures already discussed, which recognize reciprocal systems of rights, responsibilities, and obligations defined by local moral orders.

Nevertheless, such a concern does not seem to entail any form of egalitarianism. There is no reason why a recognition of the dignity and worth of persons should be tied to a belief that every person has equal rights, responsibilities, and obligations. It could be very well tied to a hierarchical system of graduated and asymmetrical rights, responsibilities, and obligations, according to one's social position within social collectives. Japanese society has for centuries been highly stratified and hierarchical, and while the upper echelons such as the feudal lords and samurai recognized the rights of lower echelons such as farmers and outcasts (such as their protected right to ownership of land and the practice of certain trades), the rights, responsibilities, and obligations of each order were quite distinct and asymmetrical (Benedict, 1967).

Nor is there any reason to presume that such a recognition will necessarily operate on principles of broad inclusion. Rather it may operate in tandem with rather rigid principles of exclusion with respect to socially devalued persons or groups that may result in the treatment of some human beings as non-persons: for example, the treatment of American prisoners of war by the Japanese; the treatment of women in some cultures; or the treatment of dishonored persons in Maori culture. Indeed, it may result in the grossest forms of destruction and cruelty, characteristic of the identity projects of medieval knights and the followers of Ghengis Khan.

Identity and Responsibility

Now oftentimes such principles of exclusion are based upon the intentional actions of agents, for which they are held responsible by other members of a social collective. The Japanese soldier who surrendered was disgraced as a soldier, citizen, and family man. He was 'dead' to his former life: these moral careers were over. This was treated by other Japanese (including his own family) as a form of failure as a person (Benedict, 1967). It is also characteristic of Western collectives to treat the achievements and failures of agents with respect to their moral careers as a product of their personal effort and application, so that agents may claim credit for their achievements and accept responsibility for their failures.

This enables agents to avoid certain threats to their identity by recourse to a variety of excuses that delimit their responsibility for failure, by appeal to external factors beyond their control. Thus my rather poor performance at a lecture or my failure to get home from work in time for my child's birthday is not held (by me or others) to reflect negatively on my identity if I have laryngitis or if my car was involved in an accident caused by the reckless driving of another. This has led one theorist to claim that: 'emotions, such as pride, ambition, guilt and remorse, imply a certain view of ourselves. They are probably not felt in cultures in which little importance is attached to individual effort and responsibility' (Peters, 1974: 402).

It is true that these sorts of distinction and these forms of excusing are not salient in some cultures. The moral order of the Maoris, for example, does not seem to make much of such distinctions. The individual is dishonored and disgraced by the defeat in battle of his tribe or himself, even if he proved to be a brave and courageous fighter, and defeat was due to factors beyond his control. There is no reason to suppose he is not ashamed, or any less ashamed, because of his individual performance, or because defeat was beyond his control (Smith, 1981). Many persons in some cultures and historical periods do appear to take genuine pride in and feel genuinely ashamed of successes and failures that are believed to be a product of fate or divine intervention, even by the most fickle of gods. Consider what is supposed to be the genuine remorse and shame of Oedipus, as described by Sophocles, despite the fact that Oedipus' actions were held to be determined by Fate.

Indeed, such a conception is hardly alien in the contemporary West: often enough we are proud of our successes however effortlessly achieved, and ashamed of our failures however hard we try to avoid them, or however much they are beyond our control. The gifted child regularly takes pride in her effortless academic achievements, and is socially honored by her peers, parents, and teachers. The child who lacks height and weight may be genuinely ashamed of his failure to make the football team, and may be cruelly scorned by his peers. The adult scientist may take pride in the easy products of his genius to the point of pomposity, and we may award him prizes and honors in recognition of his established reputation. The unemployed miner in the economic recession may be ashamed of his inability to support his family, and may be condemned by many for his failure. We may of course have good cause to question whether this is as it ought to be. Nevertheless, it appears to be a fairly well established social psychological fact of contemporary life.

Identity and Agency
This is not to devalue our concept of human agency, or to deny its explanatory utility as a theoretical psychological description. I have argued in detail elsewhere (Greenwood, 1988, 1989) that many human actions may in fact be genuine products of human agency, and that this likely state of affairs ought to be squarely faced by scientific psychologists.

An action may be said to be a product of human agency if it is within the power of the person to produce or refrain from producing that action: if the production of the action comes within the self-control of the person. In the case of actions that are the product of agency, stimulus situations provide opportunities for the exercise of a human power – such as the ability to speak Russian or solve differential equations – but do not determine particular manifestations of it. Actions that are not the product of human agency are those that are determined by stimulus-driven liabilities – such as the liability to stutter in female company – in which the (internal or external) stimulus conditions function as ontologically sufficient conditions for the production of the action. In the case of human liabilities, the person cannot refrain from acting as he does (or finds it enormously difficult to do so). Such actions are not within the self-control of the agent, but are under the control of the stimulus conditions.[11] According to this account, it is an empirical matter whether any particular action is a product of human agency or is stimulus-determined. Thus for example some acts of aggression may be exercises of human agency motivated by revenge; other acts of aggression may be determined by 'violent stimuli' (Berkowitz and LePage, 1967).

The concept of human agency plays an essential role in our Western concepts of responsibility and desert. In order for any person to be held responsible for a crime and deserving of punishment, the crime must be a product of human agency: it must have been the intentional exercise of a personal power that the agent could have refrained from exercising. It is also true that the concepts of agency and responsibility play a major role with respect to our characteristically Western (and characteristically individualistic) identity projects. It may, however, be suggested that it is doubtful if they play such a major role with respect to the identity projects of persons in other cultures (and doubted if they play as much of a role in our own as is commonly supposed), and that whatever the role they play in any particular culture or historical period, this feature is *not an intrinsic component of identity projects and their associated emotions*.

It does not seem to be a necessary condition of shame, for example, (although perhaps a common enough feature of it) that persons represent the objects of their shame as products of their agency. There seems to be no contradiction or empirical implausibility in supposing that some persons may be ashamed of their physical disabilities or their race, their own liabilities to be aggressive or offensive, or the actions of their cousins or ancestors. Indeed all these phenomena are actual in some cultures (including our own).

We should, however, be careful not to confuse this issue with another issue. The fact that many cultures have little social usage for the concept of human agency does not entail that the concept has no application in these cultures, that it is merely a (socially constructed) linguistic artifact of our particular (and perhaps peculiar) form of social life. We can properly ask of any person in any culture or historical period whether (or to what degree) their actions are exercises of agency or determined by stimulus-driven liabilities – this is simply a consequence of the general fact that the social lack of a concept of X in another culture does not preclude us from providing an objective answer to the question of whether the dimensions referenced by *our* concept of X – e.g. of anger, democracy, or agency – are instantiated in another culture. There can always be an objective answer to this empirical question because having the concept of human agency is not a necessary condition for being a human agent: it is not necessary to have the concept of human agency in order to be able to refrain from the exercise of a power. Nor of course is possession of the concept of agency sufficient for human agency: having the concept of human agency does not by itself enable me to overcome my stimulus-driven liabilities – would that it did!

One might suppose that having the concept of agency might facilitate agency. However, this is far from obviously true. What does facilitate agency is any form of social practice that promotes the expenditure of human effort in surmounting liabilities. Yet, oddly enough, the sorts of social practice that involve the steeling or training or exercise of the 'will' are regularly to be found in those cultures that are committed to forms of determinism. Muslims believe that everything that happens is the 'will of Allah,' but devote huge portions of their lives to practical rituals of self-control (such as the Ramadan fast). Those Scottish Church fathers who were most deeply committed to the predestination doctrines of extreme Calvinism were also those most brutal in their practical schemes to instill the virtues of self-control in their children. Conversely, those Western cultures that take human agency for granted often do little in practice to encourage self-control among their members – especially, and perhaps notoriously in some cases – with respect to their children.

Notes

1 Assuming, as I do, that the psychological states of persons are physically incarnated in their neurophysiology. However, precisely the same point would in fact apply if the psychological states of persons were instantiated in some form of non-physical or spiritual substance (see Greenwood, 1993b).

2 'Quasi-memory' is a term – originally introduced by Shoemaker (1970) – to describe memories of prior experiences or actions that do not presuppose that the person remembering the prior experience or action is identical to the person who had the original experience or engaged in the original action.

3 Thus Locke (1690, II, xxvii, 2), for example, claimed of thoughts that 'concerning their diversity there can be no question . . . no motion or thought considered as at different times can be the same . . .'; Reid (1785: 109) claimed that 'identity cannot, in its proper sense, be applied to our pains, our pleasures, or any operations of our minds. . . . They are all successive in their nature, like time itself, no two moments of which can be the same moment.'

4 The term 'identity project' is appropriated from Rom Harré (1983a, 1983b). However, the present account does not aim to provide any interpretation of his theoretical employment of the notion of an 'identity project'. I am sure he would not agree with many of my claims about identity projects, although I hope my account is close to the spirit of – if some miles from the letter of – his.

5 For reasons that he never gives and which I do not pretend to understand, Goffman himself denies that one can succeed or fail with respect to moral careers (1961: 127). He then goes on to document in great detail how one can succeed or fail in 'making out' in 'total institutions' such as prisons, army training camps, monasteries, and mental hospitals. He may have only meant that such moral careers cannot be treated as successes or failures in terms of the measures of conventional careers: what is at stake in a moral career is reputation and self-worth, not merely level of salary or hierarchical position *simpliciter*.

6 Although for most of the following discussion of identity projects I talk of unified and integrated identity projects encompassing a *plurality* of moral careers, there is of course no reason in principle why a person's identity should not encompass only a single moral career. Given the variety of threats to identity documented in Chapter 7, this would, however, represent a rather hazardous state of affairs for any person.

7 These remarks do not imply that it is easy for persons to abandon prior identity projects when they embark upon new ones. Persons who abandon old identity projects and adopt new ones may still retain elements of older identity projects, and some of the actions of the persons they now are may still require some reference to the identity projects of the persons they once were. Thus we may retain some of the elements of the moral careers of our childhood, early family life, schooldays, and adolescence, perhaps against our will and better judgment, or without our knowledge. This is perhaps the best way to theoretically accommodate some of the insights of the psychoanalytic literature, and many of the – less than full-blown – cases of multiple-personality.

8 Failure to make precisely these distinctions between distinctness, independence, and causal autonomy vitiates much of the classical debate about the mind–body problem.

9 The distinction between individualistically and collectivistically conceived identity projects is also independent of the recognized fact that sometimes we see ourselves in terms of the properties we share with, or sometimes identify ourselves with, other members of social collectives (psychologists, Christians, etc.) or derivatively social groups (women, persons with AIDS, etc.), in order either to distinguish ourselves from others, or to affiliate ourselves with them, on different occasions and in different circumstances (although, as argued in Chapter 7, none of these forms of 'self-labeling' or identification play any constitutive role with respect to our identity). Thus the poet Yeats revelled in his Irishness in London, and in his status as part of the English intelligentsia in Dublin – but not during the time of the Easter rebellion against the English.

10 Although not that many men in fact reach this stage, and Kohlberg (1981b) doubted if anyone – including any men – reached the highest stage – Stage 6 – involving the recognition of the universal and intrinsic value of human life.

11 There is no contradiction involved in claiming that some human *actions* are not a product of human *agency*. It is not a necessary condition of human actions that they are products of human agency, although it is a common error to suppose that this is the case. Those behaviors that are human actions are those behaviors that are intentionally directed and/or socially meaningful according to some convention. Such actions may be either products of human agency or determined by stimulus-driven liabilities. Thus my aggressive action may be intentional and my offensive action may be socially meaningful, but both forms of action may be determined by stimulus-driven liabilities to be aggressive and offensive towards certain persons. For a fuller discussion and defense of this claim, see Greenwood (1989, 1991a).

7

Identity and Social Labeling

Much of the social psychological literature on identity is avowedly concerned with the social nature of identity, but is based upon an impoverished conception of the social dimensions of identity. Most social psychological theories of identity treat identity as constituted by social labeling: by the employment of cognitive labels related to membership of social groups.[1] In this chapter I distinguish such accounts from the form of social psychological theory in terms of intrinsically social identity projects advanced in the previous chapter.

'Social labeling' accounts of identity are inadequate because they treat identity as *derivatively* social. I do not deny that social labeling plays an important role with respect to our identity, only that it plays any *constitutive* role with respect to our identity: our identities are not constituted by the employment of cognitive labels – by self or others – relating to group membership. The real significance of cognitive labeling can only be appreciated by recognizing the leading role it plays in relation to our success or failure in pursuing those intrinsically social identity projects that are constitutive of our identity.

There are many 'social' theories of identity. However, they bear only a tenuous relationship to the social psychological theory of identity in terms of identity projects. The social developmental theories of Cooley (1902) and Mead (1934), for example, stress the social origins of our sense of identity, but conceive of this as constructed out of the descriptions and interpretations of 'significant others' or 'generalized others.' Many theorists stress that our sense of identity is largely determined by our social location, but conceive of this in terms of our self-descriptions based upon our membership of certain social groups, or occupation of certain social roles (Epstein, 1973; Hoelter, 1983; Kuhn, 1964; McCall, 1977; McCall and Simmons, 1978; Rosenberg, 1981; Rosenberg and Gara, 1985; Stryker, 1980; Turner, 1987; Wicklund and Gollwitzer, 1982). We label ourselves according to the categories of groups of which we are members. Thus we may describe ourselves in terms of categories or roles such as sex, race, occupation, family position, age, social class, and the like. Kuhn's (1964) well-known twenty statements test (TST), requiring twenty answers to the question 'Who am I?', is an invitation to provide a list of such self-descriptions.

To claim that identity is constituted in this fashion is to claim that identity is merely derivatively social, in two respects. It is to claim that whatever social dimensions may be attributed to identity are a consequence of the social significance (according to a convention) of properties we ascribe to ourselves (or that are ascribed to us by others) that we share (or are held to share) with other members of aggregate groups: groups that are themselves derivatively social.

The aim of this chapter is not to deny the importance and relevance of such work on self-labeling and social comparison processes (Festinger, 1957; Tajfel, 1981) to a theoretical account of identity. Nevertheless, such theories do not appear to get to the heart of the matter. A large part of the problem is the opacity of references to the 'social groups' or 'reference groups' (Merton and Kitt, 1950), by means of which a person is supposed to fix his or her identity. Although social psychologists and sociologists do regularly distinguish between different types of social groups and populations, the significance of such distinctions is generally ignored in discussions of personal identity.

In particular there is a singular failure to distinguish between what I characterized in Chapter 5 as intrinsically social groups or social collectives, and derivatively social aggregate groups. Intrinsically social groups – or social collectives – are those populations whose members are parties to sets of arrangements, conventions, and agreements governing their behavior, such as the populations of bankers, married persons, the Azande, and Hell's Angels. Derivatively social groups are aggregate groups comprised of populations whose members share a common property (or properties) that is (or are) socially significant according to some convention or agreement, such as the populations of men, women, blacks, senior citizens, and persons who are deaf, have AIDS, or are unemployed.

The significance of this distinction for identity is as follows. Although membership of derivatively social aggregate groups – such as the populations of women, unemployed persons, or persons with AIDS – provides a basis for social labeling and social comparison, it does not provide the conceptual or practical resources for the formation and maintenance of identity. Such groups have no structural features (social or otherwise) that ensure their maintenance throughout changes in membership. They are not constituted by joint commitments by members to arrangements, conventions, and agreements, including those governing rites of passage and status elevation and reversal. They do not provide possible and potentially progressive routes for the management of reputation and self-worth, and do not conventionally define situations that represent hazards to it. In short, they do not provide the conceptual or practical resources for identity projects.

In contrast, many (although not all)[2] social collectives such as professions, families, religious organizations, street gangs, and primitive tribes manifest all these features, and are thus effective conceptual and practical vehicles for the formation and maintenance of identity, for they are effectively conceptual and practical vehicles for identity projects.

Identity and Identification

Much social psychological theory is not really concerned with identity per se, but is rather concerned with *identification* (Weinreich, 1980, 1983). This is perhaps not surprising, since the term 'identity' was introduced into the social scientific literature in the 1950s in the context of studies of ethnic, racial, and religious identification (Gleason, 1983). Most social psychological theories of identity are concerned with the members of groups that persons identify with, and the self-descriptions or 'cognitive labels' they apply to themselves as a result (and their respective priority).[3] Thus, many measures of identity are free or structured invitations to list and rank such self-categorizations, and persons regularly list descriptions (in different ranked orders) such as 'mother,' 'nurse,' 'black,' 'French,' 'deaf,' 'reader,' 'gardener,' 'woman,' 'middle-aged,' and so on (Hermans, 1976; Rosenberg and Jones, 1972; Zavalloni, 1971). Often enough, in fact, identity is simply defined in such terms: 'identity is comprised of the labels one would use to describe oneself' (Breakwell, 1983a: 13); 'ascribed categories such as gender, race, and ethnicity are forms of identity that provide a basis for self definition' (Deaux, 1993).

This appears to be quite wrong. I am proud to be Scottish, proud of my ancestors and their traditions. Being Scottish contributes significantly to my self-esteem and self-concept, and I might very well describe myself as Scottish if required to give twenty answers to the Kuhnian question. Yet I don't suppose for a moment that this has anything to do with my *identity*: it plays no generally directive role with respect to my actions. This is not a personal idiosyncrasy. Being Scottish does not enable me to fix my identity in any way. It is not something I can make a moral career of. I cannot make a success of it or fail at it. It plays no essential role in my identity, since, like other properties of aggregate group membership I share, and like the properties of aggregate group membership in general, although it undoubtedly does have significance for me, it can provide no point and purpose to my life or general direction to my actions.

Despite the familiar rhetoric, the feminist movement has not created new or richer or alternative ways for women to fix their identities. Being a woman is to be a member of a derivatively social aggregate group, since the property of gender has social significance. Yet the populations of women in most Western cultures do not form social collectives. One cannot make a moral career out of being a woman. This is largely a consequence of the feminist movement.

It used to be the case, and still is in some cultures, that one could make a moral career of being a woman, namely in those cultures where being a woman is identified with the moral careers of wife and mother. In small towns in Scotland, for example, such identifications are still strong: young girls from the age of 15 onwards go to great lengths to borrow other people's babies so that they can parade them down the local streets, ideally with their boyfriends on their arm – just like the real wives and mothers do. This form of social rehearsal is indicative of their overriding commitment to this form of moral career. Much the same is true of women in rural France and Germany, and in many Latin and Asian countries.

One sees little of this in Greenwich Village, of course. This form of identification is denied by many today who have been influenced by the feminist movement. Yet in the absence of this form of identification, being a woman does not by itself provide the social psychological basis for any other form of moral career.[4] What the feminist movement has done, to a greater or lesser degree, is to open up a number of alternative moral careers that were either closed to women or difficult for them to enter or succeed in (such as the professions, including the army, organized religion, literature, politics, and the like).

The civil rights movement has perhaps been less successful in this respect, particularly in relation to the academic world. Unlike women, many blacks seem to have had much less success in exploiting the supposedly increased educational opportunities that are now available to them, and the increased professional opportunities that are consequent to academic success. There have been many explanations of this. One popular explanation is that blacks have failed to identify with the goals and values of the white persons who tend to dominate the academic world and professions, and therefore make little effort to fix their identity in these terms.

This may or may not be the case. Yet it needs to be stressed that any alternative identification and solidarity with other blacks provides no solution to any identity problem they may have. Being black does not itself fix any form of identity, any more than being a woman or being a man does.

One used to be able to make a moral career out of being an Ndongo tribesman (of West Central Africa), because this was identified with success or failure in agriculture and cattle rearing among the Ndongo. However, it is hard to be a good Ndongo on the streets of Harlem or Atlanta. Analogously, one used to be able to make a moral career out of being a man, and no doubt this is still possible in some cultures, when and where being a man is identified with a particular kind of moral career. No such possibility exists for most modern Western men, except perhaps in the event of war.

Essentially the same point can be made by making the following contrasts. Being married is not only socially significant, but also enables persons to fix their identity by reference to the moral career structure the institution of marriage provides. Being divorced is also socially significant but does not offer a similar moral career structure for fixing identity. Someone who is married is part of a structured social collective that provides a conventional route for fixing identity. Someone who is divorced is only part of an aggregate social group. Or contrast the moral careers offered by the social institutions of most professions and trades with the merely socially significant membership of the aggregate groups of unemployed or retired persons. One can make a moral career out of being an academic psychologist or a miner. One cannot make a moral career out of being an unemployed or retired person.

This is not of course to deny that unemployed, retired, or divorced persons – or blacks, women, or Scotsmen – can have moral careers. It is just to deny that they can make a moral career out of being an unemployed, retired, or divorced person – or a black person, woman, or Scotsman – since the members of the aggregate groups with whom they share common properties do not form a social collective. They can of course pursue moral careers within social collectives of which they are members: the unemployed or retired person, for example, can fix their identity by the moral careers of family, religion, or politics. Nor is it to deny that at any point in time such aggregate groups could organize themselves into social collectives with moral career structures (and the basic point of the present discussion is not vitiated if I am wrong or out of date in claiming that certain populations – such as deaf persons – are aggregate groups rather than social collectives).

Nor do these claims involve any denial of the social significance and emotional potency of being seen by oneself and others as a woman, a black, or a Scotsman, or as an unemployed, retired, or divorced person.[5] Rather, the main point of the claims is to illustrate and stress that such social labeling and comparison phenomena generally only have significance and emotional potency in relation to socially available identity projects within social collectives. A central thesis of this work is that identity is a social phenomenon in a much stronger sense than is usually acknowledged by many 'social' theories of identity. It is not merely social in developmental origin and influenced by social labeling based upon group membership. It is an intrinsically social and strongly relational phenomenon: the product of a person's engagement in moral careers whose contents are derived from and evaluated by reference to conventionally possible passages of success and failure within social collectives. Without social collectives, and without a commitment to and engagement in the moral careers offered by them, persons have no conceptual or practical means of determining their own identities.

Social labeling plays no constitutive role with respect to identity, which is constituted by identity projects pursued within social collectives. It does, however, function as one of the most potent threats to identity.

Threats to Identity and Social Labeling

One important implication of the social psychological theory of identity in terms of identity projects is as follows. Some threats to a person's identity may be individual in origin: a person may simply come to lose her commitment to a particular moral career. She may no longer care about her performance as a lawyer or mother. However, most threats to identity will be intrinsically social in nature. These may take a variety of forms.

One form of threat is omnipresent. The very nature of moral careers ensures that persons are constantly exposed to potential and actual threats to their reputation and self-worth: our identities are determined by our success or failure in responding to them. Whatever our past achievements, our moral careers and consequent identities may be destroyed by major failures: as in the case of the academic who publishes a disastrous book, the warrior who runs away, the mother who beats her children, and the miner who fails to repay a loan from a friend and colleague.

It is of course possible to surmount such failure heroically by demonstrable future successes and the employment of excuses, although it is significantly harder for persons so stigmatized to maintain their moral careers, for more is naturally expected of them than others (Goffman, 1963). Other threats to identity cannot be so easily resolved by personal effort or renewed commitment. Sometimes identity is threatened by the destruction of the social collectives within which identity projects are pursued: this may be true of some demobilized soldiers, some committed participants in the now defunct hippie culture, some gang members or leaders when social or economic conditions lead to the abandonment of the gang by most of its members. This very real threat to identity can only be surmounted by adopting a quite different identity project in place of the old, or shifting priority of commitment to a concomitant moral career (such as family or religion).

A special case of this is the destruction of the joint identity projects of intimates such as marriage partners through the death of one of them. For many elderly persons, not only their lives but also their very identities are destroyed when they lose their spouses (particularly if they are also retired and their children lead independent lives): their lives no longer have any point or purpose. Often enough for such persons suicide appears not only a flight from grief but also a rational choice, and indeed in some cultures (such as Maori and Inuit) such an action is socially approved (and in others socially required) for just this sort of reason.

However, perhaps the greatest social threat to identity comes from the potent resources of social labeling. Another frequently offered reason for the academic failure of black persons is that too many have come to accept the racial stereotyping in terms of intellectual inferiority that is present in our society. They have not managed to overcome this as successfully as women, for example, who have been long subject to similar, although perhaps not so strongly negative, stereotyping. This may or may not be the case. Nevertheless, it is a plausible explanation, for the following reason.

Although social labeling in terms of socially significant and emotionally potent properties shared with other members of aggregate groups is not itself constitutive of identity, the social dynamics of such labeling are enormously powerful in determining the outcomes of socially available moral careers that are constitutive of identity.

Being a woman, being black, being Jewish, being working class or poor, being deaf, being old, being retired, and the like, and being labeled as such, are not constitutive of identity. However, they often function as powerful impediments to entry into many moral careers, and impediments to success in many others.[6] Analogously, being white, Christian, a Freemason, having an alumni father, being young, good-looking, and the like, and being labeled as such, are not constitutive of identity either. Yet they very often function as powerful advantages for accelerated entry and success in many moral careers. That is, such forms of social labeling do play an important role in determining our identities, but not constitutively: their role is restricted to influencing the possibilities of entry into, and success or failure in, moral careers within social collectives. Unless contemporary analyses of the self-concept and self-esteem are tied to possibilities of entry and success in particular moral careers, they will have little interesting theoretical light to shed upon the fundamental – and intrinsically social – psychological dimensions and problems of identity.

Social labeling based upon aggregate group membership may be emotionally potent, and references to the consequences of such labeling may play a role in the explanation of behavior. Self-labeling based upon aggregate group membership may encourage feelings of 'communion,' 'harmony,' or 'solidarity' (with other Italians or women, or other deaf, retired, black or unemployed persons), and a reference to such feelings may play a role in the explanation of behavior. But these forms of self-labeling and associative feelings are not constitutive of identity. The general significance of the consequences of, and feelings associated with, social labeling in terms of aggregate group membership, cannot be properly understood without recognizing the role they play in relation to identity projects pursued within social collectives.

The threats to identity discussed in this chapter have the significant consequence that certain persons may properly be said to lack an identity – or at least to all intents and purposes. They are persons because of their commitment to an identity project, but they lack an identity because they fail to achieve any degree of success with respect to their identity project. Despite their lack of identity, they remain persons because of their commitment to an identity project, and because their actions can be explained in terms of this commitment, and in terms of (albeit usually very negative) associated emotions and motives. Such cases are to be distinguished from the case of human beings who are not committed to any identity project – if any there are. Such human beings would not count as persons, since their actions could not be explained in terms of their commitment to identity projects, or in terms of associated emotions and motives.

Social Constructionism

One unfortunate consequence of the recent social psychological emphasis on social labeling processes with respect to theories of identity is that many theorists have come to accept a social constructionist account of identity, according to which our identities are constructed out of socially negotiated forms of discourse that are held to serve a variety of social, moral, and political ends: 'Identities are not the freely created products of introspection, or the unproblematic reflections of the private sanctum of the "inner self", but are conceived within certain ideological frameworks constructed by the dominant (patriarchical) order to maintain its own interests' (Kitzinger, 1989: 82).

According to the social constructionist theorist, our identities are constituted by such forms of social discourse. There are no independent facts about our identities that our social discourse putatively 'about' our identities describes, so the question of the truth or accuracy of such accounts does not arise:

> Departing from psychology's traditional interest in identity as a personal and 'subjective' account of the self (to be compared with the 'objective' account of the person's self as assessed by the psychologist), research interest within a social constructionist framework is focused not on the 'accuracy' of the identity account, but on the social and political functions it serves. (Kitzinger, 1989: 82)

The social constructionist account denies the intrinsically social nature of identity. According to social constructionism, identity is at best derivatively social, by virtue of the intrinsically social nature of our theoretical discourse putatively 'about' identity.

It may be recognized – as in the previous chapter – that identity is not determined by the continuity or continuance of a 'private' or 'inner' entity such as the 'soul,' the 'ego,' or the 'self.' It does not follow that identity is not determined by any psychological continuant. As noted in the previous chapter, there are more than two theoretical alternatives to be considered. One is not forced to accept that identity either presupposes a mysterious 'ego' or 'soul,' or is nothing more than a socially potent linguistic device. According to the social psychological theory of identity advanced in this work, identity is an intrinsically social psychological fact about persons that is fixed by the identity projects they are engaged in within social collectives.

It can also be recognized – and has been recognized – that identities are social constructions in the respect noted in Chapter 5. They are social constructions insofar and inasmuch as they are constitutive products of arrangements, conventions, and agreements governing what counts as success and failure and hazard with respect to moral careers within social collectives. Moreover, identities are also socio-linguistically constructed or created: they emerge and are forged in historical time and cultural place through the social actions of persons and their moral commentaries upon them, and are maintained and sustained by the reproduction of such actions and commentaries. The conventions of marriage, the professions, and organized religion, for example, are not to be found among non-social and non-linguistic animals.[7] However, the constitutive outcome of such actions and commentaries is the creation of certain intrinsically social facts about collectives and their conventions, including those governing identity through identity projects.

It is an established convention that achievement in the moral career of a scientist is determined in certain ways rather than others: by publication in internationally refereed journals, by peer replication of significant results, by the attainment of prestigious positions, awards, and the like. It is an objective matter whether or not this type of moral career within a social collective is established in any culture or historical period. Moreover, when such a form of moral career is socially available in any culture or historical period, it is an objective matter whether or not any particular person is committed to it, or is a success or failure according to its conventions. Given the conventions of the academic world and marriage, it is an objective matter whether any particular man, woman, black person, white person, Scotsman or Jew is committed to, and is a success or failure with respect to, such moral careers – whatever advantages or impediments they may enjoy or suffer as a consequence of social labeling.

Our theoretical descriptions of the arrangements, conventions, and agreements of social collectives within which moral careers are pursued are linguistically objective: they are true and accurate if and only if there are persons who are parties to these arrangements, conventions, and agreements and who regulate their actions in accord with them.

None of these reflections are arguments for the preservation of the status quo. If sufficient numbers of persons abandon the arrangements, conventions, and agreements that constitute the moral order of a social collective and become parties to new ones, the old moral order is destroyed and replaced with a new moral order offering different possibilities of moral career and identity determination. Where and when this occurs – and there is little doubt that it can and does occur, and that it ought to occur with respect to some contemporary moral orders – it is very often the product of socio-linguistic negotiation. However, as noted earlier, this acknowledged fact about the creation – and destruction – of the moral orders of social collectives within which identity projects are pursued does nothing to suggest that identity is nothing more than a linguistic artifact: that there is nothing more to identity than social discourse putatively 'about' it. It remains an objective matter whether particular moral careers are available in particular cultures, whether particular persons are committed to them, and whether they make a success or failure of them when they are.

It has also been recognized that social discourse plays an enormously powerful role in the determination of identity. Social labeling according to the properties of aggregate group membership frequently functions as a social device that advantages some and disadvantages others with respect to entry into and success within a variety of moral careers. Often enough these forms of social discourse do serve a variety of socio-economic and political ends, by promoting the interests as well as the individual identities of members of dominant social groups (although whether such ends are intentionally pursued by the members of dominant social groups is a quite separate question).

Sometimes these social functions become institutionalized in language, a familiar example being the frequently avowed male bias of the English language. It may be the case that the supposedly neutral use of the male personal pronoun does encourage the stereotype that successful scientists, doctors, and other professionals, for example, tend to be males. However, it seems equally clear that neither social collectives nor the power relations among social groups are constituted by such linguistic practices. As most feminists recognize, change in linguistic practice alone will not ensure the creation of alternative moral careers or improved entry and success in those that are socially available. The Hungarian language is entirely non-sexist: one can only refer to a third party by the non-gender 'o,' not by any linguistic equivalent of 'he' or 'she' (Machan, 1987). Yet Hungary is not well known for its provision of alternative moral careers for women, nor for its increased access for women to those moral careers traditionally dominated by men. On the contrary, what the feminist would define as blatant sexism is rampant within the traditional social structures of that country.

All this can be agreed without granting the essential tenet of social constructionism: that there are no facts about identity independent of our theoretical discourse putatively 'about' identity. In denying that there are any objects of theoretical discourse putatively 'about' identity, the social constructionist denies the intrinsically social nature of identity.

Social constructionists are right to maintain that there is no mysterious 'inner' or 'private' object that is the object of such theoretical discourse and self-knowledge, but wrong to deny that such forms of discourse and self-knowledge have no object. The 'selves' that we are are just the persons that we are: the embodied persons that we are with particular commitments to particular forms of identity projects. Theoretical descriptions of the 'selves' that we are are just descriptions of the persons that we are: they are descriptions of our powers, liabilities, and potential; of the identity projects to which we are committed; and of our relative success or failure in pursuing them.

Accordingly, the 'selves' that we know are just the persons that we are. We can have knowledge of our powers, liabilities, and potential. We can have knowledge of the content of the identity projects to which we are committed. We can have knowledge of our relative success or failure in pursuing them. In this respect our 'self-concept' may properly be held to be descriptive and linguistically objective: it may be more or less accurate or inaccurate, and subject to the usual biases and distortions common to any form of knowledge. We may have an unrealistic estimate of our powers, liabilities, and potential. We may deceive ourselves about our commitment to (or level of commitment to) the moral careers that comprise our identity projects. We may delude ourselves about our success in such careers in order to preserve our self-esteem.

Harré (1989: 26) claims that: '"I" is a word having a role in conversation, a role that is not referential, nor is the conversation in which it dominates typically descriptive fact-stating.' The personal pronoun 'I' does not reference any mysterious inner entity. Yet this is insufficient grounds for denying it is regularly employed to make reflexive reference to the persons that we are. It is an interesting fact that some languages (such as Japanese) appear to have no proper first person pronouns, and that others (such as Inuit) have only attenuated forms of first person reference. It does not follow that persons who speak such languages have no sense of self or only an attenuated form of selfhood (Harré, 1987), if this means that they have no identities or only attenuated forms of identity. At most this indicates that the identity projects of persons in such cultures are not individualist, or are only weakly individualist (as argued in Chapter 6).

Identity and Theory

Many social constructionists have followed Harré (1987) in characterizing the self as a 'theory' (rather than an entity): 'The "self" is not a thing but exists only as a concept. It is the central concept of a theory, which the persons who hold it use to impose order upon their thoughts, feelings, and actions' (Harré, 1987: 49). It may be agreed that our theoretical discourse about ourselves is not about any mysterious inner object or entity (such as the 'ego' or 'soul'). However, this characterization of self or identity as 'theoretical' is doubly ambiguous. It fails to distinguish between realistically and instrumentally interpreted theories, and fails to distinguish between our theories about our identity and our 'theories' about social actions and relations, only the latter of which play any role in the ordering of our 'thoughts, feelings, and actions.'

It is true that many theories, such as Bohr's theory of the atom, 'impose order' upon – or bring 'conceptual integration' to – the body of empirical phenomena putatively explained by the theory (such as the spectral emission laws explained by Bohr's theory). According to an instrumentalist account of theories, this is *all* that theories do: they serve no additional descriptive function. According to a realist account of theories, most theories have an additional descriptive function: they ascribe properties to theoretical entities. According to this account, Bohr's theory is a description of the composition, structure, and properties of the atom.

It is true that our theoretical descriptions of ourselves are not putative descriptions of the structure and properties of mysterious inner entities.

Yet our theories about ourselves are not merely linguistic devices that 'impose order' or bring 'conceptual integration' to the phenomena they purport to explain – the instrumentalist interpretation. Our theories about ourselves are linguistically objective descriptions of our powers, liabilities, and potential, our commitment to identity projects, and our success and failure in pursuing them, according to a realist interpretation of the social psychological theory of identity in terms of identity projects.

Some of our theories may be said to 'impose order' upon our 'thoughts, feelings, and actions,' insofar as they play an important role in the organization of our thoughts, feelings, and actions. *It is not our theories about our identities that play this role*, but our 'theories' about our actions and social relations, in which certain actions and social relations are represented as achievements, failures, violations of honor, humiliations, offenses, and the like, according to the conventions of the social collectives within which identity projects are pursued. These conventions of social collectives provide the social evaluative matrix within which many of our thoughts, feelings, and actions are constituted. This does not, however, require that we employ a theory *about* such matters: it is sufficient that we have the joint commitments to the conventions that are constitutive of this intrinsically social evaluative matrix.

Much the same is true of our characteristically human emotions, as I will argue in the following chapters.

Notes

1 Through this chapter and the rest of this work I use the terms 'cognitive labeling' and 'social labeling' interchangeably, on the reasonable assumption that 'cognitive labels' are socially constructed.

2 Not all arrangements, conventions, and agreements that are constitutive of social collectives provide the conceptual and practical resources for identity projects. For example, those that constitute the social collectives of Russian speakers and drivers, formed by parties to the conventions of the Russian language and the rules of the road, do not.

3 It is of course true that we can label ourselves according to properties we share with other members of social collectives: thus we may label ourselves as 'psychologist,' 'Christian,' and the like. However, this form of labeling is still based upon membership of derivatively social aggregate groups, since – as noted in Chapter 5 – most if not all social collectives are also derivatively social groups: their members also share a common property (or set of properties) that is (or are) held to be socially significant according to some convention or agreement. However, such labeling is never itself sufficient for identity – one has to be committed to, and determine one's actions in accord with, the arrangements, conventions, and agreements that are constitutive of moral careers within social collectives.

4 Although being a feminist does seem to. It appears that one can make a moral career out of being a feminist – there appear to be recognized ways of succeeding and failing at this. However – at least the last time I checked – one does not have to be a woman to be a feminist.

5 Again this is not to deny, either, that often we may associate ourselves with or distinguish ourselves from others via labeling based upon derivatively social group membership, on different occasions and in different circumstances (or that this may play a role in the explanation of our behavior), as noted in Chapter 6 (Note 9). It is simply to deny

that this form of labeling – which varies on different occasions and in different circumstances – fixes our identity, which is determined by relatively *stable* and enduring identity projects pursued within social collectives.

6 An extreme example of this is the case of the so-called 'half-Asian' child in the United Kingdom, as described by Hitch (1983), who faces 'double jeopardy' with respect to her – severely delimited – moral career options, because of her 'uncertain' race.

7 The question of whether animals have identities is left open, although it should be noted that it has nothing to do with the question of what they can or cannot do with mirrors (Gallup, 1980). Like the question of the attributability of characteristically human emotions – such as shame and pride – to animals, it depends upon the degree to which certain forms of social life and linguistic competence can be attributed to animals.

8

Emotion and Social Labeling

Many contemporary theories of emotion purport to be theories of the social nature of emotion, but in fact are not. I will argue in this chapter that 'social labeling' (Schachter, 1965), 'social inferential' (Nisbett and Ross, 1980) and 'social constructionist' (Gergen, 1985; Gergen and Davis, 1985) accounts only appear to provide theories of the social nature of emotion via unwarranted assumptions about the constitution of emotion by socially constructed cognitive labels of emotion. These theories – at best – only characterize emotions as derivatively social.

In the following chapter I argue that some emotions may be characterized as intrinsically social in nature: they may be said to be socially constituted. Contrary to many contemporary views, I maintain that a recognition of the social dimensions of emotions is entirely consistent with a realist account of the sense and reference of theoretical psychological descriptions of emotions, an account that is committed to the linguistic – and epistemic – objectivity of theoretical descriptions[1] of emotions.

Before proceeding, it might be useful to restate the definitions of linguistic objectivity in order to highlight what is at issue in debates about the role of the social labeling of emotion. A theoretical description is *linguistically objective* if it makes a claim about a putative theoretical entity and attributes properties to it: if it is true or false – or accurate or inaccurate – according to whether the entity putatively described has or has not the properties attributed to it by the description. Theoretical descriptions are linguistically objective if they are true or false by virtue of independent facts about the theoretical entity they purport to describe; if the employment of the theoretical description – by actor or observer or aggregate social group or social collective – is neither a necessary nor sufficient condition of the truth of the description. I will maintain in this chapter and the next that the employment of theoretical descriptions of emotions – or cognitive labels – is neither a necessary nor sufficient condition of the truth or accuracy of theoretical psychological descriptions of emotions. Emotions are not themselves constituted *to any degree* by our – socially constructed – descriptions of them. The truth or accuracy of such descriptions is entirely determined by independent facts about emotions.

Many avowedly linguistically objective theories of emotion conceive of these independent facts about emotion as physiological facts (Izard, 1984; Plutchik, 1980; Tomkins, 1970; Zajonc, 1984). In contrast, the present account of the social constitution of emotion maintains that these independent facts are intrinsically social facts. Unfortunately, many recent theories that concentrate on the social as opposed to the physiological dimensions of emotions have been associated with social constructionist denials of linguistic objectivity. The following chapters attempt to redress this imbalance by maintaining that it is an objective fact about many human emotions that they are socially constituted: that they are intrinsically social.

To anticipate one form of purely semantic complaint, it is perhaps worth stressing that the following chapters are primarily concerned with those human emotions that have social evaluative elements. Thus the conception of emotional phenomena is both broader and narrower than most other conceptions. Many phenomena that are frequently characterized as emotions and studied by psychologists – such as the startle response, taste aversions, and the galvanic skin response (Zajonc, 1984) – are not the object of concern of these chapters. Rather I will be concerned with psychological phenomena such as shame, envy, disappointment, pride, jealousy, sympathy, anger, and the like, that may be ascribed – intensional – contents directed upon – intentional – objects (see Chapter 2), and that provide articulable reasons for action. Thus, the analysis also includes many phenomena normally characterized as motives, such as motives of revenge, achievement, and the like.

The aim of these chapters is not to make any universal claim about all the phenomena normally characterized as emotions, far less to offer a general theory of emotions. (There are very good reasons, which I will discuss later, for avoiding any attempt to provide a general theory of emotions.) Rather, my aim is to map the intrinsically social dimensions of a class of psychological phenomena that are frequently characterized as emotions, and to argue that the recognition of the social dimensions of these emotions poses no threat to the linguistic objectivity of our theoretical descriptions of them.

Social Labeling and the Schachter–Singer Experiment

Many of those who advance theories of the social nature of emotion treat the Schachter–Singer experiment (1962) as illustrative and supportive of their theories. In this experiment subjects were artificially aroused via epinephrine injections as part of an experiment ostensibly designed to investigate the effects of a new drug ('suproxin') on vision. Those subjects who were unaware of the real cause of their sympathetic arousal (they were not informed or were misinformed of the real effects of the injection), labeled their arousal states in accord with the euphoric or angry behavior of experimental stooges in the two experimental conditions.[2] (In the euphoria condition subjects were asked to wait in a room with a stooge who acted in a very carefree and jolly manner, making paper planes and cavorting with a hula-hoop. In the anger condition subjects had to fill out an offensive questionnaire which led to angry protests from the stooge.)

Many theorists have interpreted this experiment as licensing a claim about the constitution of emotion by the cognitive labeling of emotion (Jones, 1985; Russell, 1991). Thus Heelas, for example, quoting Schachter, claims that: 'Recent theorizing in the psychology of emotions suggests that emotional experiences are in fact constituted by conceptual systems (See Schachter, 1971)' (1981: 13). This analysis is then generalized to cover a broad range of psychological phenomena: 'Our descriptions of our experience are, in part, constitutive of what we experience. ... If people raised in different cultures or sub-cultures come to internalize different ways of describing their experience, this may make what they experience different' (Mischel, 1977b: 21).

The Schachter–Singer experiment does not demonstrate or illustrate this claim. The Schachter–Singer experiment was itself only concerned with the cognitive labeling of emotion. It provides support for the experimental hypothesis that when the source of their arousal is ambiguous, subjects tend to label their arousal states in accord with situational cues, and do not base their judgments upon perceived physiological differences between anger and euphoria – *contra* the so-called 'James–Lange' theory.[3] It does not demonstrate that emotions themselves are constituted by cognitive labeling, far less that emotions are themselves social in nature. In fact neither of these unsupported claims are made by Schachter and Singer in the original experimental report (1962). They remain silent on the nature of emotion itself.

Nevertheless, it is clear that Schachter, at least, thought that the experiment illustrated something about emotion. In a later paper (Schachter, 1965), he noted that the work of Maranon (1924) and Hohmann (1966) appeared to demonstrate that cognitive labeling and sympathetic arousal are individually necessary but individually insufficient for emotion. Maranon's study dealt with subjects who had been artificially aroused via epinephrine injections, but who did not report emotional states when asked to describe their experience. Hohmann's study dealt with paraplegics and quadriplegics with spinal cord lesions who also did not report emotional states. For Schachter it was significant that both groups reported 'as if in an emotional state' experiences. This led Schachter to postulate that cognitive labeling and sympathetic arousal jointly constitute emotional states: 'It is my basic assumption that emotional states are a function of the interaction of such cognitive factors with a state of physiological arousal' (Schachter, 1965: 141).

That is, cognitive labeling and arousal are held to be jointly sufficient for emotion. Schachter also argued that different cognitive labels *constitute* qualitatively similar arousal states as different emotions: 'It could be anticipated that precisely the same state of physiological arousal could be labelled "joy" or "fury" or any of a great diversity of emotion labels, depending upon the cognitive aspects of the situation' (1965: 141). This account of emotion is clearly committed to the notion that emotions are constituted by the employment of emotion labels. It may also be said to provide an account of the social dimensions of emotion. If emotion labels are socially constructed, as they may be presumed to be, then the social dimensions of constitutive emotion labels may be ascribed to emotions themselves, albeit derivatively.

It ought, however, to be stressed again that the Schachter–Singer experiment does not demonstrate this account of emotion. Moreover, this account of emotion is inconsistent with one of the salient facts about our emotional lives, namely that we can be mistaken in our judgments about our emotional states. People who are angry and jealous are often the last to recognize that they are angry or jealous (Bedford, 1962). However, Schachter's account precludes the possibility of error. If emotion labeling is in fact constitutive of emotion, then it is logically impossible for a subject to be mistaken when he labels his own emotional state. If my labeling of my arousal state as 'anger' constitutes my arousal state *as* the emotion of anger, then I can never be mistaken in my judgment that I am angry. If my labeling of my arousal state as 'anger' or 'euphoria' *makes* it anger or euphoria, there is no logical room for error.[4]

This counter-intuitive implication is a direct consequence of Schachter's labeling-constitutive account of emotion. This account precludes a linguistically objective analysis of a person's cognitive labeling. On a linguistically objective conception of cognitive labeling, a descriptive cognitive label is true or false according to whether a psychological state has or has not the properties ascribed to it by the descriptive label. According to such a conception, a psychological state is correctly described as 'anger' if and only if it has the representational properties constitutive of anger (whatever these may be exactly, although they would normally be held to involve some representation of offense); it is incorrectly described as 'anger' if it does not. That persons ascribe descriptive cognitive labels to their emotions is neither a necessary nor sufficient condition of the accuracy of such descriptive labels. Consequently, according to a linguistically objective analysis of emotion ascriptions, we *can* be mistaken in our ascription of cognitive labels. However, if, as Schachter claims, our cognitive labeling of arousal is both necessary and sufficient to constitute an arousal state as a particular emotion, then we can never be mistaken in our emotion judgments, since there is no possibility of a mismatch between descriptive cognitive labeling and the phenomena labeled: there is no logical room for error.

As Schachter himself recognizes, the claim that emotions are physiologically homogeneous is not supported by the Schachter–Singer experiment. However, even if it were, it would not follow that such homogeneous physiological states are constituted as emotions by emotion labels. They might very well be socially rather than physiologically constituted, as maintained in the following chapter.

Emotion as Social Inference

The 'social-inferential' account (Nisbett and Ross, 1980) of emotion is a variant of the social labeling account that appears to avoid its paradoxical preclusion of error in emotion judgment. According to Nisbett and Ross, emotion discourse is employed as a set of socially learned 'a priori' theories that provide causal explanations of our behavior (for ourselves and others): 'Schachter's essential insight was that emotional experience and behavior reflect a considerable amount of what can only be termed "causal inference"' (1980: 200). This account allows for the possibility of subject error in emotion judgment, since subjects can be mistaken when they advance any form of causal explanation.

This account advances a theory of the social origin of emotion labels – conceived as causal theories. It does not advance any account of the intrinsically social nature of emotion. Even if it is accepted that emotion labels are causal theories that are socially constructed and socially learned, it does not follow that emotion is itself social in nature. This would only follow if our cognitive labeling of emotion based upon our inferences from stimuli and behavior is somehow constitutive of our emotions. However, inferential theorists leave open the possibility of error in emotion judgment by denying that emotions are constituted in the manner suggested by Schachter. According to the inferential account, emotion labeling is neither necessary nor sufficient for emotion. Such labeling is true or false according to whether the theoretical causal explanation is true or false. This account thus provides an analysis of the truth conditions of emotion labels that is independent of the employment of emotion labels. Accordingly, the social dimensions of emotion labels cannot be ascribed to emotions themselves – even derivatively – since emotion labels are not held to be in any way constitutive of emotions.[5]

Nevertheless, this account does not provide a linguistically objective realist interpretation of the theoretical meaning and truth conditions of emotion avowals. According to a realist account, the meaning and truth conditions of theoretical descriptions are independent of the meaning and truth conditions of descriptions of empirical phenomena or correlations that they may be employed to explain, and of any causal explanatory propositions in which they may figure.

The inferential account employs an *instrumentalist* interpretation of theoretical ascriptions. Apparent references to emotions are not assumed to make actual reference to emotions, but serve to bring 'conceptual integration' to a body of empirical laws relating stimuli and responses. In proper instrumentalist fashion, Nisbett and Ross remain agnostic with respect to the question of the existence of emotions (1980: 197). In claiming that subjects err in emotion judgments, they never demonstrate that persons are mistaken in the sense that they sometimes judge, for example, that they are angry when in fact they are really only disappointed. They only show that persons are regularly mistaken in their judgments about which stimuli cause which behaviors. Given their assumption that the meaning of emotion judgments is defined in terms of such putative empirical laws, it naturally follows for them that persons are regularly mistaken in their emotion avowals. Precisely the same is true even if such theoretical attributions are given a referential realist (or semantic functionalist) interpretation, as making reference to causally potent internal states that 'intervene' between empirical stimuli and behavior.

The 'social-inferential' account of emotion ascriptions also has a counter-intuitive implication, whether it is interpreted in instrumentalist or referential realist fashion. It retains a constitutive element, precluding error at precisely the points at which we would expect it. For Nisbett and Ross, error in emotion judgment is essentially – and can only be – error in the operational definition of emotion. That is, our lay emotion attributions are socially defined – via 'a priori' social theories – in terms of *inaccurate* empirical hypotheses relating stimuli and responses (with or without reference to 'intervening' internal states). If they were more scientifically defined, in terms of empirically established relations between stimuli and behavioral responses, then our emotion attributions would not be in error, if we correctly determined stimuli and responses in particular cases.

If this is the case, it precludes observer error in the case of deception by the actor, and actor error in the case of self-deception, if actor and observer understand the social meaning of the – scientifically defined – emotion label, and correctly determine stimuli and responses in particular cases. Grief, for example, might be operationally defined in terms of stimuli such as the death of a spouse that are regularly associated with behavioral phenomena such as tears and characteristic facial expression. However, not every person who responds to the death of a spouse with a public behavioral manifestation of grief is truly grieving. The murderer intent to hide his crime from others (or himself) is certainly not.

Emotion and Causal Judgment

This is not to deny that sometimes we do make causal inferences to our emotional states from the stimulus situation or our behavior, or that sometimes we are in error when we do. The recognition of these facts is entirely consistent with a linguistically objective realist account of emotion labeling, which denies that the semantics and truth conditions of psychological descriptions are determined by reference to empirical laws or causal explanatory propositions. Errors in emotion judgments may often be a *consequence* of errors in causal judgments, but errors in emotion judgments are not themselves errors *of* causal judgment. A good number of theorists (Leventhal, 1980), including social constructionist theorists (Harré, 1987), hold the view that causal judgment plays an essential role in determining the identity of an emotion, but this is a major error.

If accurate causal judgment is held to be constitutive of emotion, this precludes emotion error when our causal judgments are correct. Yet this is surely not precluded. We can be right about the source of our arousal or cause of our emotion but wrong about our emotional state. We may be correct in our judgment that the cause of our present arousal or emotional state is the news that our colleague has received unexpected promotion, but although we claim (and perhaps sincerely believe) that we are elated, we may in fact be angry, jealous, or disappointed (especially if we were expecting promotion ourselves).

We may also be wrong about the source of our arousal or cause of our emotion but right about our emotional state. I may become aroused and emotional before a sudden but obviously important meeting with my boss, but may not notice this because I am so involved in preparations. If I claim to be angry with a colleague because I feel her contribution to the meeting unjustly undermines my position, I am surely not mistaken just because I suppose my arousal or emotional state was caused by her contribution. Analogously a subject in the anger condition of the Schachter–Singer experiment who feels that the questionnaire is grossly insulting is surely not wrong in her judgment that she is angry *just* because she (falsely) believes her arousal or emotional state is caused by the questionnaire.

It might be objected that it is a necessary condition of bona fide emotion that sympathetic arousal is caused by the object of the emotion. It might be claimed, for example, that subjects in the anger condition of the Schachter–Singer experiment were angry only if their arousal was caused by the questionnaire. However, if this is correct, then subjects in the Schachter–Singer experiment were not mistaken about their emotional states, as Nisbett and Ross claim, but were mistaken in their judgment *that they were in an emotional state*.

The Schachter–Singer experiment does not itself establish this objection, and there seems to be no other good reason to accept it. It does not seem to be a general requirement of emotion that the intentional object of an emotion is identical to its cause,[6] any more than it is a general requirement of belief that the intentional object of a belief is identical to its cause – beliefs about fairies and water spirits are, I presume, rarely caused by them. My dread of the examination tomorrow is never caused by it (it is caused by my anticipation of it), although my disappointment with my exam performance is usually caused by it.

Of course many times the object and cause of an emotion will be identical, and in either case the judgments of persons may be mistaken. Still such causal judgments play no *constitutive* role with respect to the identity of the emotion. This may be best illustrated by reference to the cross-cultural and transhistorical identification of emotions. Maori warriors sometimes fear a forthcoming battle. This is natural enough, because a forthcoming battle is an appropriate object of fear in most places and times (because of the likely consequences). Maori warriors do not, however, believe that their fear is caused by the battle, or their cognitive anticipation of it (as we would naturally suppose). Rather they believe that such fears are caused by antagonistic ancestral spirits (*atua*), angered by some violation of a ritual rule (*tapu*). This belief is reflected in their ritual treatment of fear, which is thought to be removed by crawling between the legs of a high-born woman, whose sexual organs are believed to have the power to eliminate such supernatural influences (Smith, 1981). Let us suppose, as we would normally suppose, that this belief is in fact false. It surely does not follow, nor does it seem likely to be the case, that the Maori are mistaken in their judgment that they are afraid.

Social Constructionism

Social constructionists regularly reference the Schachter–Singer experiment to support their claim that emotions are in some sense constituted by socially constructed emotion labels:

> It was traditionally believed that emotion terms stand in rough correspondence to an array of independent physiological states. The major problem was to determine how many states exist and to develop an appropriate set of measures for them. Schachter's work threw this line of thinking into sharp question. To what entities or physiological states did the widely variagated vocabulary of emotions refer? With no convincing answer available to this question, the conclusion seemed inescapable that the linguistic variations were not 'mirrors' of physiological states but products of social convention. Over time the emotional language had become reified. In place of these reifications Schachter proposed that there was only a single 'entity,' a generalized and amorphous state of arousal. Suddenly the hoary problem of emotional identification was resolved; there was no set of entities to be identified. (Gergen, 1987c: 56)

However, this conclusion is escapable, for there are more than two interpretative options. It is not the case that emotion labels are either linguistically objective descriptions of independent physiological states, or nothing more than 'reified' social constructions that have no reference. There is another interpretation available, which I will advance and defend in the following chapter: emotion labels are linguistically objective descriptions of independent psychological states that are socially constituted – that are intrinsically social by virtue of their intrinsically social representational contents and objects.[7]

Social constructionists also regularly appeal to cross-cultural and historical differences in conceptions of emotion to demonstrate that emotions are socially constructed: that they are nothing more than 'reified' by-products of theoretical discourse. For example, Gergen (1985), citing different historical conceptions of romantic love (Averill, 1985) and mother's love (Badinter, 1980), and cross-cultural differences in conceptions of emotion among the Ifaluk (Lutz, 1982) and the Illongot (Rosaldo, 1980), claims that 'such differences do not appear to reflect alterations in the objects or entities of concern' (1985: 267). However, it is hard to see how Gergen could establish this claim if putative 'objects' or 'entities' are themselves nothing more than 'reified' by-products of socio-linguistic theoretical construction.

It may very well be the case that differences in historical and cross-cultural conceptions of emotion do not reference differences in physiological states (and this is in fact doubtful). However, again there are more than two interpretative options. Such differences in conception, as argued in the following chapter, may very well reference intrinsically social differences in the social constitution of emotions in different historical periods and cultures.

It is critically important to distinguish between the claim that emotions are socially *constituted* – that they are intrinsically social – and what is claimed of emotions by most social constructionist theorists. To claim that emotions are socially constituted – to claim that they are intrinsically social – is also to claim that they are social constructions, in the following respect: they are constructed or created out of the joint commitment to certain arrangements, conventions, and agreements by those who are parties to them. This is not, however, what is standardly claimed by social constructionist theorists: they claim that emotions are social constructions in the sense that they constituted by, or are nothing more than, socially constructed *theories of emotion*.

The central thesis of *social constructionism* is the denial of the linguistic objectivity of emotion ascriptions. According to social constructionism, emotion ascriptions are not true or false – or accurate or inaccurate – by virtue of independent facts about emotional states. They are 'culturally constructed concepts' (Lutz, 1982) that have no independent psychological reference. According to Gergen, what is true of emotions is true of all forms of discourse putatively 'about' psychological phenomena:

> In broad terms, it may be said that the 'contents of psyche,' those powers, motives, intentions, needs, wants, urges, tendencies and so on, that are endowed with the capacity to direct human behavior have no ontological status, but appear to do so only because they are objectified through linguistic practice. They are essentially reified by-products of human communication practices. (1982: 84)

Such accounts deny the intrinsically social dimensions of emotion by denying the linguistic objectivity of emotion descriptions. At best, such accounts treat emotion as derivatively social, by virtue of the intrinsically social dimensions of our socially constructed emotion descriptions. Yet, strictly speaking, on many social constructionist accounts, emotions cannot even be characterized as derivatively social, since according to such accounts emotion discourse makes no reference to any independent phenomena that might be partially or wholly constituted by such forms of discourse. According to such accounts, there is nothing social about emotion itself. There are only socially constructed forms of emotion discourse and their social consequences: thus, in the case of emotion discourse, as in the case of psychological discourse in general, we are 'invited to look not for their referents but for their consequences in social life' (Gergen, 1989b: 71).

Such claims or conclusions are regularly based upon general denials of the linguistic and epistemic objectivity of theoretical descriptions in natural and social and psychological science. I considered and rejected the arguments held to support these denials in Chapters 3 and 4. However, as also noted at the end of Chapter 4, many theorists who might otherwise be sympathetic to a realist position nevertheless think that there is a more intimate connection between theoretical discourse and the phenomena that such forms of discourse purport to describe in the case of social psychological phenomena such as emotions.

This is perhaps a natural error, as well as a common one. It is an error nonetheless. There is an important grain of truth in social labeling, social inferential, and social constructionist accounts of emotion, despite their myriad inadequacies. This lies in the – faint – recognition that characteristic human emotions – such as shame, remorse, pride, envy, anger, guilt, and the like – do not exist independently of, and cannot be characterized without reference to, socially constructed forms of representation. These accounts fundamentally err, however, in supposing that the forms of representation that are constitutive of emotion are forms of representation *of emotions themselves*. In the following chapter I will argue that this is not the case: that emotions are in fact socially constituted by the intrinsically social dimensions of our evaluative representations of *actions and social relations*.

Not all of those who advance social constructionist accounts of emotion base their claims upon general arguments that deny the linguistic and epistemic objectivity of theoretical descriptions in natural and social and psychological science, or draw the negative ontological conclusions popularized by Gergen. Many theorists who call themselves social constructionists do appear to offer accounts of the social dimensions of emotions themselves (Armon-Jones, 1986; Averill, 1980, 1985; Coulter, 1979; Franks and Doyle McCarthy, 1989; Harré, 1986b), based upon considerations that are often specific to theories of emotion. It is also true that many cognitive theorists of emotion do focus upon cognitive appraisals of actions and social relations, rather than upon cognitive appraisals of arousal (Frijda, 1986; Roseman, 1984; Scherer, 1984; Smith and Ellsworth, 1985; Weiner, 1985). However, although some of the accounts of some of these theorists may have some things in common with the account of the intrinsically social nature of emotion advanced in the following chapter (although I make no attempt to delineate or detail any commonalities), most if not all of these accounts remain at best ambiguous with respect to the role played by descriptive cognitive labels of emotion.

Many theorists remain inclined to the view that there is an especially intimate relation between emotion labels and emotions themselves, such that emotions are held to be at least partially constituted by socially constructed emotion labels. Thus even those theorists such as Harré (1986b) who offer accounts of the social construction of emotion, but also distance themselves from the relativist meta-theoretical version of social constructionism developed by Gergen and his associates, still seem to suppose that any transhistorical or cross-cultural differences in emotions are a constitutive *consequence* of different emotion labels to be found transhistorically and cross-culturally: 'Historians and anthropologists have established conclusively that there are historically and culturally diverse emotion vocabularies. I claim that it follows that there are culturally diverse emotions' (Harré, 1986b: 10).

In the following chapter I argue that emotions are not constituted – in any way or to any degree – by our socially constructed descriptive labels of them. Most of the interesting things that many social constructionists want to say about emotion – in opposition to standard physiological or naturalistic accounts – can be accommodated by the claim I shall advance in the following chapter: that many emotions are socially constituted by the intrinsically social dimensions of our socially constructed evaluative representations of social actions and social relations, and not by the intrinsically social dimensions of our socially constructed cognitive labels of emotion.

Notes

1 Throughout this chapter and the rest of the work, I use the terms 'emotion description,' 'emotion attribution' and 'emotion ascription' interchangeably, employing the terms 'attribution' and 'ascription' to avoid confusion when discussing the question of whether emotion discourse is descriptive and linguistically objective.

2 In this experiment there were four types of groups:
   (a) Epinephrine Informed, namely subjects who were given correct information about the normal effects of the injections
   (b) Epinephrine Misinformed, namely subjects who were given incorrect information about the normal effects of the injections
   (c) Epinephrine Ignorant, namely subjects who were given no information about the effects of the injections
   (d) Placebo, namely subjects who were given saline injections and given no information about their effects.

3 This hypothesis was supported by the experimental results. As predicted by the hypothesis, subjects in the euphoria condition who were Misinformed or Ignorant exhibited a higher degree of euphoria (as measured by self-report and behavioral indexes) than subjects who were Informed (although not all differences were statistically significant); subjects in the anger condition who were Ignorant exhibited a higher degree of anger than those who were Informed (there was no Misinformed group in the anger condition). One anomalous result not predicted by the hypotheses was that the degree of euphoria and anger exhibited by the Placebo subjects was less than that exhibited by the Ignorant and Misinformed subjects, but *greater* than that exhibited by the Informed subjects. The significance of this anomaly is discussed in Chapter 9.

4 There is some irony in this, since Nisbett and Ross (1980: 200) cite Schachter's interpretation of the Schachter–Singer experiment as support for their claim that persons are

regularly mistaken with respect to self-knowledge of their emotional states. The matter is discussed in greater detail in Chapter 10.

5 It might be said that in the case of inferential theories, as in the case of Schachter's labeling theory, emotions may also be characterized as social insofar and in as much as the self-ascription of emotions is held to be based upon social cues. However, at best this only enables us to characterize emotions as derivatively social, and in the case of inferential accounts, it remains the case that these derivatively social dimensions of emotion labels cannot be attributed to emotions themselves, since emotions are not themselves constituted by emotion labels according to the inferential account.

6 And even if this was the case, someone could still be right about the cause of their emotion and wrong about their emotional state, as in the example of our reaction to the news of our colleague's promotion. And we may still be wrong about the cause of arousal and right about our emotion: the earlier example may be modified. The man in the meeting may believe his present arousal is a result of his earlier anxiety, but his earlier arousal may have been dissipated. Although his present arousal is in fact caused by his reaction to his colleague's contribution, he can surely be right in his judgment that he is angry with his colleague.

7 This is not to endorse Schachter's claim that different emotions are physiologically homogeneous. I doubt very much if this is in fact the case. It is merely to claim that many emotions are not themselves constituted as different emotions by physiological differences. If such emotions are in fact physiologically heterogeneous or homogeneous, this is an additional interesting but independent fact about them.

9

The Social Constitution of Emotion

In this chapter I argue that characteristically human emotions such as shame, remorse, pride, envy, jealousy, anger, guilt, disappointment, and the like are socially constituted. They are intrinsically social forms of evaluative representation of actions and social relations.

Emotion and Social Evaluation

Many human emotions are essentially constituted *as* emotions by intrinsically social forms of evaluative representation directed upon socially appropriate objects. They are socially constructed in the following respect: they are created or constructed out of arrangements, conventions, and agreements concerning the evaluation of actions and social relations, including those concerning the appropriate objects of such forms of evaluation. They are socially negotiated in historical time and cultural place by parties to these arrangements, conventions, and agreements, and consequently can, and often do, vary transhistorically and cross-culturally. These forms of intrinsically social evaluative representation of actions and social relations are also socio-linguistically constituted. The intrinsically social intensional contents of emotions – of intrinsically social forms of evaluative representation – are appropriated from intrinsically social forms of moral commentary on actions and social relations – forms of moral commentary that are also socially negotiated by parties to arrangements, conventions, and agreements about what is honorable, degrading, offensive, admirable, and the like in different historical times and cultural places. In these respects many human emotions may be said to be *socially constituted*: they are constituted as emotions by their intrinsically social dimensions, and are theoretically individuated by reference to these dimensions.

Many human emotions are intrinsically social evaluative representations that are constituted as emotions by intrinsically social *intensional contents* directed upon socially appropriate *intentional objects*. Thus for example I may be said to be ashamed if and only if I represent my action (or failure to act) as degrading and humiliating.[1] This form of evaluative representation of my action (or failure to act) is constitutive of my shame. Analogously, I may be said to be motivated by revenge if and only if I represent my contemplated action as restitution for some prior injury. This form of evaluative representation is constitutive of my motive of revenge. The forms of representation and evaluation that are constitutive of emotion – and, as suggested above, constitutive of some form of motivation – are generally forms of representation and evaluation of *social reality*:[2] of the actions and social relations of ourselves and others. They are not forms of representation or evaluation of emotions themselves. Emotions are not constituted – in any way or to any degree – by our representations, theories, or cognitive labels *of* emotions, or of any other 'internal' states.

Our theoretical descriptions of human emotions are linguistically objective: they are true or false – or accurate or inaccurate – according to whether or not psychological states have the intrinsically social properties attributed to them by our descriptions. Thus a psychological state may be accurately described as shame if and only if it involves the representation of an action (or failure to act) as personally degrading and humiliating. Analogously, a psychological state may be accurately described as a motive of revenge if and only if it involves the representation of an action as restitution for a prior injury. It is neither a necessary nor sufficient condition of shame or motive of revenge that it is described or represented by the actor or any observer – or social group or collective – as 'shame' or 'motive of revenge.' It is necessary and sufficient that it involves the representation of an action (or failure to act) as degrading and humiliating, or as restitution for a prior injury: that it has the properties attributed by the descriptions 'shame' and 'motive of revenge.'

Our theoretical descriptions of emotions are themselves intrinsically social and socially constructed: they are created or constructed out of conventions of – theoretical – descriptive meaning, which may of course be linguistically constructed in different ways in different cultures and historical periods. However, the intrinsically social dimensions of emotions are not a constitutive consequence of the intrinsically social dimensions of our theoretical descriptions of them. Our theoretical descriptions of atoms and DNA are intrinsically social linguistic constructions. It does not follow, nor is it true to say, that atoms and DNA are intrinsically social or are socially constructed or constituted: they do not have any social dimensions by virtue of the social dimensions of our descriptions of them. Precisely the same is true of human emotions such as shame and pride: they do not have social dimensions by virtue of the social dimensions of our descriptions of them. The intrinsically social dimensions of emotions – their intrinsically social evaluative representational contents – are logically and ontologically independent of the intrinsically social dimensions of our theoretical descriptions of them.

Our socially constructed theoretical descriptions of atoms and DNA are descriptions of phenomena that are constituted or *preformed* as atoms and DNA by their physical and biological dimensions, independently of our descriptions of them. Analogously our socially constructed theoretical descriptions of emotions are descriptions of phenomena that are constituted or *preformed* as emotions by their intrinsically social psychological dimensions, independently of our descriptions of them.

Emotion and Social Learning

Perhaps the best way to illustrate these points is by considering the fashion in which characteristically human emotions are learned. These emotions, unlike sensations such as pain, itches, or hunger, do not occur independently of intrinsically social forms of evaluative representation. Shame, for example, does not occur in us spontaneously and independently of evaluative representations of social reality. Rather, we have to learn to *be ashamed*, which means that we have to come to represent and treat certain actions and social relations as degrading and humiliating – we have to become parties to conventions and agreements that stipulate the degrading and humiliating nature of these actions and social relations.

Hippocrates describes how the epileptic child originally reacts with distress and fear towards his attacks, and only later learns to be ashamed. The child does not learn to be ashamed of his epileptic attacks either by being taught to label his arousal as 'shame,' or by learning that the source of his arousal is his epileptic attack, or by learning that his skulking behavior is caused by a mysterious 'inner' state called 'shame' (or any combination of these). Rather the child learns to be ashamed when he comes to represent and treat his epileptic behavior as degrading and humiliating: when he comes to adopt and accept – when he becomes party to – these conventional forms of evaluative representation.

Analogously we have to learn – and are taught – to be angry, proud, disappointed, envious, remorseful, jealous, and the like. In order to do this, we have to adopt and accept – become parties to – the arrangements, conventions, and agreements that are constitutive of the moral orders of social collectives. The language of emotion is essentially our intrinsically social language of moral commentary upon our own and others' actions in social collectives: it characterizes certain forms of action and social relations as degrading, insulting, cruel, achievements, failures, and the like. When we have learned this language of moral commentary, and appropriated its (intensional) contents to such a degree that we come to represent and treat our own and others' actions as degrading, insulting, cruel, achievements, failures, and the like, then we may be said to be capable of having characteristically human emotions such as shame, anger, remorse, pride, disappointment, and the like, and be motivated by their intrinsically social contents.

Once a child has learned to be ashamed and be proud, and has manifested her shame or pride in appropriate public actions and moral commentaries, then she can learn that this is what we call 'shame' and 'pride' in our form of social life: she can learn the correct usage of these cognitive labels. However, emotions do not require a language descriptive *of* emotion: a language comprising descriptions such as 'shame,' 'anger,' 'jealousy,' and the like. A child or adult can be ashamed or proud even if they do not recognize that these emotions are described as 'shame' and 'pride' in our form of social life. Analogously many Americans may experience angst without recognizing that this emotion is described as 'angst' in another form of social life.

This is simply a reflection of the linguistic objectivity of psychological descriptions. Acids and carbon would still exist even if we did not employ the descriptions 'acid' and 'carbon': there would still be solutions and elements that have the properties ascribed by our descriptions 'acid' and 'carbon.' Shame and angst could still exist even if we did not employ the descriptions 'shame' and 'angst' (or any translational equivalents): there could still be psychological states that have the intrinsically social representational properties ascribed by our descriptions 'shame' and 'angst.'

Emotion and Belief

If emotions such as shame, jealousy, pride, anger, and the like are constituted by their intrinsically social evaluative representational contents, then such emotions can be rationally and morally appraised in terms of the beliefs upon which they are based, and the appropriateness of the emotion given such beliefs. In consequence many emotions are modifiable – at least in principle – by rational persuasion.[3] An angry lover may represent the other's failure to arrive on time as an intentional rebuke. This may be incorrect: the other may be delayed by a traffic accident in which he was injured. If she learns this fact, she may change her evaluation, and become anxious and guilty instead. An unmarried mother may be ashamed: she may represent her situation as degrading and humiliating. This may be considered inappropriate and unreasonable in this day and age. In consequence she may be persuaded to change her evaluation and come to feel proud and elated instead.

However, the falsity or inappropriateness of such beliefs makes no constitutive difference. The original lover who represents the other's failure to arrive on time as an intentional rebuke really is angry. Her actions – such as kicking the lamppost and dropping his love locket down the nearest drain – may be readily explained in these terms. The mother who inappropriately and perhaps unjustifiably represents her situation as degrading and humiliating really is ashamed. Her self-deprecating actions – and perhaps her suicide attempt – may also be readily explained in these terms.

The same logic applies to subjects in the Schachter–Singer experiment who had mistaken beliefs about the cause of their arousal. An originally deceived subject who was later informed of the real cause of his arousal would remain angry if he continued to represent the questionnaire – in the anger condition – as insulting and offensive. Indeed, even though it may be true that the cognitive labeling of subjects in this experiment was influenced by social cues, there is a plausible interpretation of this experiment according to which most subjects were correct in their emotion labeling. The questionnaire was genuinely offensive: it asked questions concerning the ablutive and sexual habits of one's parents, for example. It is thus not implausible to suppose that many of the subjects in the anger condition were genuinely angry: that is, that they treated the questionnaire as an offense to their dignity and rights. Analogously, many of the subjects in the euphoria condition may have been genuinely elated: they may have genuinely enjoyed joining in the fun with the experimental stooge.

This interpretation is in fact suggested by one result of the experiment that Schachter and Singer found anomalous. The placebo group who were not artificially aroused by epinephrine injections, but who participated in the 'anger condition,' also claimed to be angry and exhibited the appropriate behavioral responses. In fact such subjects were judged by themselves and others to be *more* angry than those who were injected with epinephrine and informed of its effects. This strongly suggests that at least these subjects were genuinely angry, and that the experimental conditions were themselves sufficient to generate anger and euphoria in most subjects.

Contrary to social constructionist accounts, the Schachter–Singer experiment does not demonstrate or illustrate that emotions are constituted by our employment of socially constructed descriptions of emotion. On the contrary, it is entirely consistent with a linguistically objective account of emotion descriptions that treats emotions as independently constituted by their intrinsically social evaluative representational contents directed upon actions and social relations.

This is not to deny the causal potency of erroneous emotion labeling, or the explanatory utility of references to it. It is rather to insist upon the denial of the constitutive role of emotion labeling, and the fact that agents can be genuinely mistaken in their emotion labeling. For example, Schachter (1965) makes approving comments on Bruch's (1962) account of chronic obesity. He makes the theoretically significant observation that obese persons may not have successfully learned to discriminate between hunger and emotional states such as fear, anger, and anxiety:

> She describes such cases as characterized by a confusion between intense emotional states and hunger. During childhood these patients have not been taught to discriminate between hunger and such states as fear, anger, and anxiety. If correct, these people are, in effect, labeling a state of sympathetic activation as hunger. Small wonder that they are both fat and jolly. (Schachter, 1965: 173)

While this may provide a legitimate explanation of some forms of obesity – some persons may eat more than they need because they misidentify their psychological state as hunger rather than anxiety – it follows neither that such persons are not anxious, nor that they are jolly. In fact

Bruch herself documents in great detail the various manifestations of social anxiety in obese persons.

A similar sort of point can be made about Schachter's interpretation of Wrightsman's (1960) studies, which found that levels of anxiety tend to increase when one is waiting with others to take part in a psychology experiment involving electric shocks, or waiting to visit the dentist. Schachter suggests that these studies demonstrate that many persons become anxious – or more anxious – as a result of labeling their arousal state in accord with the social cues provided by other anxious subjects. The results of such studies do not, however, oblige us to conclude that emotions such as anxiety are constituted by descriptive labeling. The manifest anxiety of other persons waiting with us (for the experiment or dental visit) may cause us to represent our situation as more threatening than we would if we were waiting alone. Thus the subjects in the Wrightsman study may have correctly described their emotional state and correctly estimated its intensity. Anxiety is constituted by our evaluative representation of situations as threatening, not by our representation of our emotional state as 'anxiety.'

The Ontological Diversity of Emotion
The claim that emotions are intrinsically social has one significant implication that is much stressed by social constructionist theories – albeit for different reasons – and is worth stressing: the possible cultural and historical diversity of emotions. If some emotions are constituted by their intrinsically social (intensional) contents and (intentional) objects, we ought to expect cultural and historical variations with respect to the objects and contents of emotions.

We frequently do mark cross-cultural and transhistorical differences in emotions in terms of socially diverse objects and contents. Thus we may note that the English characteristically take pride in their homes while Italians take pride in their sisters' virginity. Middle-class Western children characteristically take pride in their academic achievements and stamp collections (or at least they used to), while Nepalese children are more likely to take pride in the birds they have bred and raised (Harris, 1989). In sexually promiscuous ages and cultures persons may be envious of the castles and cattle of others, but not of their husbands and wives. The anthropologist Prince Peter of Greece, for example, reports that the polyandrous tribes of the eastern Himalayas are not envious of the mates but only of the property of others (Harré et al., 1985).

More interesting perhaps are more fundamental differences with respect to intensional contents. Western anger appears to be different from the *tu nu* of the Brazilian Kaingang Indians (Averill, 1980), because anger involves some perceived moral transgression and *tu nu* does not, although both are directed against rivals and enemies. Japanese *amae* appears to be quite different from Western love because it involves a 'fawning' dependency that contrasts starkly with Western notions of reciprocal support (Doi, 1973; Morsbach and Tyler, 1976), although both are directed upon the same objects (spouses, lovers, friends). The early medieval emotion of 'accidie' involved a form of disgusted boredom with the world (Altschule, 1965) that seems quite different from the dark visions of 'the skull beneath the skin' characteristic of the Jacobean emotion of 'melancholia.' These, in turn, appear to be quite different from the representations of 'helplessness' and 'hopelessness' characteristic of much contemporary depression (Abramson et al., 1978; Abramson et al., 1989).

There is nothing theoretically or scientifically suspect about the fact that some intrinsically social emotions may not be reidentifiable in other forms of social life. Some of the ontological items that form the subject matter of natural sciences are reidentifiable in different regions of space and time – such as atoms and planets, but others are not – such as species and viruses. It is an open and empirical question in any science whether any ontological particulars are reidentifiable in space and time.

According to the present account, the possible cross-cultural and transhistorical diversity of emotions is a properly objective and empirical question, since whatever diversity exists is a product, not of the social diversity of intrinsically social descriptions of emotions, but of the social diversity of intrinsically social forms of evaluative representation of actions and social relations. The empirical discrimination of such diversity requires the determination of the intrinsically social intensional contents of the forms of evaluative representation of actions and social relations to be found in diverse forms of social life.

Thus accidie, for example, is not constituted as accidie by the employment of the classificatory description 'accidie.' It was not created by the social construction of the intrinsically social theoretical description 'accidie' or its social employment, nor was it eliminated from our repertoire of emotions when persons ceased to employ the theoretical description 'accidie.' There is some evidence that the intrinsically social form of evaluative representation that used to be characterized as 'accidie' may be reidentifiable in contemporary times, despite the fact that only very few would represent or describe it as 'accidie.' The psychiatrist Robert Findley-Jones (1986) suggests that the General Health Questionnaire (Goldberg, 1962) and the Present State Examination (Wing et al., 1974) can be employed to discriminate accidie from contemporary forms of depression, and that accidie appears to be presently prevalent among housewives and the unemployed.

This point must be insisted upon against the social constructionist, for it has important methodological implications. The cross-cultural and transhistorical diversity of emotions is a product of the social diversity of intrinsically social forms of evaluative representations of actions and social relations, and not a product of the social diversity of intrinsically social descriptions of emotions. Western anger is different from *tu nu* because of differences in the intrinsically social intensional content of these forms of evaluative representation (the former involves a perceived moral transgression while the latter does not), not because there is no description employed by the Kaingang Indians that is near synonymous with 'anger.' The Kaingang Indians may very well be angry on occasions, even though they have no descriptive label for anger, just as Americans may experience angst even though they have no descriptive label for angst, and children may be ashamed even though they lack the descriptive label 'shame' – or before they come to learn it.

This is not to deny that some emotions may be absent in some cultures: it is just to deny that this is a necessary consequence of the absence of descriptive labels of emotions. A good many theorists have made much of the claim that there is no descriptive label for depression to be found in many non-Western cultures (Marsella, 1981): for example, no such descriptive emotion label can be found among the Yoruba of Nigeria (Leighton et al., 1963), the Fulani of Africa (Reisman, 1977), or the Kaluli of Papua New Guinea (Schieffelin, 1985). It simply does not follow that persons in such cultures are never depressed, any more than it follows that we never experience accidie, just because we lack the descriptive label for it. It may, however, be the case that persons in such cultures are never depressed, not because they lack a descriptive label for depression, but because – perhaps for philosophical or spiritual reasons – they are not inclined to represent themselves as 'helpless' or their situation as 'hopeless': the forms of evaluative representation constitutive of contemporary Western depression.

Geertz (1959) claims that the emotion of *sungkan* is 'peculiarly Javanese.' It refers to 'a feeling of respectful politeness before a superior or an unfamiliar equal, an attitude of constraint, a repression of one's own impulses and desires, so as not to disturb the emotional equanimity of one who may be spiritually higher' (1959: 233). Although Westerners or other Easterners perhaps do not have a descriptive label for this, it is very doubtful if Geertz's account describes an emotion that is completely alien or unknown to them. This appears to be an attitude that many Irish adopt towards their priests, that many students adopt towards their famous professors, that many Malays adopt towards their mullahs, and that many Chinese adopt to their 'elders and betters.'

There may well be intrinsically social emotions described in some cultures or historical periods that are alien to us, not only in the sense that we recognize the intensional dimensions but deny their prevalence in our cultural or historical setting, but also in the sense that we find it hard to get any conceptual grip on these intensional dimensions themselves. For example, we may very well understand the intensional dimension described by the German word *Schadenfreude* – which describes the pleasure taken in another's displeasure or suffering – but may like to think that it plays no role in our own emotional lives imbedded within our distinctive moral careers, even if this is in fact most doubtful (it can be observed commonly enough in children's – often cruel – games and occasionally at departmental meetings). However, it is hard to grasp the intensional dimension referenced by the emotion description *fago* of the Ifaluk, as characterized by Lutz (1982). It is hard to grasp just what form of evaluative representation is common to the representation of someone dying, being needy, being ill, going on a journey *and* being in the presence of someone admirable or receiving a gift.

There is no good reason to suppose that there will be descriptive labels for every emotion in every form of social life. We might anticipate a temporal lag between the social construction of novel emotions – the development of novel forms of evaluative representations of actions and social relations – and the social construction of novel descriptive labels. It is in fact extremely doubtful that there is a descriptive label for every human emotion. This much at least is suggested by Kemper's (1978) social psychological analysis of emotions. Despite the fact that Kemper limits his analysis to the dimensions of represented power and status, his theoretical matrix generates combinations of evaluative dimensions that are intuitively familiar but for which there are no conventional descriptions, or only a loosely related assortment of names and phrases in a variety of different languages: *Gemütlichkeit*, *Weltschmerz*, *élan*, *brio*, and the like.

These points indicate the deep ambiguity of contemporary references to the 'indigenous psychology' (Heelas and Lock, 1981) of a form of social life. This may refer to the emotions and motives referenced by the descriptive cognitive labels employed by participants in a form of social life, or it may refer to the emotions and motives articulated and expressed in participants' moral commentaries on actions and social relations. An indigenous psychology in the latter sense is almost certainly bound to be richer and more extensive than an indigenous psychology in the former sense.

If this is the case, then theoretical psychologists – and philosophers – ought not to concern themselves with the proper definition of emotion labels such as 'anger,' 'shame,' and 'envy,' or the question of whether there are cognitive labels that are more or less translationally equivalent to them in different cultures and historical periods. This is not the route to a proper understanding of emotional phenomena, or a proper appreciation of emotional diversity. Rather, theoretical psychologists ought to document the intrinsically social evaluative dimensions of representations of actions and social relations expressed in – and appropriated from – the possibly diverse languages of moral commentary on actions and social relations. For the same reason, emotions in our own culture are not best studied through the employment of self-report measures employing descriptive cognitive labels, but rather through the employment of instruments that may be exploited to tap the semantic contents of evaluative representations of actions and social relations, such as the repertory grid (Collett, 1979) and multidimensional scaling (Forgas, 1979).

Some emotion researchers do employ such measures (for example, Corraliza, 1987; Gehm and Scherer, 1988; Lutz, 1982), but unfortunately restrict their employment to analyses of emotion labels, rather than analyses of the evaluative dimensions of representations of actions and social relations. Nonetheless, even these limited studies are suggestive of the inadequacies of standard attempts to find translational equivalents for emotion terms. For example, Tanaka-Matsumi and Marsella (1976) employed standard translational techniques to select '*yuutsu*' as the Japanese translation for the English language term 'depression.' However, when Tanaka-Matsumi and Marsella (1977) (and Imada et al., 1991) rated '*yuutsu*' and 'depression' on semantic differential scales, their analyses yielded quite different factor structures.

If this course were pursued, it might – or it might not – reveal that the apparent cross-cultural and transhistorical diversity of emotions is an illusion generated by the social diversity of descriptive labels in diverse forms of social life. It may turn out that there are a number of basic evaluative representational dimensions – such as representations of reputation, power, honor, dignity, responsibility, obligation, and the like – that can be reidentified in all ages and cultures. They may simply be differentially combined in different ages and cultures (thus we may recognize the dimensions of *amae*, even though they are not combined in the manner of *amae* in our culture), or their descriptions may be differentially defined in different ages and cultures (thus, for example, the Ifaluk word '*song*' appears to reference the dimensions referenced by the English words 'anger' and 'sadness' (Lutz, 1988); the Gidjingali aborigine word '*gurakadj*' appears to reference the dimensions referenced by the English words 'shame' and 'fear' (Hiatt, 1978)). This is an open and objective question, but it cannot be seriously addressed until researchers focus in much more detail upon the intrinsically social evaluative representational dimensions of emotions. Contemporary analyses based upon 'semantic primitives' such as 'want,' 'think,' 'good,' and 'bad' (Wierzbicka, 1986), while able to formally accommodate most emotions, simply ignore the intrinsically social forms of representation of reputation, honor, and power that are integral to those emotions associated with moral careers within social collectives – they are blind to the intrinsically social dimensions of what is considered 'good' and 'bad' in any form of social life.

Emotion and Language

These remarks suggest that there would be no great loss to our emotional lives if we did not employ theoretical descriptions of our emotions. Some cultures seem to have little social interest in theoretical reflections upon their psychological states. As Hallpike notes, 'the realm of purely private experience and motives, *as distinct from the evaluation of actual behavior*, is given little attention in many primitive societies'

(1979: 392; my emphasis). Some cultures, such as the Pintupi Aborigines of Western Australia (Myers, 1979) and the Ommura of Papua New Guinea (Hallpike, 1979) have few descriptive labels of emotions. It does not follow, nor is there any evidence to suggest that it is the case, that the psychological lives of such persons are emotionally impoverished. The Taiwanese language has approximately 750 emotion labels (Boucher, 1979) and the English language only about 400[4] (Davitz, 1969). It does not follow, nor is there any evidence to suggest that it is the case, that in consequence the Taiwanese lead richer emotional lives than the English.

The richness and diversity of emotions in any historical period or culture is a direct function of the richness and diversity of the – indigenous – intrinsically social forms of evaluation of actions and social relations that are constitutive of human emotions, and not a function of the number of linguistic labels that may be employed to describe emotions. It is a consequence of the richness and diversity of the language of moral commentary on actions and social relations to be found in any culture or historical period, from which the contents of intrinsically social emotions are appropriated. There is no good reason to suppose that the richness and diversity of emotional life when and where it occurs will be necessarily paralleled by a similar richness and diversity of descriptive emotion labels. There is no conceptual absurdity or empirical implausibility about a possible form of social life that is productive of emotional richness, but which eschews any form of discourse about emotions.

It might be objected that discourse about emotions plays an essential role in moral commentary, and is in this sense constitutive of emotion (Harré, 1989). It is hard to see how this could be the case. Emotion labels are not necessary for moral commentary on our actions and social relations: actions and social relations may be characterized as offensive, degrading, humiliating, obligatory, great achievements, and miserable failures, without any reference to psychological states. Emotion labels are necessary neither for discourse about emotions themselves, nor for moral commentary upon them, for these may be designated directly by reference to the intensional contents of evaluative representations. Thus in commenting upon an action, we may characterize it as offensive or object that it is not really offensive (according to the conventions of that place and time). Instead of claiming that a person's 'anger' is inappropriate, we may simply complain that her treatment of another's action as offensive is inappropriate, unreasonable, and the like.

This is not to claim that the employment of emotion labels is causally impotent: that it is a mere linguistic epiphenomenon. When and where emotion labels are available, they may be employed to reference emotions in the social negotiation of moral commentaries. That is, descriptive references to emotions may feed into discourse about the appropriateness of certain emotions in particular situations or the appropriateness of

particular emotions themselves. This in turn may lead to the transformation of forms of moral commentary on actions and social relations,
and consequently the transformation of emotions themselves. The
employment of descriptive labels may play a causal role in the
transformation of emotions in this fashion, but emotions are not
constitutively created or transformed (or eliminated) by the employment
of such emotion labels.

Nor is the employment of emotion labels causally necessary for the
creation or transformation of emotions. Since the intrinsically social
contents of emotions are appropriated from the contents of our moral
commentaries on actions and social relations, it is ultimately our
discourse about actions and social relations, and not about emotions
themselves, that is critical to the creation or transformation of emotions.
Discourse about the appropriateness of certain forms of evaluations of
actions in certain situations, or discourse about the appropriateness of
certain forms of evaluations themselves, *may* proceed via the employment
of emotion labels, but may instead directly reference such evaluations
themselves.

Moreover, although it may be the case that – at least on some
occasions – the employment of emotion labels facilitates the development
or transformation of emotions by facilitating the development or
transformation of our moral commentaries on actions and social
relations, this is not obviously the case – and may not be generally the
case. Indeed, it may be argued (for reasons to be discussed in more
detail in Chapter 10) that the employment of emotion labels may
constitute an *impediment* to the development or transformation of
intrinsically social forms of evaluative representation appropriated from
moral commentaries on actions and social relations: that is, when
theoretical discourse about emotions *directs attention away from the
evaluation of actions and social relations.* Thus cultures that focus their
theoretical attention upon the evaluation of actions and social relations
rather than the theoretical descriptions of emotions, such as the Pintupi
Aborigines and the Ommura, may develop richer forms of emotional life
– through richer forms of moral commentary on actions and social
relations – than cultures that focus their theoretical attention upon
emotions themselves.

It is particularly important to avoid the gratuitous assumption that
those cultures with more developed forms of theoretical discourse about
emotions – that employ developed folk theories or indigenous
psychologies or scientific psychologies referencing a large number of
emotions – necessarily have richer emotional lives than cultures that do
not (Russell, 1991). Fischer and Frijda claim, for example:

> It makes a considerable difference whether or not a labelled category exists for
> a particular type of emotion. The presence of a label more or less implies the
> existence of an *emotion script* (Fisher, 1991). Emotion scripts are culturally and
> individually based knowledge structures, providing emotional reactions in

certain situations with meaning, and making certain aspects of emotional situations more salient than others. The nature and occurence of emotions is deeply influenced, we believe, by the presence of a particular category and its script. (1992: 26)

It may well be the case that many of our emotions are governed by intrinsically social 'emotion scripts' (Fischer, 1991) or 'emotion rules' (Hochschild, 1983) – conventions and agreements relating to appropriate occasions for emotions and their behavioral expression. The employment of descriptive emotion labels *may* causally facilitate the development of such scripts – or may impede it. However, the employment of descriptive emotion labels is not necessary for the development or employment of emotion scripts. The conventions and agreements governing appropriate occasions for and behavioral expression of emotions may directly cite forms of evaluative representation of actions and social relations. Thus, there may very well be complex conventions and agreements governing responses to represented offenses in cultures that do not have any descriptive labels that translate as 'anger,' and persons in such cultures may have richer emotional lives – and may employ more detailed 'emotion scripts' or 'emotion rules' – than persons in cultures that have richer vocabularies of emotion labels.

These are properly theoretical questions about the causal role of emotion descriptions in the development and transformation of the forms of intrinsically social evaluative representation that are constitutive of emotion, and in the development of intrinsically social 'scripts' or 'rules' regulating these forms of intrinsically social evaluative representation (their appropriate occasions and behavioral expression). Yet whatever causal role such emotion descriptions play, they play no constitutive role with respect to intrinsically social emotions: none of the various possible causal roles for emotion descriptions considered above do anything to suggest that intrinsically social emotions are constituted by our intrinsically social descriptions of them.

It might be objected that emotion labeling plays an important role in our *experience* of emotion. Thus Lewis and Saarni claim that 'emotional experience . . . requires that organisms possess a language of emotion' (1985: 8), and Malatesta and Haviland claim that 'the emotion words of a culture exert a powerful influence on the actual experience of emotion' (1985: 110) – compare Mischel, 1977b. However, it is hard to see how this could be the case. The employment of emotion labels can add nothing to the intensional contents of our emotions, since they are merely descriptive of them. It can add nothing to our experience of sympathetic arousal for the same reason (assuming, which may be doubted, that emotion labels are also descriptive of sympathetic arousal). Our emotional lives are, however, enormously enriched by our developing appreciation and understanding of the subtleties of the distinctions employed in our moral commentaries on actions and relations (of the sort provided by Sabini and Silver (1982), for example).[5] The only 'language of emotion' necessary for emotional experience is the language of moral commentary on actions and social relations.

To deny the constitutive role of linguistic descriptions of emotions is not to deny the critically important role played by language in the social construction of intrinsically social emotions. What I take to be the basic socio-linguistic truth of social constructionist analyses of emotion (although not all – and perhaps few – avowed social constructionists would endorse it) is that the intrinsically social intensional contents of representational states such as shame and pride are appropriated from the intrinsically social linguistic contents of our moral commentaries upon actions and social relations. Such characteristically human emotions evolve in particular forms of social life when particular forms of social life develop these forms of moral commentary on actions and social relations, and persons in these forms of social life come to represent actions and social relations in terms of them – when they become party to the sets of arrangements, conventions, and agreements that ground them. The recognition of this important truth about intrinsically social human emotions is entirely consistent with the denial of the standard social constructionist claim that such emotions are constituted by our socially constructed linguistic descriptions of them.

Emotions and Identity Projects

It is also important to stress the precise respects in which the social constitution of human emotions is linguistically grounded in moral commentaries on actions and social relations. A good many forms of psychological states attributable to persons, such as many – linguistically informed – beliefs and attitudes, may also be said to be socially constituted, at least to the degree that they depend upon a person being party to conventions governing the semantics of descriptions, from which the contents of linguistically informed beliefs – or opinions[6] – are appropriated. Thus only linguistic agents – parties to conventions of descriptive meaning – can have beliefs that presidents never represent the electorate, or have attitudes towards abortion on demand. However, persons do not need to be party to any other arrangements, conventions, or agreements in order to have these beliefs or attitudes.

Intrinsically social emotions such as shame and pride do depend upon persons being parties to the conventions governing the semantics of moral commentaries on actions and social relations, but they also depend upon something more: that persons to whom such emotions are attributable are also party to the conventions and agreements about the evaluation of actions and social relations expressed by these forms of moral commentary.

It is not sufficient for the emotion of anger that I simply understand the language of moral commentary on actions and social relations that represents certain actions as offensive: nor is it sufficient that I recognize certain actions as satisfying conventional criteria for offensive actions according to the semantics of such forms of moral commentary. In order to be angry, I have to *take offense* at another's action. I have to treat the other's action as reflecting negatively upon my reputation and self-worth – on my *identity*. I have to accept and be committed to – be party to – the conventions governing the moral order of the social collectives within which I pursue my identity project, which are expressed in the forms of moral commentary on action from which the evaluative content of my anger is appropriated. That is, such emotions are ultimately individuated by reference to the conventions of identity projects pursued within social collectives.

Cooley (1902) emphasized how emotions such as shame and pride depend upon a social audience: 'The thing that moves us to pride and shame is not the merely mechanical reflection of ourselves, but an imputed sentiment, the imagined effect of this reflection upon another's mind' (1902: 93). Recent research on the development of such emotions in children (Harter and Whitesell, 1989; Harter et al., 1987) demonstrates that they originally depend upon the actual presence of a social audience (e.g. parents and teachers), but eventually become independent of it, while retaining a conceptual link to the imagined response of a social audience. Thus one may be proud or ashamed even if no other is aware of one's success or failure: it is often enough to know how they would appraise our actions if they were. I may be proud of my prize-winning essay for a long time before its announcement or publication, even if modesty prevents me from mentioning it to anyone. I may be ashamed of cheating in a critical exam, even though prudence suggests silence.

However, not any old social audience – real or imagined – will do. Such emotions are also tied very specifically to moral careers within identity projects pursued within social collectives. I have to care about the actual or possible or imagined appraisals of those who constitute the collectives within which my moral careers are embedded: that is, I have to be committed to specific moral careers. Thus I will not be ashamed even though my performance in a friendly soccer match is by all conventional standards pitiful, nor will I be angry if it elicits comments from the devout that are by conventional standards abusive and offensive (and that I recognize as such), if I do not care about my performance or their appraisals: if I am in no way committed to this form of moral career. Analogously a construction worker will not be ashamed of the patently poor job he has done, or angered by the critical comments of his colleagues, if he does not care about his performance or their opinion of him (if his job is protected by the union and his identity is fixed by another form of moral career).

Conversely, if I am committed to an academic moral career, I will be ashamed if my invited address is pitiful by conventional standards, and angry if I represent offensive complaints of my colleagues as unjustified. Yet a student who does not care a jot about his performance in a math test will not be ashamed of his miserable performance, or angered by the teacher's abusively offensive remarks; in fact in the moral order of the gang of which he is a member this may be a source of pride and satisfaction.

The Kinds of Things that Are Emotions

I have claimed in this chapter that many human emotions are socially constituted: that they are intrinsically social representational phenomena that are constituted as emotions by their intensional contents appropriated from intrinsically social forms of moral commentary on actions and social relations – the forms of moral commentary that create the possibilities of identity projects pursued within social collectives. I maintain these claims in the strong sense that such emotions are theoretically individuated by such forms of intrinsically social evaluation of actions and social relations.

It might be objected that the analysis of emotions offered is biased and one-sided because it focuses exclusively upon paradigmatically social emotions such as 'shame,' 'jealousy,' 'pride,' and the like that do seem to be grounded in developed forms of socio-linguistic life, but ignores more primitive or basic emotions such as rage and fear that we share with non-social, non-linguistic animals. It might also be objected that it has ignored the biological grounding and phylogenetic continuity of emotions, and evidence for the fact that the forms of cognitive appraisal involved in some emotions may be innate (Leventhal and Scherer, 1987).

The analysis presented in this chapter makes no pretense of offering a general theory of all emotions. It does not claim that all emotions are socially constituted, or that emotions can only be attributed to socio-linguistic agents. It assumes that there are many emotional states that are not socially constituted – such as *some* forms of rage and fear – that can be attributed both to non-social, non-linguistic animals and to socio-linguistic human agents – with the qualification that *other* forms of rage and fear that can be attributed to human agents are socially constituted, being based upon the intrinsically social dimensions of moral career frustrations (because of race or color, for example) or threats to one's reputation. The question of whether socially constituted emotional states such as 'shame' and 'pride' can be attributed to non-human animals has not been considered, but it suffices to note that the answer to this open and empirical question depends upon the degree to which certain forms of social life and linguistic competence can be attributed to certain animals.

The primary aim of the analysis is to recognize the legitimate respects in which some emotional phenomena may be said to be socially constituted – to be intrinsically social in nature – and to argue that this poses no threat to the linguistic – or epistemic[7] – objectivity of our theoretical psychological descriptions of them. If it is a fact that some emotional phenomena are socially constituted, then it is an entirely objective fact. The reason for focusing upon the most plausibly socio-linguistic examples of emotions is precisely that these are the sort of examples that are usually cited in support of the standard social constructionist analysis of emotions – according to which emotions are constituted by our socially constructed descriptions of them – which I have been at pains to deny.

None of these claims entail any denial of the biological basis or phylogenetic continuity of emotional phenomena. The recognition that some emotions are socially constituted is entirely consistent with the recognition of the biological basis and phylogenetic continuity of emotional phenomena. It is no doubt also true that the forms of cognitive appraisal involved in some emotions are innate (Leventhal and Scherer, 1987); which is not to endorse the view that all the forms of cognitive appraisal involved in all emotions are innate – those involving representations of reproachful responsibility that are constitutive of guilt seem to be absent in many cultures (Gerber, 1975).

However, the recognition of these points is entirely consistent with the view that certain forms of evaluative representation that are constitutive of some emotions are neither innate nor individual. The intrinsically social forms of evaluative representation that are constitutive of human emotions such as shame, jealousy, pride, guilt, and the like, are based upon intrinsically social and socially diverse forms of moral commentaries on actions and social relations.

I have argued that a certain class of representational phenomena – including emotional phenomena such as shame, pride, jealousy, and guilt – that play an important role in the explanation of human action are socially constituted – are intrinsically social. Within the class of such socially constituted representational phenomena are also many phenomena often classified as motives – such as motives of revenge or ambition, with intrinsically social intensional contents that are socially directed and socially located within identity projects. This has the theoretical consequence (already suggested in the previous discussion) that there is no interesting difference between many human emotions and motives – a consequence that I believe ought to be embraced by psychologists.

I have studiously tried to avoid getting embroiled in debates about the general nature of emotion: debates about the social versus the cognitive or physiological nature of emotion. Emotions do not form a natural kind, or indeed *any kind of thing at all* – which is why some are indistinguishable from motives. The types of phenomena referenced by the English language term 'emotion,' for example, range from purely physiological non-intensional and non-intentional states such as the galvanic skin response (having no content or object); through intentional but non-intensional states such as conditioned aversion (with an object but not a content), and intensional but non-intentional states such as vague anxiety (with a content but not an object); to intensional and intentional states such as shame (with a content and object).[8] For this reason most debates about the 'real' nature of emotion degenerate into purely semantic debates concerning competing normative recommendations for restricting the reference of the term 'emotion' – such as the recent *American Psychologist* exchange between Zajonc (1980, 1984) and Lazarus (1981, 1984) concerning physiological versus cognitive accounts of emotion.

To deny that emotions form a natural kind is not to deny the biological basis or phylogenetic continuity of emotions. It is rather to stress that biological basis and phylogenetic continuity are perhaps *all* that emotional phenomena have in common – which is not to claim that the best form of theoretical individuation of all emotional phenomena is physiological. For to deny that emotional phenomena form a natural kind is not to deny that the diverse types of phenomena we classify as particular emotions do form *individual kinds*. Although it is no doubt true that some emotional phenomena – such as forms of rage and fear in most animals and young children – are constituted by physiological arousal and/or innate cognitive appraisal, the present account is committed to the strong claim that human emotions such as shame, jealousy, pride, guilt, and the like are constituted by their intrinsically social intensional contents, *and not by anything else*.

This is not to deny that we may identify evolutionary or developmental precursors of such intrinsically social emotions, such that intrinsically social emotions may be held to be cultural elaborations of these evolutionary and developmental precursors (Averill, 1986). Thus we might identify evolutionary precursors of shame in the distress or urges to hide that animals appear to feel when rejected by other members of their herd or troop (Scheff, 1988), or developmental precursors of jealousy in the spontaneous desires of children for desirable objects held by other children. Yet – adult – human emotions such as shame and jealousy are only elaborations of these evolutionary or developmental precursors in the sense that speeches may be elaborations of remarks, or statues may be elaborations of drawings: that is, in the sense where elaboration does not presuppose identity in kind. Adult human shame and jealousy are grounded in intrinsically social evaluative representations of actions and social relations that may – or may not (Ratner, 1989) – contain elements of their evolutionary and developmental precursors, but which are no more to be identified with their evolutionary and developmental precursors than speeches are to be identified with remarks or statues with drawings. The distress that epileptic children originally feel when rejected by others may be grounded in such evolutionary or developmental precursors of shame; yet, as Hippocrates noted, children have to learn to be ashamed, by becoming parties to conventions governing evaluative representations of their epileptic behavior as degrading and humiliating.

Similar sorts of considerations apply to biologically grounded forms of physiological arousal. Intrinsically social emotions such as shame, jealousy, or anger are often accompanied by physiological arousal, which may enhance or impede our social actions directed by the intrinsically social contents and objects of our emotions. Thus the physiological arousal associated with anger may enhance or impede my response directed to restitution for, or reaction to, a represented offense (according to its intensity and other factors). I do not deny that such arousal plays an important role with respect to our intrinsically social emotions constituted within the moral careers that make up our identity projects. On the contrary, arousal and associated stress are bound to play a very large role in our emotional lives, as we face the myriad social threats and hazards to our identity, via the so-called General Adaption Syndrome (Seyle, 1950, 1974) – but I stress that the forms of evaluative representation of actions – as hazards or threats to our identities – that generate such forms of arousal are intrinsically social in nature.

All these matters may be granted while at the same time insisting that the theoretical identity of such emotions is fixed by their intrinsically social contentful dimensions rather than by their physiological dimensions: that intrinsically social emotions such as shame, jealousy, and anger cannot be identified with forms of physiological arousal. Indeed, a stronger claim can be made and supported: physiological arousal plays *no* constitutive role with respect to these emotions.

Such arousal is plainly not sufficient for such emotions, as evidenced by Maranon's (1924) subjects, who were artificially aroused and who reported no emotional states. However, *contra* Schachter and others, it is not obviously necessary for intrinsically social emotions either – even though arousal is a *de facto* common concomitant of shame, anger, jealousy, pride, and the like. There appears to be nothing logically paradoxical about the ascription of such emotions to possible beings that might not be physiologically aroused. Despite perhaps rather dramatic differences in their physical composition, we would attribute anger and shame to such beings – such as Martians, complex robotic computers, or other aliens – if we came to believe that they represented some of their actions and social relations in ways that we consider to be socially appropriate for anger and shame, and if their actions were best explained by reference to the intensional contents of such intrinsically social psychological states.

Similarly there is nothing paradoxical about 'calm' joy or 'cold' anger: that is, joy and anger without arousal. The intrinsically social forms of evaluative representation of actions and social relations are sufficient for these forms of emotion. They continue to motivate our actions in the absence of arousal, and many of our 'cool-headed' actions may be explained by reference to them. Consider the comments of some of the paraplegic and quadriplegic patients studied by Hohmann who did not experience physiological arousal:

It's sort of cold anger. Sometimes I act angry when I see some injustice. I yell and cuss and rage hell ... but it just doesn't have the heat to it that it used to. It's a mental kind of anger.

Seems like I get thinking mad, not shaking mad, and that's a lot different. (Cited in Schachter, 1965: 165–6)

Anger without arousal retains its identity *as* anger through its intrinsically social content and ability to motivate by virtue of its intrinsically social content. Although instances of such 'calm' or 'cold' emotions are perhaps rare at present (and perhaps only occur in clinical contexts), they might become common in a future age when we have learned to control our arousal through biofeedback techniques or synthetic drugs. Such intrinsically social emotions without arousal would still promote the appropriate forms of action. Thus I might coldly refuse your request for additional funds because I am angry at your squandering of previous financial support. The calm but emotionally potent performance of Sydney Carton on the guillotine is perhaps presently a fictional idea to be aspired to (or not, according to one's taste in such matters), but it is not a logically incoherent one.

It might be objected that the presence of physiological arousal is precisely what distinguishes emotions from motives. Yet this is doubtful: motives of revenge are often accompanied by high levels of physiological arousal. Although there is a significant sense in which we characterize persons as emotionally involved when their actions are promoted or impeded by physiological arousal, there is also an equally significant sense in which we characterize persons as emotionally involved when their actions are a product of social engagement and commitment, irrespective of their levels of physiological arousal – in fact, precisely when their actions are a product of the forms of social engagement and commitment that are integral to human identity projects pursued within social collectives.

This last point is worth stressing to forestall another possible objection. Those emotional – and motivational – phenomena that I claim to be socially constituted have been characterized as representational states. It might be objected that this sort of analysis ignores the dynamic aspects of emotion. However, the characterization of such emotional phenomena as representational *states* is entirely neutral with respect to the question of their dynamic or static nature.

The present analysis of socially constituted emotions is not inconsistent with accounts of such emotions as 'action tendencies' (Frijda, 1987; Fischer and Frijda, 1992). On the contrary, emotions are conceived within the present analysis as – intrinsically social and linguistically informed – *dispositional states*[9] that promote various forms of action. Whether or not such emotions are dispositional states or action tendencies is not really at issue – few would deny that they are. What is at issue is the question of which dimensions ought to be cited in a theoretical analysis of such emotions employed to provide psychological explanations of human actions.

Certainly not dispositions, tendencies, and the like. They explain nothing, since they are defined in terms of the sorts of actions produced by dispositions or tendencies. A mere reference to a disposition to engage in aggressive actions no more explains why people engage in aggressive actions than a reference to the solubility of salt explains why salt dissolves. Of course both dispositions are real enough, but they are explanatory duds. Dispositions themselves require theoretical grounding in order, for example, to explain why salt is disposed to dissolve and why persons who are ashamed are disposed to act in some directed ways rather than others. In the case of the solubility of salt, the theoretical explanation looks to the composition and structure of salt. In the case of emotions such as shame, it would look to the intrinsically social content of the evaluative representation that is constitutive of shame. An account of shame in terms of this representational content, in conjunction with auxiliary assumptions about 'emotion scripts' and other action conventions, can provide an explanation of why such an emotion regularly leads to certain forms of action (or inaction). This seems a very good reason for treating such intrinsically social representational contents as the constitutive dimensions of emotions such as shame.

It has a number of theoretical advantages. One is that it enables us to preserve our intuition that shame and jealousy can be reidentified cross-culturally and transhistorically, even though persons in different times and places who are ashamed or jealous may act in different ways because of differences in local 'display rules' (Ekman, 1980; Harris, 1989) or 'emotion rules' (Hochschild, 1983). They remain the same emotions, just as chemical elements remain the same chemical elements even though they behave differently in different physical environments, and at different temperatures and pressures.

Explanatory Kinds

I noted earlier that it cannot be presumed that particular emotions can be reidentified cross-culturally and transhistorically, and suggested that we may anticipate ontological differences in emotions in different cultures and historical periods: *amae* is rare in the West, and accidie is rare these days. I stressed that the possible ontological diversity of emotions in different cultures and historical periods poses no threat to the linguistic (or epistemic) objectivity of theoretical psychological descriptions of emotions. The degree to which some emotions can be reidentified cross-culturally and transhistorically is an entirely open and empirical question.

It is always an objective and empirical question whether emotions such as shame, *amae*, and accidie can be reidentified in our own or another form of social life. The presence of such emotions in our own or another form of social life does not depend upon the availability of descriptive labels such as 'shame,' *'amae,'* and 'accidie' in our own or another form of social life. It entirely depends upon whether there are psychological states that have the intrinsically social representational properties referenced by these or other forms of theoretical psychological description.

Analogous points can be made about the possible non-universality of explanations that reference intrinsically social emotional phenomena. We may anticipate that there are unlikely to be any universal or general laws governing emotions, and relating them to invariant antecedents and consequents. We are able to reidentify instances of shame and pride in our own and other cultures, even though different persons may be ashamed of and take pride in different things (and their arousal may be caused in different ways), and may act in different ways even when the contents and objects of their emotions correspond.

The possible and likely lack of universality or generality of psychological explanations that make reference to emotions does not entail or imply any form of explanatory inadequacy. An explanation is universal if it applies to each and every instance of a reidentifiable phenomenon (no matter how rare or common its frequency of occurrence). However, a lack of universality does not entail the inadequacy of an explanation: a reference to the regular inhalation of tobacco smoke may be an entirely adequate explanation of some instances of lung cancer but not others (which may be genetically determined), and a reference to social pressures to conform may be an entirely adequate explanation of some instances of 'destructive obedience' (Milgram, 1974) but not others (which may be a product of violent coercion). Analogously a reference to anger may provide an entirely adequate explanation of some aggressive actions but not others (which may be caused by the presence of 'violent stimuli' (Berkowitz and LePage, 1967)).

Nor does a lack of universality entail or imply a lack of generality, which is a quite different matter. An explanation is general if it applies to a range of different phenomena. Thus a reference to the regular inhalation of tobacco smoke may not only adequately explain some instances of lung cancer, but may also explain some instances of heart disease and bronchitis, and a reference to social pressures to conform may adequately explain not only some instances of 'destructive obedience,' but also some instances of racism and teenage pregnancies. Analogously a reference to shame may not only provide an adequate explanation of some instances of altruism (as a form of restitution), but also an adequate explanation of some instances of spiritual devotion and suicide. The ultimate criterion of the adequacy of any explanation is its accuracy, and the only measure of its accuracy is the quality of the empirical evidence in favor of it. The *scope* of an explanation is an entirely separate and independent empirical question.

This is not to deny that some of these psychological explanations may turn out to be universal (and/or general). This is a properly empirical matter. The point is that we should not be surprised if they do not, and should not conclude that our explanations are necessarily inadequate if they do not turn out to be universal. There may very well be different causes and consequences of anger and depression in our own and other cultures (mediated by intrinsically social forms of representation of appropriate objects of, and responses to, such forms of evaluation). We obscure our real explanatory achievements if we presume that there must be unitary explanations of such phenomena, or that a reference to such phenomena must furnish a unitary explanation of some form of action.

Universality is a common but contingent feature of many explanations in the natural sciences. It is not an intrinsic feature of an adequate explanation. Whether the best explanation of a set of physical states or events is universal or not depends upon whether that set of states or events is causally produced by a singular type of physical state or event, or by multiple types of physical state or event. Although many explanations in the natural sciences are universal in scope, there are perfectly adequate natural scientific explanations that are not. Many of the motions of physical bodies are best explained in terms of gravitational forces. Yet some are clearly not: the motion of a pin moving towards a magnet is best explained in terms of magnetic forces.

It is true that those emotions that are socially constituted form what may be termed *social psychological* rather than *natural kinds*: they are constituted as emotions by their intrinsically social psychological dimensions rather than their biological or physical dimensions. It is also true that many explanations of the behavior of natural kinds of thing are universal in scope, although others are not. Yet the significant theoretical issue is not whether such emotions form social psychological or natural kinds. The important question is whether such emotions form *explanatory kinds*, whatever the scope of explanations that reference their intrinsically social psychological dimensions. I have suggested in the last few chapters that we have very good grounds for supposing that they do form explanatory kinds: that many forms of human action require an explanation in terms of characteristically human intrinsically social emotions – and motives – located within identity projects.

Although many explanations referencing intrinsically social human emotions may turn out to be non-universal, it may also be the case that universal explanations apply at fairly high levels of abstraction. Although the specific details of individual lives and conventions of social life may vary from person to person and place and time, identity projects, which provide the intrinsically social evaluative matrix for human emotions and motives, may very well be a universal element. In this respect the form and basic theoretical explanatory dimensions of all human lives may be the same, even though the detailed causal stories to be told about particular actions and particular emotions in particular places and times may be as diverse as we care to imagine.

I suspect that this is very probably true. If so, then a developed form of social psychological science might look very much like some theoretical branches of the physical sciences, which may be strong on causal understanding through a grasp of basic theoretical explanatory dimensions, but delimited with respect to prediction and control, because of either the complexity of the phenomena (as in meteorology), or our inability to control through intervention (as in astronomy), or our moral reluctance to do so (as in human genetics). It would be unsurprising if we discovered this was the case with intrinsically social psychological phenomena such as human emotions, which are complex phenomena over which we have limited degrees of control that we are morally reluctant to increase.

It may well turn out that a broad theoretical picture of emotions may reference basic theoretical dimensions that undermine our traditional distinctions between drives, emotions, motives, and the like. But such a broad theoretical picture will need to cite intrinsically social psychological and relational as well as individual psychological and physiological dimensions. There is simply no a priori reason to suppose that the best theoretical form of explication and integrative explanation of human emotions will be individualistically psychological or reductively physiological in nature, and there are very good reasons for anticipating that it will involve an essential reference to the intrinsically social and relational dimensions of many emotions.

Notes

1 I do not claim that this characterization will do as a theoretically adequate account of shame, nor is theoretical adequacy claimed for most of the characterizations of particular emotions offered in this work. These characterizations are rather offered as economical approximate characterizations that are sufficient for the purposes of the present analysis. A theoretically adequate account of such emotions would be much more sophisticated and detailed, particularly via its specification of the subtly different ways in which different emotions are tied to identity projects. The best contemporary analysis of emotions within the general framework of the present account is to be found in Sabini and Silver (1982).

2 This is not to deny that many socially constituted emotions may be directed towards non-social intentional objects: thus I may be ashamed of my disfigurement and jealous of my brother's physique. Nor is it to deny that such socially constituted emotions can be directed upon emotions themselves: I may be ashamed of my jealousy or indeed of my shame. It is, however, to deny that any emotion is constituted as that particular emotion by the representation *of that particular emotion itself*.

3 It does not of course follow from the fact that emotions are rationally appraisable that they can be modified by rational persuasion. Thus some rationally inappropriate feelings of hopelessness and helplessness, or some rationally inappropriate phobic fears, may not be eliminable by 'verbal' therapies: persons may instead require some form of behavioral treatment if such emotions are to be altered. The essential point of the analysis is however supported by the fact that it is these rationally appraisable contentful states that need to be modified or eliminated if the depression is to be relieved or the fear surmounted.

4 This figure may be disputed. Wallace and Carson (1973) claim that there are over 2,000 words for categories of emotion in the English language, although they also suggest that only about 200 are regularly employed by English speakers. Yet this sort of dispute seems to have

no bearing on the question of the emotional richness or poverty of the lives of English speakers. In order to determine the latter question, one would be better advised to look to the descriptions of and moral commentaries on actions and social relations produced by English speakers – in everyday life or in literature – rather than looking to dictionaries and surveys.

5 It is unfortunate that Sabini and Silver misleadingly characterize their own social psychological explorations as a form of 'conceptual analysis.' Their work is in large part devoted to detailed articulations of the content of the forms of social representation and evaluation based upon moral commentaries that are constitutive of those phenomena we call 'anger,' 'envy,' 'jealousy,' and so on in our particular form of social life. That is, their analysis is properly empirical: it is a contingent matter of fact whether persons in our own or other cultures represent social reality in the ways they so illuminatingly describe. One way of illustrating this point is by noting that one could engage in a Sabini–Silver type of inquiry in a culture that employed no emotion labels, and could employ this form of inquiry to answer the question of whether persons in another culture lead similar or different emotional lives to ourselves, quite independently of questions about the inter-translatability of emotion labels.

6 To employ Dennett's (1978) term for 'linguistically infected' beliefs. The claims made in this chapter are not presumed to apply to those basic – 'sub-doxic' – representational states involved in basic perceptual and cognitive processing which, although they may be properly ascribed contents by virtue of their intentional direction, cannot be presumed to have linguistically informed contents.

7 Although issues concerning epistemic objectivity are not discussed in this chapter, having been sufficiently covered – I hope – in Chapter 4, and because the recognition of the intrinsically social nature of emotions appears to introduce no new epistemic problems.

8 It is far from obvious that all cultures recognize a psychological category for emotion, and many that may be said to do so almost invariably deploy it in somewhat different ways from each other and from us – for a useful discussion, see Russell (1991).

9 To recognize that emotions *are* – intrinsically social and linguistically informed – dispositions is not to endorse any form of semantic functionism – it is not to claim that the meaning of theoretical descriptions of emotions must be operationally defined in terms of such dispositions.

It is perhaps also worth noting at this stage – to avoid possible confusion – that to claim that emotions and other psychological phenomena are linguistically informed, and to claim that our theoretical ascriptions of emotions to self and others are modeled upon the properties of linguistic utterances (their sense and reference), is not to claim that theoretical descriptions of linguistically informed psychological states are descriptions of internal sentences or sentence-like phenomena (Fodor, 1975). Whether or not linguistically informed psychological states are best explicated in this fashion is a separate – and much disputed – theoretical question.

10

Self-Knowledge and Accounting

One potentially very powerful exploratory resource in the theoretical analysis of human psychology is the ability of human agents to provide accounts of their emotions, motives, beliefs, and other psychological states. This resource has, however, been historically neglected by psychologists, and remains underdeveloped and underexploited. Of course, like any other exploratory resource in any science, the epistemic viability of agent accounts is ultimately an empirical question. However, most of the reasons advanced by psychologists for ignoring this exploratory resource are thoroughly bad reasons, and there are rather good grounds for supposing that human agents are generally authoritative and reliable with respect to their self-knowledge of emotions and other psychological states.

In order to avoid unnecessary confusions, it may be useful to state clearly in advance what I am *not* claiming with respect to agent accounts of their psychological states. I do not claim that persons are epistemic authorities on the causal explanation of their actions or their modes of cognitive processing. If this *were* the case, then of course psychological experimentation and other forms of empirical adjudication of causal explanations would be redundant. Agents undoubtedly do err regularly in advancing causal explanations of their actions (Nisbett and Wilson, 1977) and logical reasoning processes (Johnson-Laird, 1983). However, the recognition of this fact is entirely consistent with the claim that agent accounts of their psychological states are generally accurate and reliable and ought to be exploited as an integral component of experimental and other forms of empirical evaluation of putative causal explanations of behavior.

This is not merely to suggest that agent accounts of their psychological states may be employed as useful heuristic devices that suggest possible causal explanations of action – although they plainly can be, and have been, employed for this purpose (Secord and Greenwood, 1993). Rather a stronger claim is maintained in this chapter: agent accounts of their psychological states enable us to *identify* their psychological states. In social psychological science, they provide observers with a form of empirical access to the psychological states of agents, which ought to be exploited in experimental or other forms of empirical evaluation of causal explanations of human behavior.

The present chapter does not, however, advance or defend any thesis about the privileged nature of 'introspection,' 'self-perception' or 'cognitive monitoring.' On the contrary, my aim is to reject the ancient and popular conception of self-knowledge of psychological states as internally directed, and to argue that the authority and reliability of self-knowledge of psychological states is not grounded in any form of 'direct access' to 'internal states,' but derives from the intrinsically social nature of our self-knowledge of psychological states such as beliefs, emotions, motives, and the like.

Most psychological accounts of self-knowledge presuppose the homogeneity of the mental, and in particular the original empiricist identification of sensation and cognition. In the classical empiricist accounts advanced by Locke, Berkeley, and Hume, thoughts or 'ideas' were held to be 'fainter copies' or 'images' of sense-impressions: ideas and sense-impressions were held to differ in degree (of intensity), but not in kind.

This analysis enabled early philosophers and psychologists to base their analysis of self-knowledge of psychological states upon the supposed paradigm of our self-knowledge of simple sensations such as pain. Our self-knowledge of such sensations was held to be direct and certain. This analysis was then uncritically generalized to cover intentional psychological states such as beliefs, emotions, motives, and the like.

As noted earlier, contemporary cognitive psychologists no longer identify concepts and images (Simon and Kaplan, 1989). Consequently, there is no longer any reason to maintain the homogeneity assumption. In actual fact, mental states form a rather heterogeneous lot (Rorty, 1979; Margolis, 1984). There is a fundamental difference between sensations such as pains and tickles, and intentional psychological states such as beliefs, emotions, and motives. Intentional psychological states such as beliefs, emotions, and motives have (intensional) contents and (intentional) objects. Sensations such as pains and tickles do not (although, like beliefs, emotions, and everything else, they do have causes). If I am deep in thought, it makes sense to ask me what I am thinking *of* and what I am thinking *about*. If I am in pain, it makes no sense to ask me what my pain is *of* or what I am in pain *about*.

Given the heterogeneity of sensations and intentional psychological[1] states such as beliefs, emotions, and motives, our self-knowledge of psychological states cannot be modeled upon our self-knowledge of sensations, and much of the contemporary debate about self-knowledge is vitiated because it remains firmly based upon the homogeneity assumption. Although there is some point in talking about 'internal perception' in the case of sensations such as pains or tickles (or sense-impressions of color and sound), there is none in the case of self-knowledge of psychological states such as beliefs, emotions, and motives. At least this is the argument of the present chapter.

The notion that agent accounts of their psychological states might enable us to identify their psychological states is anathema to most contemporary psychologists. In support of their general skepticism about the accuracy and reliability of self-knowledge of psychological states, many psychologists cite the failure of 'introspective psychology,' and the empirical studies documented by Nisbett and Wilson (1977) and Nisbett and Ross (1980) that are held to demonstrate that self-knowledge is regularly inaccurate:[2] 'The accuracy of subject reports is so poor as to suggest that any introspective access that may exist is not sufficient to produce generally correct or reliable reports' (Nisbett and Wilson, 1977: 233).

Introspective Psychology

However, the failure of 'introspective psychology' is simply irrelevant to questions about the accuracy and reliability of our self-knowledge of psychological states. The experimental studies conducted by W. Wundt and E.B. Tichener were exclusively concerned with introspection of the 'elements' of sensory experience. None of these studies were concerned with the introspection of psychological states such as beliefs and emotions. The failure of introspecting subjects to reach agreement on accounts of their introspection of sensory elements has simply no bearing on the issue of the abilities of persons to provide accounts of their psychological states, if, as already noted, sensations and psychological states are different in kind, and if, as I will argue, self-knowledge of psychological states does not involve any form of internal perception.[3]

It is of course true that some of the studies of the so-called 'Wurzburg School' and E.B. Titchener were avowedly concerned with 'thoughts.' Yet this only serves to illustrate further the present point. Such studies were directed towards 'thoughts' conceived in traditional empiricist terms as mental images: they presupposed the homogeneity of sensations and psychological states. Thus the 'imageless thought' and other controversies that led to the demise of 'introspective psychology.' An 'imageless thought' is only a theoretical paradox given the traditional empiricist equation of sensation and cognition.

In fact, Wundt himself did not conceive of psychological states such as emotions and motives as analogous to sensations, and denied that they could be studied via experimental introspective methods. In the *Völkerpsychologie* (1920) he argued that such intrinsically social and relational phenomena could only be studied through their social products, including accounting practices: 'There are other sources of objective psychological knowledge, which become accessible at the very point where the experimental method fails us. These are certain products of common mental life, in which we trace the operation of determinate psychical motives: chief among them are language, myth, and custom' (Wundt, 1897: 22).

Self-Knowledge as Theoretical Inference

Of the numerous empirical studies documented by Nisbett and Wilson (1977) and Nisbett and Ross (1980), only *two* are directly concerned with self-knowledge of psychological states, and these two studies provide no evidence at all that persons are *ever* mistaken, far less regularly mistaken, with respect to their self-knowledge of psychological states.

These two studies are the Schachter–Singer experiment (1962), and Bem's experimental analysis of attitude avowals (1967). Citing these studies, Nisbett and Ross claim that: 'Knowledge of one's own emotions and attitudes, though believed by the layperson (and many philosophers) to be direct and certain, has been shown to be indirect and prone to serious error' (1980: 227). However (as noted in Chapter 8), the Schachter–Singer experiment does not itself demonstrate that subjects are ever mistaken with respect to self-knowledge of emotion, far less regularly mistaken. It provides support for the experimental hypothesis that subjects will label their arousal states in accord with social cues when the source of arousal is unknown or ambiguous, but remains silent on the question of whether subjects in the experiment were in fact angry or euphoric.

Although Schachter (1965) did later provide an account of emotion according to which homogeneous states of physiological arousal are constituted as emotions by emotion labeling, one of the counter-intuitive implications of this constitutive account is that it *precludes the possibility of error*. If my physiological arousal is constituted as anger by my labeling it as 'anger' – if my labeling it as 'anger' *makes* it anger – then I can never be mistaken. Such a constitutive account cannot be employed to support the claim that persons regularly err with respect to self-knowledge of emotion.

As noted in Chapters 8 and 9, errors in emotion judgment cannot be identified with errors in causal judgment about source of arousal, since such causal judgments are not integral elements of those evaluative representations of actions and social relations that are constitutive of emotions. Accordingly we may be wrong in our judgment about our source of arousal, but correct in our judgment about our emotional state (and vice versa). For example, according to one plausible interpretation of the Schachter–Singer experiment, subjects in the experiment were genuinely angry and euphoric, since they were genuinely offended by the questionnaire (in the 'anger' condition) and genuinely enjoyed the jolly company (in the 'euphoria' condition). If this was the case, then subjects in that experiment did in fact describe their psychological states accurately, despite possible (and perhaps likely) errors in their judgment about the cause of their arousal.

Much the same considerations apply to Bem's analysis of attitude avowals, based upon his alternative interpretation of some of the results of 'forced compliance' experiments (Festinger and Carlsmith, 1959; Aronson and Carlsmith, 1963). In these experiments subjects are required to engage in counter-attitudinal behavior (e.g. making a counter-attitudinal speech) under conditions of insufficient justification (low reward or mild threat), and appear to change their attitude as a result, as evidenced by their attitude reports before and after their counter-attitudinal behavior. According to the standard cognitive dissonance interpretation (Festinger, 1957), subjects change their attitude to reduce cognitive dissonance. According to Bem's alternative interpretation of the outcome – in terms of 'self-perception' theory – subjects make an inference about attitude change as the most plausible causal explanation of their counter-attitudinal behavior: 'An individual's attitude statements may be viewed as inferences from observations of his own behavior and its accompanying stimulus variables' (Bem, 1967: 185).

Whatever the plausibility of this account, it does nothing to suggest that subjects are regularly mistaken in their attitude judgments. Being a good behaviorist, Bem makes no claim about the accuracy or inaccuracy of attitude avowals, since he makes no claim about the nature of attitudes themselves. If he adopted a constitutive labeling account in line with Schachter's account of emotion – which he does not – this would preclude error in the case of attitude judgments. Nothing Bem claims is in fact inconsistent with the assumption (presupposed by the cognitive dissonance account) that subjects in these experiments are correct in their attitude judgments (that they do in fact change their attitudes as a result of their counter-attitudinal behavior).

Neither of these studies provides any support for an even mildly skeptical conclusion about self-knowledge of psychological states. All the other studies documented by Nisbett and Wilson and Nisbett and Ross are concerned, not directly with self-knowledge of psychological states, but with the accuracy of our judgments about the stimulus determinants of our behavior. Nisbett and Wilson and Nisbett and Ross convincingly argue that a multiplicity of experiments in social psychology suggest that persons regularly err with respect to their causal judgments about the stimulus determinants of their behavior. They cite many studies that seem to demonstrate that persons regularly fail to identify causally efficacious stimuli, and regularly appeal to causally inert stimuli in explanations of their behavior. These studies include the failure to recognize semantic cuing effects, position effects, and anchoring effects, and erroneous reports on the emotional impact of literary passages, the effects of distraction on reaction to a film, and the effect of reassurance on willingness to take electric shocks.

These claims – and the methodologies upon which they are based – have been contested (for a comprehensive review, see White (1988)). Yet it may be readily granted that agents regularly err with respect to the causal explanation of their behavior. Nothing follows or is implied about the accuracy of self-knowledge of psychological states: the two questions are logically independent. There is no contradiction involved in supposing that agents may regularly err with respect to the causal explanation of their behavior but may regularly advance accurate accounts of their psychological states.

The reason why such studies are often held to cast doubt upon self-knowledge of psychological states is not difficult to discern. Many psychologists follow Nisbett and Wilson (1977) in treating self-knowledge of psychological states as a form of causal explanatory 'theoretical inference' from behavior and stimulus situation. Self-knowledge of such states is held to involve the employment of socially learned 'a priori' theories relating observable stimulus variables and behavioral responses, the constructs of which are operationally defined in terms of such stimulus–response sequences. Nisbett and Ross acknowledge that their general account of self-knowledge of psychological states is essentially a generalization of Bem's behaviorist analysis of attitude avowals: 'Such knowledge is based in large part on inferences about the causes of behavior. Frequent errors in the self-ascription of emotions and attitudes would appear to be inevitable, given the inadequacy and inaccuracy endemic to causal explanations of one's own behavior' (1980: 227).

Given this account, the skeptical conclusion immediately follows. If self-knowledge involves theoretical inference; if the meaning and truth conditions of theoretical psychological descriptions are specified in terms of stimulus–response sequences; and if the experimental studies demonstrate that we regularly err with respect to our judgments of stimulus causality, then it follows that we regularly err with respect to self-knowledge of psychological states.

However, according to the realist account of the semantics and truth conditions of theoretical psychological descriptions advanced in Chapter 2, the truth conditions of such descriptions are independent of the truth conditions of any empirical laws that such descriptions may be employed to explain, or the truth conditions of any causal explanatory propositions in which they may figure. If this is the case, then a conclusion about the regular inaccuracy of self-knowledge simply does not follow from experimentally demonstrated inaccuracies with respect to agents' causal explanations of their behavior.

It can be consistently maintained that agents can accurately describe their psychological states even if they regularly employ such descriptions in advancing inaccurate causal explanations of their behavior in terms of such states. Thus for example I might accurately avow my love for my wife or hatred of my boss, but inaccurately claim that my decision to marry her or quit my job was caused (even in part) by these emotions (the former may be in fact caused by need for security or Freudian mother identification, and the latter may be caused by fear of failure in my job). The possibly regular inaccuracy of our causal explanations of our behavior does not entail or imply that our self-knowledge of psychological states is regularly inaccurate.

In fact, Nisbett and Ross themselves acknowledge that subjects may fail to identify causal factors but may correctly identify psychological states. In the Wilson and Nisbett study (1977), for example, subjects were asked to rate the quality of four pairs of identical nylon pantyhose. Although the rightmost pantyhose were heavily preferred, most subjects denied that their choice was influenced by position. Nevertheless Nisbett and Ross note that:

> The subjects' reports (for example, I liked item 4 because it 'felt softest' or 'seemed most carefully constructed') may actually be accurate. What such a subject is not recognizing is the role that the experimenter's manipulation had played far earlier in the chain (for instance, the influence of 'position' on 'examination time' which influenced 'thresholds, associations, and decision criteria,' which ultimately influenced subjective experience of 'softness' or 'care in construction'). Thus the subjects may indeed have had introspective access to important mediating events, that is to the last 'links' in the causal chain. (1980: 212)

Another study cited by Nisbett and Ross (1980: 210) demonstrated that reassurance by the experimenter that electric shocks would cause 'no permanent damage' did not influence subjects' willingness to receive electric shocks, although most subjects claimed that it did. This study, however, gives us no reason to suppose that subjects were inaccurate or unreliable in avowing their belief that the shocks would cause 'no permanent damage.'

The notion that self-knowledge is itself a form of theoretical inference – the first premiss of the skeptical argument – is also extremely doubtful. No doubt we sometimes do make inferences about our psychological states on the basis of our behavior. However this is only usually on the relatively rare occasions that our behavior is *anomalous* to us. Thus, for example, I might infer that I am envious of my colleague's promotion when I realize that I have no good reason for my hostile behavior towards her, or I might infer that I am afraid of the challenge when I recognize that I have no good reason for turning down a more lucrative but more demanding position elsewhere. Yet to suppose that these sorts of example are the rule rather than the exception would be to suppose that one's behavior is *usually* anomalous to oneself. This is hard to do. I do not normally recognize that I want to secure a new position as an inference from the observed behavioral fact that I am filling out an application form for it. Nor do I normally recognize that I am in love as an inference from the observed fact that I am getting married, or recognize my grief as an inference from my behavior in the cemetery.

Self-Knowledge as Perception

These arguments do not, however, get to the heart of the matter. They misleadingly suggest that self-knowledge of emotion, belief, and other psychological states involves a form of direct internal perception – as opposed to some form of theoretical inference. This, unfortunately, plays directly into the hands of the skeptic. Thus Paul Churchland (1979, 1984), for example, claims that self-knowledge of psychological states is a form of 'internal perception' – 'the perception of our internal states' – which, like all forms of perception, is 'theory-informed.' Unfortunately, according to Churchland, it is informed by 'stagnant science,' by a body of regularly inaccurate and inadequate 'folk-psychological' theories referencing psychological states such as beliefs, emotions, and motives employed in the 'folk-psychological' explanation of human behavior. This body of 'folk-psychological' theory is socially learned 'at our mother's knee,' and provides the conventional theoretical interpretation of our perception of our internal states.

According to this account, self-knowledge is a learned form of perceptual discrimination that improves with increased experience and superior theory:

> Accordingly, the self-awareness of a young child, though real, will be much narrower or coarser than that of a sensitive adult. What is simply a dislike for someone, for a child, may divide into a mixture of jealousy, fear, and moral disapproval of someone, in the case of an honest and self perceptive adult. (Churchland, 1984: 73)

Consequently, Churchland argues that our self-knowledge would be much improved if it came to be informed by theories that advance more adequate and accurate causal explanations of our behavior, namely neurophysiological theories. Just as we can be taught to observe the heavens in ways informed by Copernican rather than Ptolemeic theory, we can be taught to observe our internal states in ways informed not by 'folk-psychological' theories, but by superior neurophysiological theories.

This is not the place to discuss Churchland's claim that our lay and scientific psychological explanations of human behavior in terms of contentful psychological states such as beliefs, emotions, and motives are generally inaccurate and inadequate, and inferior to contemporary neurophysiological accounts. I have criticized these claims in detail elsewhere (Greenwood 1991a, 1992).

Churchland's account of self-knowledge is also based upon a number of assumptions concerning theories and theory-informity that have been criticized in earlier chapters. These need not be considered here, however, for there is a much more fundamental problem with this account: it presupposes that self-knowledge of psychological states is a form of internal perception. It is based upon traditional assumptions about the homogeneity of the mental: in particular, it assumes that our self-knowledge of psychological states such as beliefs, emotions, and motives is analogous to our self-knowledge of sensations such as pain.

This account of self-knowledge as theory-informed internal perception, while it may furnish a reasonably plausible account of our self-knowledge of sensations such as pain, is not remotely plausible in the case of self-knowledge of psychological states. Unlike pain, emotions such as shame, jealousy, and disappointment do not occur and recur in us independently of any form of representation. Rather they are constituted as particular emotions precisely by forms of intrinsically social evaluative representation of actions and social relations.

Shame, for example, unlike pain, does not occur and recur in us spontaneously and independently of any form of representation (parents would wait a lifetime for purely spontaneous expressions of shame in their children), and then become revealed to us by our correct internal discrimination according to some socially learned theoretical description. Rather we have to learn to *be ashamed*, which means that we have to learn to represent and come to treat certain classes of actions (or failures to act) as degrading and humiliating, as reflecting negatively on our identity: we have to become parties to the arrangements, conventions, and agreements governing this form of evaluative representation. Once we have learned to be ashamed, we know our shame as children or adults when we know that we represent our action (or failure to act) in just this socially meaningful way. This is essentially what we know, *and all that we need to know*, when we know our shame.

Self-knowledge in children and adults is not informed by any sort of theory. Children have beliefs and emotions and can articulate the intrinsically social contents and objects of these beliefs and emotions before they come to form any theory *of* these beliefs and emotions. Two-year-olds can articulate their belief and fear that there is a big dog in their bedroom before they come to represent their psychological state *as* belief and fear. At least my two-year-old could.

Contra Churchland, the reason very young children cannot discriminate jealousy, adult fear, and moral disapproval is not that they lack introspective skills, nor that they lack sophisticated theoretical descriptions *of* these phenomena that purportedly inform adult judgments. The reason is simply that very young children are not jealous, are not afraid in adult ways, and do not express moral disapproval. They have to learn to be jealous, have adult fears, and express moral disapproval. This does not mean that they have to learn theoretical descriptions *of* jealousy, adult fear, and moral disapproval, in order that they can make finer discriminations of their already rich and complex psychological lives. Rather they have to learn to lead richer and more complex psychological lives by learning to represent actions and social relations in the conventional ways that are constitutive of these forms of emotion in any form of social life. When they come to represent *social reality* in these ways, knowing that they do so – on particular occasions – is all that is involved in self-knowledge of these emotions.

This is not to deny that the learning of emotions, and consequent determinations of emotional states, is based upon the learning of a sort of 'theory.' As noted in Chapter 7, however, it is a 'theory' about the social world – about our own and others' actions and social relations within moral careers – *not* a theory about our emotional states themselves. In order to learn emotions such as pride, anger, shame, and the like, we have to come to accept the 'theories' about what is honorable, degrading, offensive, and the like expressed in moral commentaries on actions and social relations within social collectives, from which the contents of our emotions are appropriated.

Churchland's strategy for the advancement of self-knowledge is misconceived. In order to have self-knowledge of psychological states such as emotions via theory-informed perception, I must be able to articulate the contents of the theories that inform my internal perceptions. However, this presupposes the very ability that Churchland's account is designed to deny or replace, or presupposes an infinite regress of theoretically informed perceptions to account for our ability to articulate their contents. Much the same is true of contemporary defenses of the accuracy or reliability of internal perception in terms of 'cognitive monitoring' (Pope and Singer, 1978; von Cranach, 1982). In order for my monitoring of my internal states to generate knowledge, I must be able to articulate what I have monitored. However, this presupposes the ability such accounts are designed to explain, or presupposes an infinite regress of monitorings of monitorings to account for our ability to articulate what we have monitored.

What this demonstrates is that self-knowledge of emotion and other psychological phenomena is not analogous to any form of theory-informed perception or theoretical inference, but is rather identical to our knowledge of the contents and objects of the theories that regularly do inform our perceptions and inferences: it is nothing more or less than our *ability to articulate the contents of our representations of reality – of external and social reality*. Accounts in terms of 'internal perception' and 'cognitive monitoring' distort the content of self-knowledge. In order to know my shame, I do not need to know the properties of any internal objects, or how I represent them. I need to know how I represent external social reality: how I represent my action – or failure to act. That is, in the case of self-knowledge of emotion and other psychological states, any form of internal perception informed by any sort of theory would be necessarily *focused in the wrong direction*.

Self-Knowledge: Looking in the Wrong Direction

The above analysis suggests that the 'internal focus' metaphor usually employed by both defenders and critics of self-knowledge is fundamentally misguided. Self-knowledge of emotion and other psychological states is not the product of any inward 'looking.' I do not discover my shame, motive of revenge, or belief that the value of the dollar will fall by looking inwards – 'in vacant or in pensive mood.' Rather I determine these matters by articulating the content of my representations of *external* and *social* reality.

There is a fundamental error common to all accounts of self-knowledge of psychological states in terms of 'introspection' or 'internal perception.' This is the ancient view that being in a psychological state involves having some sort of internal object before the mind: an idea, image, sense-impression, or whatever. This is perhaps most explicit in classical empiricist accounts, with their ontology of 'impressions' and 'ideas,' which have long dominated academic psychology. Thus Hume, for example, claimed that (1739: 103): 'The mind is a kind of theatre, where several perceptions successively make their appearance; pass, repass, glide away, and mingle in an infinite variety of postures and situations.'

As noted earlier, psychologists have recently abandoned the identification of concepts and images. Consequently there is no longer any good reason to maintain the doctrine that psychological states are constituted by some relation to internal objects. If we abandon this 'inner-theater' conception of psychological phenomena, then we also ought to abandon its natural corollary: that self-knowledge of psychological phenomena is a form of knowledge of the properties of internal objects.

There are no such objects to be known in the case of self-knowledge of psychological states: there are only the objects in the natural and social world to which our emotions, motives, beliefs, and the like are directed. What I know in the case of self-knowledge is not the actual properties of these objects, nor the actual properties of any additional internal objects, but the content of my representation of these objects. I know *what* I believe about these historical events, *how* I feel about these actions, *what* I intend to achieve by means of this behavior. What do I know when I know that I love my wife and hate my boss? I know what I think and feel about them. What do I focus on when I know this? My wife and boss of course. What else? There is nothing else.

Articulation and Description

Self-knowledge of psychological states is nothing more than the ability to articulate the contents of our representations of external and social reality. In recognizing this, we must recognize that *there is no such thing as consciousness of psychological phenomena*. We are of course conscious of tables and trees, persons and their promises, our actions and social relations, our stomach upsets and other sensations. However, we are never conscious of our emotions, motives, beliefs, and the like. In the case of self-knowledge of these phenomena there are no discriminable internal objects whose properties we are conscious of. To suppose otherwise is the illusion of many epochs. We can of course articulate the contents and objects of our psychological states, and may care to call this 'consciousness of psychological states.' However, that is a quite different matter.

Self-knowledge of emotions, motives, and other psychological states is just our ability to articulate the content and objects of our emotions, motives, and other psychological states. It is not an ability based upon any form of inference or internal perception. This is not, however, to deny that agents can advance linguistically and epistemically objective theoretical descriptions of their psychological states: only that our self-ascription of such theoretical descriptions is based upon any form of inference or internal perception.

To make this clear, it is perhaps useful to distinguish two senses in which we may talk of self-knowledge of psychological states. We may talk about our knowledge *that we have particular beliefs, emotions, and motives*: our ability to theoretically describe our beliefs, emotions, and motives. Or we may talk about our knowledge *of the contents and objects of our particular beliefs, emotions, and motives*: our ability to articulate these contents and objects (for ourselves and others). Then a central claim of this chapter may be expressed as follows. Our knowledge *that we have a particular belief, emotion, or motive* is not usually based upon an inference from behavior,[4] nor is it a product of any form of perception of internal states. It is usually based upon *our ability to articulate the contents and objects of our beliefs, emotions, and motives*. Our ability to articulate these contents and objects is not itself based upon any form of inference or perception.

This latter form of knowledge does not itself involve any form of theoretical description *of* psychological states. It involves the articulation of how an agent represents and evaluates external reality. Consider the following fictional but unremarkable example of this form of psychological accounting: 'I ought not to have cheated in the exam. . . . I regret it more than anything else in my life. It offended the hell out of me to see them rich kids get higher grades than me. They have all the advantages . . .. they don't have to work as well, and they got all them fancy tutors. Still I shouldn't have cheated . . . it makes me less of a person than them.' In this account the speaker reveals her shame and anger by articulating their contents and objects. She does not *describe* her shame and anger. Moreover, her ability to articulate their contents and objects does not presuppose her ability to describe them as instances of 'shame' and 'anger.' Children can articulate their shame long before they learn to classify it as 'shame,' and many Americans can articulate their angst without recognizing that it is described as 'angst' in another culture.

In this respect self-knowledge of emotions and other psychological states may be said to be direct, if only by default: in the sense that it is not based upon any form of theoretical inference or theory-informed perception. Upon what, then, is it based? It is an intrinsically social ability based upon our intrinsically social abilities to have psychological states and employ language.

Our beliefs, emotions, and motives are developmentally derived from our forms of descriptive and moral commentary on the natural and social world. Only those persons who have grasped the content of descriptions such as 'grandmother' and 'grey-haired' can come to believe that all grandmothers are grey-haired; only those persons who have grasped the content of moral commentaries on actions in terms of humiliation and degradation – and have become party to the evaluative conventions encapsulated within them – can be ashamed; and only those persons who have grasped the content of descriptions such as 'harm' or 'property' can engage in acts of aggression and theft. The intrinsically social contents of our beliefs, emotions, and many of our intentional behaviors are appropriated from the intrinsically social contents of our descriptions of the world and moral commentaries on actions and social relations. Consequently our general socio-linguistic competence and our ability to articulate the contents and objects of our beliefs, emotions, and intentional behaviors cannot be conceived as discrete psychological achievements.

Our intrinsically social ability to articulate our beliefs, emotions, and representations of behavior is an aspect of our general and intrinsically social ability to engage in descriptive and evaluative commentaries, based upon accepted conventions of meaning and the moral orders of social collectives: it is an intrinsic component of our general socio-linguistic competence. This is why it is scarcely intelligible to suppose that competent participants in social life could be generally inaccurate and unreliable with respect to their articulation of their beliefs, emotions, and forms of representation of behavior: to suppose that their articulations of their beliefs, emotions, and forms of representation of behavior – which themselves embody descriptions of the world and evaluations of their actions and social relations – could be generally incongruent with their actual beliefs, emotions, and representations of behavior.

The point might be expressed in the following fashion. According to the model we exploit in attributing theoretical psychological states to self and others, psychological states such as emotions, motives, beliefs, and the like are analogous to linguistic utterances insofar as they have a sense (intensional content) and putative reference (intentional object). If this is the case, then the best analogue of our self-knowledge of psychological states is our knowledge of the sense and intended reference of our linguistic utterances, which is but an aspect of our general and intrinsically social grasp of the conventions of language use. This demonstrates the absurdity of supposing that our articulation of the contents and objects of our emotions, motives, beliefs, and the like might be regularly false or unreliable. This would be like supposing that we regularly err – and that we all regularly err – with respect to our knowledge of the sense and (intended) reference of our linguistic utterances.

Self-knowledge of emotions and motives is formally identical to our self-knowledge of our actions. In order to know my shame, I need to know the content of my evaluative representation of my action. In order to know that I am stealing, being aggressive, warning a neighbor, or proposing marriage, I need to know the content of my representation of my behavior and its intentional direction. It follows that to suppose that our self-knowledge of psychological phenomena is regularly inaccurate and unreliable is to suggest that we regularly *do not know what we are doing*. Yet this is hard to accept, since as Giddens (1979: 19) notes, this form of self-knowledge constitutes 'the very ontological condition for human life in society.'

Agreement on this point comes from a perhaps surprising quarter. Nisbett and Ross claim that:

> Many stimuli and many responses are to a degree ambiguous, that is, they *mean* different things to different people. The actor often enjoys unique knowledge of the meaning he attaches to a stimulus or his own behavior. Moreover . . . such subjective accounts of stimuli and response may often be crucial to understanding and explaining the actor's behavior. (1980: 233)

Nisbett and Ross simply err in supposing that self-knowledge of emotion and other psychological phenomena is something different – a form of 'theoretical inference' to internal states; and in failing to recognize that its reliability is grounded in its intrinsically social nature rather than being based upon any form of private inner access. According to the present account, self-knowledge of emotion and other psychological states is just intrinsically social knowledge of the contents ('meaning') and objects ('stimuli' and 'behaviors') of such psychological states.

Accounting and Social Psychological Science

This is not to claim that self-knowledge is immune from error: agent accounts of their psychological states – based upon their ability to articulate their contents and objects – can be inaccurate and distortive. But the errors are not generally errors of perception or inference: when we err, it is rather through motivated self-deception or failure to attend to our actions and social relations. Agent accounts are often governed by a variety of self-presentational or rhetorical demands that discourage accuracy and honesty. However, if there are no general epistemic or empirical grounds for doubting self-knowledge, as has been argued in this chapter, then this acknowledged feature of agent accounts is not an object of concern. On the contrary, knowledge of self-presentational and rhetorical demands may be exploited to facilitate accurate and honest accounts (or accurate and honest 'disclosure' (Jourard, 1968)).

The intrinsically social nature of self-knowledge of psychological states ensures its general accuracy and reliability, which justifies its employment as an exploratory resource in social psychological science.

The general accounting practices of social agents – their moral commentaries on actions and social relations – reveal the psychological ontology of their form of social life: the forms of evaluative representation of actions and social relations, and the conventions of moral careers within social collectives available to social agents in their form of social life. The general virtues of this resource deserve to be stressed. The availability of agent accounts of their psychologies drastically reduces the number of epistemically viable theoretical psychological explanations of human behavior. These accounts provide a measure of the intrinsically social psychological dimensions of human agents who fix their identities in diverse forms of social life. The determination of these intrinsically social psychological dimensions of persons in particular forms of social life serves to eliminate many theoretical psychological explanations in terms of the different social psychological dimensions of different forms of social life.

Thus, for example, explanations of human actions and social practices in contemporary Europe in terms of emotions such as *amae* and the moral careers of witch-doctor or harem-master are non-starters, because agent accounts reveal that the necessary forms of moral commentary and social collectivity are absent in contemporary Europe. In this respect social psychological theories based upon agent accounts have distinct epistemic advantages over standard forms of theoretical explanation in the natural sciences. This epistemic advantage is real enough: it is just so obvious that we tend to take it for granted.

Given the general accuracy and reliability of agent accounts, they ought to be regularly exploited in experimental studies and other forms of empirical inquiry in social psychological science, with the following methodological qualification. The accounts that persons ought to be asked to provide to enable researchers to identify their psychological states and actions should be accounts of how they represent their behavior and the social context: they should not be asked to provide accounts – or 'reports' or 'labels' – of their 'internal states.' Ironically, many researchers who treat agent accounts seriously as an exploratory resource – for example, those engaged in the study of attitudes and emotions – generally employ 'self-reports' that are internally directed, whereas researchers who do employ agent accounts of their representation of behavior and social context – such as experimenters who employ quasi-controls (Orne, 1962) – tend not to take them seriously as an exploratory resource. Quasi-controls are generally employed to identify experimental demands so that these can be eliminated from or attenuated in real experiments. They are not employed to discriminate the intrinsic demands of the experimental setting from those of the social situation that are the putative objective of experimental study: for example, by comparison with agent accounts in non-experimental settings.

This is not to suggest that agent accounts should be treated as a substitute for the empirical evaluation of theoretical causal explanations of human action. Rather, as in the case of other exploratory resources in other sciences, they should be treated as yet another empirical constraint on the epistemic viability of explanatory theories.

Looking in the Right Direction
A central aim of this chapter has been to deny the ancient and popular conception of self-knowledge of psychological states as a form of internal

perception, and to advance an alternative account of self-knowledge and agent accounting that enables us to resist the skeptical challenges of contemporary psychologists, and justify the employment of agent accounts as an exploratory resource in social psychological science. According to this account, self-knowledge of our psychological states is to be identified with our intrinsically social ability to articulate the contents and objects of our representations of external and social reality, the general accuracy and reliability of which is grounded in its intrinsically social nature. The main point of the argument has been to validate the use of accounting as an exploratory resource in social psychological science. In doing so, I have tried to focus attention in a quite different direction, away from traditional and contemporary concerns with 'inner' states and our 'inner' psychological lives. In conclusion I want to stress the significance of doing so, for the present account of self-knowledge has implications for our everyday lives as well as for our forms of social psychological science.

I argued earlier that it was not necessary to employ any form of theory to have self-knowledge of psychological states. Children can know their shame before they come to learn the descriptive label 'shame,' or embrace any theories about their shame; Americans can know their angst without knowing that it is described as 'angst' in another language, and without having formed or embraced any theory about their angst. However, it might be supposed that, although not necessary, it is surely useful to have descriptive labels or theories about our emotions, for example, and that such labels and theories cannot help but advance and enhance our self-knowledge of psychological states such as emotions.

We commonly assume, and with very considerable justification, that our epistemic advances are largely a product of the increased richness and sophistication of our conceptual and theoretical resources: of our theoretical descriptions of phenomena based upon our perception of them or theory-informed inferences from perception. We justifiably believe that our increasingly superior knowledge of diseases is largely a function of the increasing superiority of our theoretical taxonomies of diseases based upon our increasingly superior empirical discriminations. We consequently tend to believe not only that the richness and diversity of emotional life in a culture or historical period will be a function of the sophistication of the theories of emotion employed, but that this will also hold true for the general level of self-knowledge of emotion in any culture or historical period.

We tend to value our knowledge of psychological theory not only as (justifiably) enabling us to know our fellows better, but also as enabling us to have self-knowledge of our psychological states that is superior to that of previous generations and other cultures. We are thus tempted to suppose that our self-knowledge of our psychological states will be advanced and improved by greater theoretical attention being paid to our psychological lives. However, this temptation must be steadfastly resisted in the case of self-knowledge of emotions and other psycho-logical states.

Many primitive cultures appear to have little use for theories about psychological states, and indeed rarely concern themselves with such matters. To recall Hallpike's remark, noted in Chapter 8: 'the realm of purely private experience and motives, *as distinct from the evaluation of actual behaviour*, is given little attention in many primitive societies' (1979: 392; my emphasis again). It does not follow that persons in such cultures are unable to articulate the contents and objects of their psychological states, or that their accounts are necessarily more impoverished than ours. It does not follow from the fact that some cultures employ few words that are descriptive of emotion – such as the Pintupi Aborigines of Western Australia or the Ommura of Papua New Guinea – that either their emotional lives or their self-knowledge of them are impoverished.

As noted in Chapter 9, the richness and diversity of emotions in any historical period or culture is a direct function of the richness and diversity of the indigenous and intrinsically social forms of evaluative representation of actions and social relations that are constitutive of human emotions. This is itself a product of the richness and diversity of the indigenous and intrinsically social forms of moral commentary on actions and social relations to be found in any culture or historical period. It is not a product of the richness and diversity of our theoretical descriptions of emotions, and there is no a priori reason to suppose that the social mechanisms responsible for a rich diversity of intrinsically social forms of evaluative representation of actions and social relations will also necessarily produce a multiplicity of theoretical descriptions of this rich diversity. In consequence, although there are no studies that I know of concerning the cultural conditions that promote the ability of agents to articulate the contents and objects of their psychological states, there is certainly no conceptual absurdity or empirical implausibility about a form of social life that is productive of emotional richness and self-knowledge, but that also eschews any form of theoretical discourse about emotions, and treats any concern with 'inner states' as a psychological aberration that requires some form of treatment – by the local witch-doctor, for example.

Furthermore, even when the social mechanisms of a form of life that are responsible for a rich diversity of emotions also promote a high degree of sophisticated theoretical discourse about emotion, there is no guarantee that this will promote self-knowledge of emotions. On the contrary, it may effectively impede it. For conceptual and theoretical refinements of our thought and discourse about emotion will only advance self-knowledge *if they are focused in the right direction*. That is, they will only advance self-knowledge if they provide conceptual and theoretical resources that promote the *articulation* of the subtly different forms of intrinsically social evaluative representation of actions and social relations that are constitutive of subtly different emotions.[5] Not all concepts and theories of emotion will serve this end. Sophisticated Western accounts in terms of internal phenomenological or neuro-physiological objects (or more primitive accounts in terms of colors and bodily organs) may in fact distort the picture by directing the focus of inquiry in completely the wrong direction.

We may be inclined to be dismissive of primitive cultures that eschew discourse about psychological states, or employ a limited number of descriptive psychological labels, just because they are primitive. However, it may be our own sophisticated modern age that has gone astray. Indeed, it may be suggested that our contemporary introverted concern with ourselves and our emotions is historically the greatest impediment to self-knowledge of emotions, by focusing our attention in completely the wrong direction. The existential anxieties of modern and post-modern Western men and women may be a direct function of the utterly hopeless focus on the 'inner life' (Logan, 1987), a focus that is utterly hopeless because there are no inner objects or properties that can be discriminated via any form of internal searching.

Kant claimed in the *Anthropologie* (1798) that introspection is not only distorting but downright dangerous: it leads to madness. One can sympathize with his sentiment. If there are no internal objects to be introspected, one is likely to go crazy searching for them. Whatever the complexity of their emotional lives, at least the Tahitians appear to have got it right. Their 'theories' of emotion, expressed in their discourse 'about' emotion, are not descriptions of the properties of any hypothetical internal objects. They are 'theories' about the self in social action and social relation, and are focused upon such matters: they are employed 'to convey and represent information about one's mode of relationship as a total individual to the social and non-social environ-ment' (Levy, 1984: 230). Perhaps South Sea islands are good for the soul after all.

Notes

1 Throughout the rest of this chapter I reserve the term 'psychological' for representational states that have (intensional) contents and (intentional) objects, such as beliefs, emotions, and motives.

2 Freudian critiques of self-knowledge are not discussed in this chapter, for essentially two reasons. First, most skeptical critics of self-knowledge rarely appeal to Freud, possibly because of familiar doubts about the scientific status of Freudian theory. Secondly, Freud did not in fact deny the primary ability of agents to have self-knowledge of their psychological states. Rather he postulated various motivated forms of impediment to it, such as repression, which it is the business of psychotherapy to surmount.

3 Strictly speaking, most of the experimental studies conducted by Wundt were studies of attention span and mental chronometry. The former were successfully replicated (Miller, 1956), and although the latter were not (Cattell, for example, obtained different results), this failure also has no bearing on the question of the ability of agents to provide accounts of their psychological states.

4 Recognizing that persons occasionally do make inferences about their psychological states on the basis of their behavior, as noted earlier, although, as also noted earlier, such inferences are exceptions rather than the rule.

5 As noted earlier, Sabini and Silver (1982) are the best source of enlightenment on these matters.

Epilogue

In this work I have argued the case for a realist meta-theory for social psychological science, and have tried to illustrate the virtues of a realist interpretation of psychological theory by exploring the possibilities it allows for theories of the social dimensions of mind, and specifically for theories of the social dimensions of identity and emotion. The present work is primarily directed to those researchers dissatisfied with the sterility of traditional empiricism but disinclined to embrace the relativism of more radical forms of social constructionism – I hope realism will appeal to them as an attractive and viable alternative.

One of the regularly advertised virtues of the social constructionist account is its ability to legitimize those alternative theoretical 'voices' – and particularly those concerned to emphasize the social dimensions of human life, and their moral and political implications – that have been denied or ignored by traditional empiricist forms of social psychological science. These theoretical 'voices' are legitimized by social construction-ism, but at the cost of the impoverishment of their accounts of the social dimensions of human life, by restricting them to accounts of the social dimensions of theoretical discourse. The legitimization of these alternative theoretical 'voices' is also a salient virtue of realism: for the realist, all theoretical options are open. The difference, of course, is that for the realist, only some theoretical options are epistemically viable.

In a hostile intellectual environment, it is perhaps natural for these neglected theoretical 'voices' to align themselves with social construc-tionism, when empiricism is seen as the only alternative. Yet empiricism and social constructionism are not the only meta-theoretical alternatives, and these neglected theoretical 'voices' do themselves a disservice by aligning with social constructionism. In the absence of any serious attempt to demonstrate their epistemic viability, they are likely to remain, and deserve to remain, neglected by mainstream social psychological science.

In the case of those who offer putative theories of the social dimen-sions of mind and behavior, alignment with social constructionism only perpetuates the historical neglect of the social by social psychological science. Realism is in fact the *only* meta-theoretical position that enables theorists to recognize the social dimensions of human life, and thus ultimately the only meta-theoretical position that enables us to develop substantive and epistemically viable theories of the social dimensions of mind and behavior – the only types of theories that can have any genuine bearing on moral and political issues.

I am too much of a mundane realist to suppose that many will be moved by these considerations, but hope that a few at least will engage the intellectual challenge that this work aims to present to those committed to empiricism or social constructionism, and – more optimistically – to those dissatisfied with both these distorting and debilitating meta-theoretical positions.

References

Abramson, L.Y., Metalsky, G.I. and Alloy, L.B. (1989) Hopelessness depression: A theory-based subtype of depression. *Psychological Review*, 96, 358–72.

Abramson, L.Y., Seligman, M.E.P., and Teasdale, J. (1978) Learned helplessness in humans: Critique and reformulation. *Journal of Abnormal Psychology*, 87, 49–74.

Alexander, C.N. and Knight, G.W. (1971) Situated identities and social psychological experimentation. *Sociometry*, 34, 65–82.

Alexander, C.N. and Scriven, G.D. (1977) Role playing: An essential component in experimentation. *Personality and Social Psychology Bulletin*, 3, 455–66.

Allport, F. (1924) *Social Psychology*. Boston: Houghton Mifflin.

Allport, F. (1933) *Institutional Behavior*. Chapel Hill: University of North Carolina Press.

Allport, F. (1961) The contemporary appraisal of an old problem. *Contemporary Psychology*, 6, 195–6.

Allport, G. (1985) The historical background to modern social psychology. In G. Lindzey and E. Aronson (eds), *A Handbook of Social Psychology, Vol. 1*. 3rd edition (1st edition 1954). Cambridge, MA: Addison-Wesley.

Altschule, M.D. (1965) Acedia: its evolution from deadly sin to psychiatric syndrome. *British Journal of Psychiatry*, 111, 117–19.

Anderson, J.R. (1981) Concepts, propositions, and schemata: What are the cognitive units? In J.H. Flowers (ed.), *Nebraska Symposium on Motivation: Cognitive Processes. Vol. 28*. Lincoln: University of Nebraska Press.

Argyle, M. (1976) Personality and social behaviour. In R. Harré (ed.), *Personality*. Oxford: Basil Blackwell.

Armon-Jones, C. (1986) The thesis of constructionism. In R. Harré (ed.), *The Social Construction of Emotions*. Oxford: Basil Blackwell.

Aronson, E. and Carlsmith, J.M. (1963) Effect of the severity of threat on the devaluation of forbidden behavior. *Journal of Abnormal and Social Psychology*, 66, 584–8.

Asch, S.E. (1951) Effects of group pressure upon the modification and distortion of judgements. In H. Guetzkow (ed.), *Groups, Leadership, and Men*. Pittsburgh: Carnegie Press.

Austin, J.L. (1962) *How to Do Things with Words*. Oxford: Oxford University Press.

Averill, J. (1980) A constructivist theory of emotion. In R. Plutchik and H. Kellerman (eds), *Emotions: Theory, Research and Experience*. New York: Academic Press.

Averill, J. (1985) The social construction of emotion: With special reference to love. In K.J. Gergen and K.E. Davis (eds), *The Social Construction of the Person*. New York: Springer-Verlag.

Averill, J. (1986) Acquisition of emotion during adulthood. In R. Harré (ed.), *The Social Construction of Emotions*. Oxford: Basil Blackwell.

Badinter, E. (1980) *Mother Love, Myth and Reality*. New York: Macmillan.

Bain, A. (1855) *The Senses and the Intellect*. London: Longmans, Green.

Barnes, B. (1982) *Interests and the Growth of Knowledge*. London: Routledge and Kegan Paul. 2nd edition.

Bechtel, W. (1988) *Philosophy of Mind: An Overview for Cognitive Science*. Hillsdale, NJ: Lawrence Erlbaum Associates.

Bedford, E. (1962) Emotions. *Proceedings of the Aristotelian Society*, 57, 281–304.

Bem, D.J. (1967) Self-perception: An alternative interpretation of cognitive dissonance phenomena. *Psychological Review*, 74, 183–200.

Benedict, R. (1967) *The Chrysanthemum and the Sword: Patterns of Japanese Culture*. London: Routledge and Kegan Paul.

Berkowitz, L. and LePage, A. (1967). Weapons as aggression-eliciting stimuli. *Journal of Personality and Social Psychology*, 7, 202–7.

Berne, E. (1970) *Games People Play*. London: Penguin.

Best, E. (1924) *Spiritual and Mental Concepts of the Maori*. Wellington, New Zealand: Dominion Museum Bulletin No. 2.

Bhaskar, R. (1975) *A Realist Theory of Science*. Leeds: Leeds Books.

Blackburn, S. (1991) Losing your mind: Physics, identity and folk burglar prevention. In J.D. Greenwood (ed.), *The Future of Folk Psychology*. Cambridge: Cambridge University Press.

Bleier, R. (1984) *Science and Gender: A Critique of Biology and its Theories of Women*. New York: Pergamon.

Bloor, D. (1976) *Knowledge and Social Imagery*. London: Routledge and Kegan Paul.

Boucher, J. (1979) Culture and Emotion. In J. Marsella, R.G. Tharp, and T.V. Ciborowski (eds), *Perspectives on Cross-Cultural Psychology*. London: Academic Press.

Braithwaite, R.B. (1953) *Scientific Explanation*. Cambridge: Cambridge University Press.

Breakwell, G. (1983a) Formulations and searches. In G. Breakwell (ed.), *Threatened Identities*. New York: Wiley.

Breakwell, G. (ed.) (1983b) *Threatened Identities*. New York: Wiley.

Breakwell, G. (ed.) (1992) *Social Psychology of Identity and the Self-Concept*. London: Academic Press.

Brewer, M.B. (1991) The social self: On being the same and different at the same time. *Personality and Social Psychology Bulletin*, 17, 475–82.

Bridgeman, P.W. (1927) *The Logic of Modern Physics*. New York: Macmillan.

Broadbent, D.E. (1957) A mechanical model for human attention and immediate memory. *Psychological Review*, 64, 205–15.

Brock, A. (1992) Was Wundt a 'Nazi'?: Völkerpsychologie, racism, and anti-semitism. *Theory and Psychology*, 2, 205–23.

Brown, H.I. (1979) *Perception, Theory and Commitment*. Chicago: University of Chicago Press.

Bruch, H. (1962) Transformation of oral impulses into eating disorders: a conceptual approach. *Psychiatric Quarterly*, 35, 458–81.

Burge, M. (1991) A critical examination of the new sociology of science, Part 1. *Philosophy of the Social Sciences*, 21, 524–60.

Burge, M. (1992) A critical examination of the new sociology of science, Part 2. *Philosophy of the Social Sciences*, 22, 46–76.

Campbell, N.R. (1920) *Physics, The Elements*. Cambridge: Cambridge University Press.

Chalmers, A.F. (1976) *What is this Thing Called Science?* Queensland: University of Queensland Press.

Cherryholmes, C.H. (1988) Construct validity and the discourses of research. *American Journal of Education*, 96, 421–57.

Churchland, P.M. (1979) *Realism and the Plasticity of Mind*. Cambridge: Cambridge University Press.

Churchland. P.M. (1984) *Matter and Consciousness*. Cambridge, MA: MIT Press.

Clark, J.M. and Paivio, A. (1989) Observational and theoretical terms in psychology. *American Psychologist*, 44, 500–12.

Collett, P. (1979) The repertory grid in psychological research. In G.P. Ginsburg (ed.), *Emerging Strategies in Social Psychological Research*. New York: Wiley.

Collins, H.M. (1981) Stages in the empirical programme of relativism. *Social Studies of Science*, 11, 3–10.

Collins, H.M. (1982) Special relativism: The natural attitude. *Social Studies of Science*, 12, 139–43.

Collins, H.M. (1983) An empirical relativist programme in the sociology of scientific knowledge. In K.D. Knorr-Cetina and M. Mulkay (eds), *Science Observed*. London: Sage.

Cooley, C.H. (1902) *Human Nature and the Social Order*. New York: Charles Scribner's Sons.

Corraliza, J.A. (1987) *La Experiencia del ambiente*. Madrid: Tecnos.

Coulter, J. (1979) *The Social Construction of Mind*. London: Macmillan.

Craib, D. (1986) Review of M. Mulkay, 'The Word and the World'. *Sociology*, 20, 483–4.

Dashiel, J.F. (1935) Experimental studies of the influence of social situations on the behavior of individual human adults. In C. Murchison (ed.), *A Handbook of Social Psychology*. Worcester, MA: Clark University Press.

Davitz, J.R. (1969) *The Language of Emotion*. New York: Academic Press.

Dawkins, R. (1976) *The Selfish Gene*. Oxford: Oxford University Press.

Deaux, K. (1993) Reconstructing social identity. *Personality and Social Psychology Bulletin*, 19, 4–12.

Dennett, D. (1975) Conditions of personhood. In A.E. Rorty (ed.), *The Identities of Persons*. Berkeley: University of California Press.

Dennett, D. (1978) *Brainstorms*. Cambridge, MA: MIT Press.

De Waele, J.P. (1971) *La Méthode des Cas Programmes*. Brussels: Dessart.

De Waele, J.P. (1992) Personal communication.

Doi, T. (1973) *The Anatomy of Dependence*. Tokyo: Kodansha International.

Duhem, P. (1906) *La Théorie physique: son objet et sa structure*. Paris.

Durkheim, E. (1895) *The Rules of Sociological Method*. In S. Lukes (ed.) and W.D. Halls (trans.), *Durkheim: The Rules of Sociological Method and Selected Texts on Sociology and Its Method*. New York: Macmillan (1982).

Durkheim, E. (1897) *Suicide*. J.A. Spaulding and G. Simpson (trans.). New York: Free Press (1951).

Durkheim, E. (1901) Preface to the second edition of *The Rules of Sociological Method*. In S. Lukes (ed.), and W.D. Halls (trans.), *Durkheim: The Rules of Sociological Method and Selected Texts on Sociology and Its Method*. New York: Macmillan (1982).

Eco, U. (1992) Overinterpreting texts. In S. Collini (ed.), *Umberto Eco: Interpretation and Overinterpretation*. Cambridge: Cambridge University Press.

Edwards, D., Ashmore, M., and Potter, J. (1993) Death and furniture: the rhetoric, politics and theology of bottom line arguments against relativism. Manuscript.

Ekman, P. (1980) *The Face of Man: Expressions of Universal Emotions in a New Guinea Village*. New York: Garland STPM Press.

Epstein, S. (1973) The self-concept revised or a theory of a theory. *American Psychologist*, 28, 405–16.

Farganis, S. (1986) *Social Construction of the Feminine Character*. Totowa, NJ: Rowman and Littlefield.

Farr, R.M. and Moscovici, S. (eds) (1984) *Social Representations*. Cambridge: Cambridge University Press.

Farrington, D.P. and Kidd, R.F. (1977) Is financial dishonesty a rational decision? *British Journal of Social and Clinical Psychology*, 16, 139–46.

Feigl, H. (1970) Beyond peaceful coexistence. In R.H. Steuwer (ed.), *Minnesota Studies in the Philosophy of Science: V*. Minneapolis: University of Minnesota Press.

Festinger, L. (1957) *A Theory of Cognitive Dissonance*. Evanston, IL: Row, Peterson.

Festinger, L. and Carlsmith, J.M. (1959) Cognitive consequences of forced compliance. *Journal of Abnormal and Social Psychology*, 47, 382–9.

Feyerabend, P.K. (1975) *Against Method*. London: New Left Books.

Findley-Jones, R. (1986) Accidie and melancholy in a clinical context. In R. Harré (ed.), *The Social Construction of Emotions*. Oxford: Basil Blackwell.

Fischer, A.H. (1991) *Emotion Scripts: A Study in the Cognitive and Social Nature of Emotions*. Leiden: DSWO Press.

Fischer, A.H. and Frijda, N.H. (1992) The emotion process as a whole: A response to Greenwood. *New Ideas in Psychology*, 10, 23–7.

Fiske, S.T. and Taylor, S.E. (1991) *Social Cognition*. 2nd edition. New York: McGraw-Hill.

Flanagan, D.J. and Adler, J.E. (1983) Impartiality and particularity. *Social Research*, 50, 576–96.

Fletcher, G.J.D. (1993) Realism versus relativism in psychology. Manuscript.

Fodor, J.A. (1975) *The Language of Thought*. Cambridge, MA: Harvard University Press.

Fodor, J.A. (1984) Observation reconsidered. *Philosophy of Science*, 51, 23–43.

Forgas, J.P. (1979) Multidimensional scaling: A discovery method in social psychology. In G.P. Ginsburg (ed.), *Emerging Strategies in Social Psychological Research*. New York: Wiley.

Foster, J. (1987) An appeal for objectivism in psychological metatheory. In H.J. Stam, T.B. Rogers and K.J. Gergen (eds), *The Analysis of Psychological Theory: Metapsychological Perspectives*. Washington, DC: Hemisphere.

Fox, R. (1977) The inherent rules of violence. In P. Collett (ed.), *Social Rules and Social Behaviour*. Oxford: Basil Blackwell.

Frager, R. (1970) Conformity and anti-conformity in Japan. *Journal of Personality and Social Psychology*, 15, 203–10.

Franks, D.D. and Doyle McCarthy, E. (eds), (1989) *The Sociology of Emotions: Original Essays and Research Papers*. London: JAI.

Frijda, N.H. (1986) *The Emotions*. Cambridge: Cambridge University Press.

Frijda, N.H. (1987) Emotion, cognitive structure, and action tendency. *Cognition and Emotion*, 1, 115–43.

Gallup, G.A. (1980) Chimpanzees and self-awareness. In M.A. Roy (ed.), *Species Identity and Attachment: A phylogenetic evaluation*. New York: Garland.

Garth, T.R. (1931) *Race Psychology: A Study of Racial Mental Differences*. New York: Whittelsey House.

Geertz, H. (1959) The vocabulary of emotion: A study of Javanese socialization processes. *Psychiatry*, 22, 225–37.

Gehm, T.L. and Scherer, K.R. (1988) Factors determining the dimensions of subjective emotional space. In K.R. Scherer (ed.), *Facets of Emotion: Recent Research*. Hillsdale, NJ: Lawrence Erlbaum Associates.

Gerber, E. (1975) The cultural patterning of emotions in Samoa. Unpublished doctoral dissertation. University of California, San Diego.

Gergen, K.J. (1973) Social psychology as history. *Journal of Personality and Social Psychology*, 26, 309–20.

Gergen, K.J. (1982) *Towards Transformation in Social Knowledge*. New York: Springer-Verlag.

Gergen, K.J. (1985) The social construction movement in modern psychology. *American Psychologist*, 40, 266–75.

Gergen, K.J. (1987a) Introduction: Towards metapsychology. In H.J. Stam, T.B.Rogers and K.J. Gergen (eds), *The Analysis of Psychological Theory: Metapsychological Perspectives*. Washington, DC: Hemisphere.

Gergen, K.J. (1987b) The language of psychological understanding. In H.J. Stam, T.B. Rogers and K.J. Gergen (eds), *The Analysis of Psychological Theory: Metapsychological Perspectives*. Washington, DC: Hemisphere.

Gergen, K.J. (1987c) Towards self as relationship. In K.M. Yardley and T. Honess (eds), *Self and Identity: Psychosocial Perspectives*. London: Wiley.

Gergen, K.J. (1988) The concept of progress in psychological theory. In W.J. Baker, L.P. Mos, H.V. Rappard and H.J. Stam (eds), *Recent Trends in Theoretical Psychology*. New York: Springer-Verlag.

Gergen, K.J. (1989a) Social psychology and the wrong revolution. *European Journal of Social Psychology*, 19, 463–84.

Gergen, K.J. (1989b) Warranting voice and the elaboration of the self. In J. Shotter and K.J. Gergen (eds), *Texts of Identity*. London: Sage.

Gergen, K.J. and Davis, K.E. (eds) (1985) *The Social Construction of the Person*. New York: Springer-Verlag.

Gergen, M. (1990) 'Doing theory' in psychology: Feminist reactions. In W.J. Baker, M.E. Hyland, R. van Hezewijk, and S. Terwee (eds), *Recent Trends in Theoretical Psychology, Vol. II*. New York: Springer-Verlag.

Giddens, A. (1979) *Central Problems of Social Theory*. Berkeley: University of California Press.

Giddens, A. (1981) *A Contemporary Critique of Historical Materialism*. Berkeley: University of California Press.

Gilbert, M. (1989) *On Social Facts*. London: Routledge and Kegan Paul.

Gilligan, C. (1982) *In a Different Voice*. Cambridge, MA: Harvard University Press.

Gilligan, C. (1986) Reply by Carol Gilligan. *Signs: Journal of Women in Culture and Society*, 11, 324–33.

Gilman, D. (1992) What's a theory to do . . . with seeing? or Some empirical considerations for observation and theory. *British Journal for the Philosophy of Science*, 43, 287–309.

Gleason, P. (1983) Identifying identity: a semantic history. *Journal of American History*, 69, 910–31.

Goffman, E. (1959) *The Presentation of Self in Everyday Life*. New York: Doubleday.

Goffman, E. (1961) *Asylums*. New York: Doubleday.

Goffman, E. (1963) *Stigma*. Harmondsworth: Penguin.

Goldberg, D.P. (1962) *The Detection of Psychiatric Illness by Questionnaire*. Oxford: Oxford University Press.

Gould, S.J. (1981) *Ever Since Darwin*. Harmondsworth: Penguin.

Grant, M. (1916) *The Passion of the Great Race*. New York: Scribner.

Greenwald, A.G. (1975) On the inconclusiveness of 'crucial' cognitive tests of dissonance versus self-perception theories. *Journal of Experimental Social Psychology*, 11, 490–9.

Greenwood, J.D. (1988) Agency, causality and meaning. *Journal for the Theory of Social Behaviour*, 18, 371–89.

Greenwood, J.D. (1989) *Explanation and Experiment in Social Psychological Science*. New York: Springer-Verlag.

Greenwood, J.D. (1990) Two dogmas of neo-empiricism: the 'theory-informity' of observation and the Quine–Duhem thesis. *Philosophy of Science*, 57, 553–74.

Greenwood, J.D. (1991a) *Relations and Representations*. London: Routledge.

Greenwood, J.D. (1991b) Reasons to believe. In J.D. Greenwood (ed.), *The Future of Folk Psychology*. Cambridge: Cambridge University Press.

Greenwood, J.D. (1992) Against eliminative materialism: From folk psychology to Völkerpsychologie. *Philosophical Psychology*, 5, 349–67.

Greenwood, J.D. (1993a) Situated persons: Review of L. Ross and R.E. Nisbett 'The Person and the Situation'. *Informal Logic*. In press.

Greenwood, J.D. (1993b) *Folk Psychology and Personal Identity*. Manuscript.

Hacking, I. (1983) *Representing and Intervening*. Cambridge: Cambridge University Press.

Hallpike, C. (1979) *Foundations of Primitive Thought*. Oxford: Clarendon Press.

Hanson, N.R. (1958) *Patterns of Discovery*. Cambridge: Cambridge University Press.

Harding, S. (1986) *The Science Question in Feminism*. London: Cornell University Press.

Harding, S. (1987) The curious coincidence of feminine and African moralities: Challenges for feminist theory. In E.F. Kittay and D.T. Meyers (eds), *Women and Moral Theory*. Totowa, NJ: Rowman and Littlefield.

Harré, R. (1981) Psychological variety. In P. Heelas and A. Lock (eds), *Indigenous Psychologies*. London: Academic Press.

Harré, R. (1983a) *Personal Being*. Oxford: Basil Blackwell.

Harré, R. (1983b) Identity projects. In G.M. Breakwell (ed.), *Threatened Identities*. New York: Wiley.

Harré, R. (ed.) (1986a) *The Social Construction of Emotions*. Oxford: Basil Blackwell.

Harré, R. (1986b) An outline of the social constructionist movement. In R. Harré (ed.), *The Social Construction of Emotions*. Oxford: Basil Blackwell.

Harré, R. (1987) The social construction of selves. In K.M. Yardley and T. Honess (eds), *Self and Identity*. London: Wiley.

Harré, R. (1989) Language games and texts of identity. In J. Shotter and K. Gergen (eds), *Texts of Identity*. London: Sage.

Harré, R., Clarke, D., and De Carlo, N. (1985) *Motives and Mechanisms*. London: Methuen.

Harris, P.L. (1989) *Children and Emotion*. Oxford: Basil Blackwell.

Harter, S. and Whitesell, N. (1989) Developmental changes in children's emotion concepts. In C. Saarni and P.L. Harris (eds), *Children's Understanding of Emotions*. New York: Cambridge University Press.

Harter, S., Wright, K., and Bresnick, S. (1987) A developmental sequence of the understanding of shame and pride. Paper presented at the Society for Research in Child Development Biennial Meeting, Baltimore, MD, April.

Hayek, F.A. (1954) *The Counter Revolution in Science*. Indianapolis: Liberty.

Heelas, P. (1981) Introduction: Indigenous psychologies. In P. Heelas and A. Lock (eds), *Indigenous Psychologies*. London: Academic Press.

Heelas, P. and Lock, A. (eds) (1981) *Indigenous Psychologies*. London: Academic Press.

Hempel, C.G. (1965) *Aspects of Scientific Explanation*. New York: Free Press.

Hempel, C.G. and Oppenheim, P. (1948) Studies in the logic of explanation. *Philosophy of Science*, 15, 135–75.

Hermans, H.J. (1976) *Value Areas and Their Development*. Amsterdam: Swets and Zeitlinger.

Hesse, M.B. (1974) *The Structure of Scientific Inference*. London: Macmillan.

Hesse, M.B. (1976) Models versus paradigms in the natural sciences. In L. Collins (ed.), *The Use of Models in the Social Sciences*. London: Tavistock Press.

Hiatt, L.R. (1978) Classification of the emotions. In L.R. Hiatt (ed.), *Australian Aboriginal Concepts*. Princeton, NJ: Humanities Press.

Hitch, P. (1983) Social identity and the half-Asian child. In G. Breakwell (ed.), *Threatened Identities*. New York: Wiley.

Hochschild, A.R. (1983) *The Managed Heart*. Berkeley: University of California Press.

Hoelter, J. (1983) The effects of role evaluation and commitment on identity salience. *Social Psychology Quarterly*, 46, 140–7.

Hogg, M.A. and Abrams, D. (1988) *Social Identifications*. London: Routledge and Kegan Paul.

Hohmann, G.W. (1966) Some effects of spinal chord lesions on experienced emotional feelings. *Psychopsychology*, 3, 143–56.

Hume, D. (1739) *A Treatise on Human Nature*.

Imada, H., Araki, M., and Kujime, Y. (1991) Comparisons of concepts of anxiety, fear, and depression in English and Japanese languages. Manuscript in preparation. Cited in Russell (1991).

Isaac, J. (1987) *Power and Marxist Theory: A Realist View*. Ithaca: Cornell University Press.

Izard, C. (1984) Emotion–cognition relationships and human development. In C. Izard, J. Kagan, and R. Zajonc (eds), *Emotions, Cognition, and Behavior*. New York: Cambridge University Press.

Johansen, J.P. (1954) *The Maori and his Religion in its Non-Ritualistic Aspects*. Copenhagen: Munksgaard.

Johnson-Laird, P.N. (1983) *Mental Models*. Cambridge: Cambridge University Press.

Jones, E.E. (1985) History of social psychology. In G.A. Kimble and K. Schlesinger (eds), *Topics in the History of Psychology, Vol. 2*. Hillsdale, NJ: Lawrence Erlbaum Associates.

Jourard, S.M. (1968) *Disclosing Man to Himself*. New York: Litton.

Kant, I. (1798) *Anthropologie in pragmatischer Hinsicht*.

Keller, E.F. (1985) *Reflections on Gender and Science*. London: Yale University Press.

Kemper, T.D. (1978) *A Social Interactional Theory of Emotions*. New York: Wiley.

Kendler, H.H. (1952) 'What is learned?' – A theoretical blind alley. *Psychological Review*, 59, 269–77.

Kimble, G.A. (1989) Psychology from the standpoint of a generalist. *American Psychologist*, 44, 491–9.

Kitzinger, C. (1987) *The Social Construction of Lesbianism*. London: Sage.

Kitzinger, C. (1989) Liberal humanism as an ideology of social control: The regulation of lesbian identities. In J. Shotter and K.J. Gergen (eds), *Texts of Identity*. London: Sage.

Knorr-Cetina, K.D. (1981) *The Manufacture of Knowledge: An Essay on the Constructivist and Contextual Nature of Science*. Oxford: Pergamon.

Knorr-Certina, K.D. and Mulkay, M. (eds) (1983) *Science Observed*. London: Sage.

Kohlberg, L. (1981a) *Essays on Moral Development: The Theory of Moral Development*. San Francisco: Harper and Row.

Kohlberg, L. (1981b) From ought to is: How to commit the naturalistic fallacy and get away with it in the study of moral development. In L. Kohlberg, *Essays on Moral Development*. San Francisco: Harper and Row.

Kohler, W. (1924) *Static and Stationary Physical Configurations*. Erlangen: Verlag der Philosophischen Akademie.

Kolak, D. and Martin, R. (eds), (1990) *Self and Identity: Contemporary Philosophical Issues*. New York: Macmillan.

Kuhn, M. (1964) Self and self-conception. In J. Gould and W. Kolb (eds), *A Dictionary of the Social Sciences*. New York: Free Press.

Kuhn, T. (1970) *The Structure of Scientific Revolutions*. 2nd edition. Chicago: University of Chicago Press.

Lachman, R., Lachman, J., and Butterfield, E. (1979) *Cognitive Psychology and Information Processing*. New Jersey: Lawrence Erlbaum Associates.

Lakatos, I. (1970) Falsification and the methodology of scientific research programmes. In I. Lakatos and A. Musgrave (eds), *Criticism and the Growth of Knowledge*. Cambridge: Cambridge University Press.

Latané, B., and Darley, J.M. (1970) *The Unresponsive Bystander: Why Doesn't He Help?* New York: Appleton-Century-Crofts.

Latour, B. (1983) Give me a laboratory and I will raise the world. In K.D. Knorr-Cetina and M. Mulkay (eds), *Science Observed*. London: Sage.

Latour, B. (1987) *Science in Action: How to Follow Scientists and Engineers Through Society*. Cambridge, MA: Harvard University Press.

Latour, B. and Woolgar, S. (1986) *Laboratory Life: The Construction of Scientific Facts*. Princeton: Princeton University Press.

Lauden, L. (1977) *Progress and its Problems*. Berkeley: University of California Press.

Lazarus, R.S. (1981) Thoughts on the relations between emotion and cognition. *American Psychologist*, 37, 1019–24.

Lazarus, R.S. (1984) On the primacy of cognition. *American Psychologist*, 39, 124–9.

Leahey, T.H. (1992) *A History of Psychology*. 3rd edition. Englewood Cliffs: Prentice-Hall.

Ledwidge, B. (1978) Cognitive behavior modification: a step in the wrong direction? *Psychological Bulletin*, 85, 353–75.

Leighton, A.H., Lambo, T.A., Hughes, C.C., Leighton, D.C., Murphy, J.M., and Macklin, D.B. (eds) (1963) *Psychiatric Disorder among the Yoruba*. Ithaca: Cornell University Press.

Leplin, J. (1984) Introduction. In J. Leplin (ed.), *Scientific Realism*. Berkeley: University of California Press.

Leslie, A.M. (1988) Some implications of pretense for mechanisms underlying the child's theory of mind. In J.W. Astington, P.L. Harris, and D.R. Olson (eds), *Developing Theories of Mind*. Cambridge: Cambridge University Press.

Leventhal, H. (1980) Towards a comprehensive theory of emotion. In L. Berkowitz (ed.), *Advances in Experimental Social Psychology*, 13. New York: Academic Press.

Leventhal, H. and Scherer, K.R. (1987) The relations of emotion and cognition: A functionalist approach to a semantic controversy. *Cognition and Emotion*, 1, 3–28.

Lévi-Strauss, C. (1960) The family. In H.L. Shapiro (ed.), *Man, Culture, and Society*. New York: Oxford University Press.

Levy, R. (1984) Emotion, knowing and culture. In R. Shweder and R. LeVine (eds), *Culture Theory: Essays on Mind, Self, and Emotion*. Cambridge: Cambridge University Press.

Lewin, K. (1951) *Field Theory in Social Science*. New York: Harper.

Lewis, D. (1972) Psychophysical and theoretical identifications. *Australian Journal of Philosophy*, 50, 249–58.

Lewis, M. and Saarni, C. (1985) Culture and emotion. In M. Lewis and C. Saarni (eds), *The Socialization of Emotion*. London: Plenum.

Locke, J. (1690) *An Essay Concerning Human Understanding*.

Logan, R.D. (1987) Historical change in prevailing sense of self. In H.M. Yardley and T. Honess (eds), *Self and Identity: Psychosocial Perspectives*. London: Wiley.

Louch, A. (1967) *Explanation and Human Action*. Oxford: Basil Blackwell.

Lukes, S. (1973) Methodological individualism reconsidered. In A. Ryan (ed.), *The Philosophy of Social Explanation*. Oxford: Oxford University Press.

Lutz, C. (1982) The domain of emotion words in Ifaluk. *American Ethnologist*, 9, 113–28.

Lutz, C. (1988) *Unnatural Emotions*. Chicago, IL: University of Chicago Press.

Lyons, J.O. (1978) *The Invention of the Self*. Carbondale: Southern Illinois University Press.

McCall, G.C. (1977) The social looking-glass: A sociological perspective on self-development. In T. Mischel (ed.), *The Self: Psychological and Philosophical Issues*. Oxford: Basil Blackwell.

McCall, G.C. and Simmons, J.L. (1978) *Identities and Interactions* (rev. ed.). New York: Free Press.

MacCorquodale, K. and Meehl, P.E. (1948) On a distinction between hypothetical constructs and intervening variables. *Psychological Review*, 55, 95–107.

McDougall, W. (1920) *The Group Mind*. New York: Putnam.

McDougall, W. (1921) *Is America Safe for Democracy?* New York: Scribner.

Machan, T.R. (1987) Letter to the Editor. *Proceedings and Addresses of the American Philosophical Association*, 60, 515.

Malatesta, C.Z. and Haviland, D.R. (1985) Signals, symbols and socialization. In M. Lewis and C. Saarni (eds), *The Socialization of Emotion*. London: Plenum.

Manicas, P.T. and Secord, P.F. (1983) Implications for psychology of the new philosophy of science. *American Psychologist*, 38, 399–413.

Maranon, G. (1924) Contribution à l'étude de l'action émotive de l'adrénaline. *Revue Française d'Endocrinologie*, 21, 301–25.

Margolis, J. (1984) *Philosophy of Psychology*. Englewood Cliffs: Prentice-Hall.

Markus, H., and Nurius, P. (1986) Possible selves. *American Psychologist*, 41, 954–69.

Marsella, A.J. (1981) Depressive experience and disorder across cultures. In H. Triandis and J. Draguns (eds), *Handbook of Cross-Cultural Psychology*. Boston: Allyn and Bacon.

Marsh, P., Rosser, E., and Harré, R. (1978) *The Rules of Disorder*. London: Routledge and Kegan Paul.

Marx, M. (1951) Intervening variable or hypothetical construct? *Psychological Review*, 58, 235–47.

Mead, G.H. (1934) *Mind, Self, and Society*. Chicago: University of Chicago Press.

Merton, R.K. and Kitt, A.S. (1950) Contributions to the theory of reference group behavior. In R.K. Merton and P.F. Lazarsfeld (ed.), *Continuities in Social Research*. Glencoe, IL: Free Press.

Milgram, S. (1974) *Obedience to Authority*. New York: Harper and Row.

Miller, G.A. (1956) The magical number seven, plus or minus two: Some limits on our capacity for processing information. *Psychological Review*, 63, 81–97.

Minsky, M. (1981) K-lines: a theory of memory. In D. Norman (ed.), *Perspectives on Cognitive Science*. Norwood, NJ: Ablex.

Mischel, T. (ed.) (1977a) *The Self: Psychological and Philosophical Issues*. Oxford: Basil Blackwell.

Mischel, T. (1977b) Conceptual issues in the psychology of the self: An introduction. In T. Mischel (ed.), *The Self: Psychological and Philosophical Issues*. Oxford: Basil Blackwell.

Mixon, D. (1972) Instead of deception. *Journal for the Theory of Social Behaviour*, 2, 145–77.

Morris, C. (1972) *The Discovery of the Individual, 1050–1200*. New York: Harper and Row.

Morris, I. (1975) *The Nobility of Failure*. London: Secker and Warburg.

Morsbach, H. and Tyler, W.J. (1976) Some Japanese–Western linguistic differences concerning dependency needs: the case of 'amae'. In R. Harré (ed.), *Life Sentences*. New York. Wiley.

Moscovici, S. (1976) *La Psychoanalyse: son image et son public* 2nd ed. Paris: Presses Universitaires de France.

Moscovici, S. (1989) Preconditions for explanation in social psychology. *European Journal for Social Psychology*, 19, 407–30.

Myers, F. (1979) Emotions and the self. *Ethos*, 7, 343–70.

Nagel, E. (1961) *The Structure of Science*. New York: Harcourt, Brace, and World.

Newell, A., Shaw, J.C., and Simon, H.A. (1958) Elements of a theory of problem-solving. *Psychological Review*, 65, 151–66.

Nicolson, L. (1991) The arrogance of social theory. Paper presented at the Thirtieth Oberlin Colloqium in Philosophy, Oberlin, OH, April.

Nisbett, R.E. and Ross, L. (1980) *Human Inference: Strategies and Shortcomings of Social Judgment*. Englewood Cliffs, NJ: Prentice-Hall.

Nisbett, R.E. and Wilson, T.D. (1977) Telling more than we can know: Verbal reports on mental processes. *Psychological Review*, 84, 231–59.

Nuttin, J.R. (1984) *Motivation, Planning, and Action: A Relational Theory of Behavior Dynamics*. Hillsdale, NJ: Lawrence Erlbaum Associates.

Olson, D. and Astington, J. (1986) Children's acquisition of metalinguistic and metacognitive verbs. In W. Demopoulos and A. Marras (eds), *Language and Concept Acquisition*. Norwood, NJ: Ablex.

Orne, M.T. (1962) On the social psychology of the psychological experiment: with particular reference to demand characteristics and their implications. *American Psychologist*, 17, 776–83.

Paivio, A. (1986) *Mental Representations: A Dual Coding Approach*. Oxford: Oxford University Press.

Parfit, D. (1984) *Reasons and Persons*. Oxford: Oxford University Press.

Perner, J. and Wilde-Astington, J. (1993) The child's understanding of mental representation. *Proceedings of the Twentieth Anniversary Symposium of the Jean Piaget Society*. In press.

Perry, J. (1975) The problem of personal identity. In J. Perry (ed.), *Personal Identity*. Berkeley: University of California Press.

Peters, R.S. (1974) *Psychology and Ethical Development*. London: Allen and Unwin.

Pickering, A. (1984) *Constructing Quarks: A Sociological History of Particle Physics*. Edinburgh: Edinburgh University Press.

Plutchik, R. (1980) *Emotion: A Psychoevolutionary Synthesis*. New York: Harper and Row.

Pope, K.S. and Singer, J.L. (eds) (1978) *The Stream of Consciousness*. New York. Plenum Press.

Popper, K.R. (1945) *The Open Society and its Enemies, Vols 1 and 2*. London: Routledge and Kegan Paul.

Popper, K.R. (1959) *The Logic of Scientific Discovery*. London: Hutchinson.

Popper, K.R. (1963) *Conjectures and Refutations*. London: Routledge and Kegan Paul.

Porpora, D.V. (1989) Four concepts of social structure. *Journal for the Theory of Social Behaviour*, 19, 199-211.

Potter, J. (1992) Constructing realism: Seven moves (plus or minus a couple). *Theory and Psychology*, 2, 167–73.

Potter, J. and Wetherell, M. (1987) *Discourse and Social Psychology: Beyond Attitudes and Behaviour*. London: Sage.

Prilleltensky, I. (1989) Psychology and the status quo. *American Psychologist*, 44, 795–802.

Prilleltensky, I. (1990) On the social and political implications of cognitive psychology. *Journal of Mind and Behavior*, 11, 127–36.

Prince, M. (1905) *The Dissociation of a Personality*. London: Longmans, Green.

Quine, W.V.O. (1953) Two dogmas of empiricism. In *From a Logical Point of View*. Cambridge, MA: Harvard University Press.

Quine, W.V.O. and Ullian, J.S. (1970) *The Web of Belief*. New York: Random House.

Rachels, J. (1986) *Elements of Moral Philosophy*. New York: Random House.

Ratner, C. (1989) A social constructionist critique of the naturalist theory of emotion. *Journal of Mind and Behavior*, 10, 211–30.

Regan, T. (1986) *Matters of Life and Death*. New York: Random House.

Reid, T. (1785) *Essays on the Intellectual Powers of Man*. Chapter 4, 'On memory'. Reprinted in J. Perry (ed.), *Personal Identity*. Berkeley: University of California Press (1975).

Reisman, P. (1977) *Freedom in Fulani Social Life: An Introspective Ethnography* (trans. M. Fuller). Chicago: University of Chicago Press.

Rorty, A. (ed.) (1975) *The Identities of Persons*. Berkeley: University of California Press.

Rorty, A. (1979) *Philosophy and the Mirror of Nature*. Oxford: Basil Blackwell.

Rosaldo, M.Z. (1980) *Knowledge and Passion: Ilongot Notions of Self and Social Life*. Cambridge: Cambridge University Press.

Rosch, E. (1975) Cognitive representations of semantic categories. *Journal of Experimental Psychology: General*, 104, 192–233.

Roseman, I.J. (1984) Cognitive determinants of emotion: A structural theory. In P. Shaver (ed.), *Review of Personality and Social Psychology: Vol. 5. Emotions, Relationships and Health*. Beverly Hills, CA: Sage.

Rosenberg, A. (1988) *Philosophy of Social Science*. Boulder, CO: Westview.

Rosenberg, M. (1981) The self concept: Social product and social force. In M. Rosenberg and R.H. Turner (eds), *Social Psychology: Sociological Perspectives*. New York: Basic Books.

Rosenberg, S. and Gara, M. (1985) The multiplicity of personal identity. *Review of Personality and Social Psychology*, 6, 87–113.

Rosenberg, S. and Jones, R.A. (1972) A method of investigating and representing a person's implicit personality theory. *Journal of Personality and Social Psychology*, 22, 372–86.

Ross, L. and Nisbett, R.E. (1991) *The Person and the Situation: Perspectives on Social Psychology*. Philadelphia: Temple University Press.

Rumelhart, D.E. and McClelland, J.L. (eds) (1986) *Parallel Distributed Processing: Explorations in the Microstructure of Cognition. Vols. 1 and 2*. Cambridge, MA: MIT Press.

Russell, B. (1924) The relation of sense-data to physics. Reprinted in *Mysticism and Logic*. London: Allen and Unwin (1962).

Russell, J.A. (1991) Culture and the categorization of emotions. *Psychological Bulletin*, 110, 426–50.

Sabini, J. and Silver, M. (1982) *Moralities of Everyday Life*. Oxford: Oxford University Press.

Salner, M. (1988) Epistemic beliefs and their developmental relationship to post-positivist psychology. In W.J. Baker, L.P. Mos, H.V. Rappard and H.J. Stam (eds), *Recent Trends in Theoretical Psychology*. New York: Springer-Verlag.

Sampson, E.E. (1977) Psychology and the American ideal. *Journal of Personality and Social Psychology*, 35, 767–82.

Sampson, E.E. (1981) Cognitive psychology as ideology. *American Psychologist*, 36, 730–43.

Sartre, J.P. (1948) *Existentialism and Humanism* (trans. P. Mairet). London.

Schachter, S. (1965) The interaction of cognitive and physiological determinants of emotional state. In P.H. Leiderman and D. Shapiro (eds), *Psychobiological Approaches to Social Behaviour*. London: Tavistock.

Schachter, S. (1971) *Emotion, Obesity, and Crime*. New York: Academic Press.

Schachter, S. and Singer, S. (1962) Cognitive, social and physiological determinants of emotional state. *Psychological Review*, 69, 379–99.

Scheff, T. (1988) Hiding behavior: Toward resolving the shame controversy. Paper presented at the Conference on Shame Research, Asilomar.

Scheman, N. (1983) Individualism and the objects of psychology. In S. Harding and M.B. Hinkitta (eds), *Discovering Reality*. Dordrecht: Reidel.

Scherer, K.R. (1984) On the nature and function of emotion: A component process approach. In K.R. Scherer and P. Ekman (eds), *Approaches to Emotion*. Hillsdale, NJ: Lawrence Erlbaum Associates.

Schieffelin, E.L. (1985) The cultural analysis of depressive affect: An example from New Guinea. In K. Kleinman and B. Good (eds), *Culture and Depression*. Berkeley: University of California Press.

Schlesinger, G. (1961) The prejudice of micro-reduction. *British Journal for the Philosophy of Science*, 12, 215–24.

Schlick, M. (1936) Meaning and verification. *Philosophical Review*, 45.

Secord, P.F. and Greenwood, J.D. (1993) Self-knowledge of psychological states: The status of subjects' accounts. In P.E. Shrout and S.T. Fiske (eds), *Advances in Personality Research, Methods, and Theory*. Hillsdale, NJ: Lawrence Erlbaum Associates.

Sen, A. (1982) *Choice, Welfare, and Measurement*. Cambridge, MA: MIT Press.

Seyle, H. (1950) *The Physiology and Pathology of Exposure to Stress*. Montreal: Acta, Inc.

Seyle, H. (1974) *The Stress of Life*. New York: McGraw-Hill.

Shapere, D. (1964) The structure of scientific revolutions. *Philosophical Review*, 73, 383–94.

Shapin, S. and Schaffer, S. (1985) *Leviathan and the Air Pump: Hobbes, Boyle, and the Experimental Life*. Princeton: Princeton University Press.

Shoemaker, S. (1970) Persons and their pasts. *American Philosophical Quarterly*, 7, 269–85.

Shotter, J. (1984) *Social Accountability and Selfhood*. Oxford: Basil Blackwell.

Shotter, J. (1985) Social accountability and self-specification. In K.J. Gergen and K.E. Davis (eds), *The Social Construction of the Person*. New York: Springer-Verlag.

Shotter, J. (1987) The rhetoric of theory in psychology. In W.M. Baker, M.E. Hyland, H.V. Rappard, and A.W. Staats (eds), *Current Issues in Theoretical Psychology*. Amsterdam: Elsevier.

Shotter, J. (1989) Social accountability and selfhood. In J. Shotter and K.J. Gergen (eds), *Texts of Identity*. London: Sage.

Shotter, J. (1992) Social constructionism and realism. Adequacy or accuracy? *Theory and Psychology*, 2, 175–82.

Shotter, J. and Gergen, K.J. (eds) (1989) *Texts of Identity*. London: Sage.

Simon, H.A. and Kaplan, C.A. (1989) Foundations of cognitive science. In M.I. Posner (ed.), *Foundations of Cognitive Science*. Cambridge, MA: MIT Press.

Skinner, B.F. (1938) *The Behavior of Organisms*. New York: Appleton-Century-Crofts.

Skinner, B.F. (1953) *Science and Human Behavior*. New York: Macmillan.

Skinner, B.F. (1974) *About Behaviorism*. New York: Knopf.

Skinner, B.F. (1984) Representations and misrepresentations. *Behavioral and Brain Sciences*, 7, 655–67.

Smith, C.A. and Ellsworth, P.C. (1985) Patterns of cognitive appraisal in emotion. *Journal of Personality and Social Psychology*, 48, 813–38.

Smith, J. (1981) Self and experience in Maori culture. In P. Heelas and A. Lock (eds), *Indigenous Psychologies*. London: Academic Press.

Stoddard, L. (1920) *The Rising Tide of Color Against White-World Supremacy*. New York: Scribner.

Stryker, S. (1980) *Symbolic Interactionism: A Social Structural Version*. Menlo Park: Benjamin/Cummins.

Swinburne, R. (1986) *The Evolution of the Soul*. Oxford: Clarendon Press.

Tajfel, H. (1981) *Human Groups and Social Categories*. Cambridge: Cambridge University Press.

Tanaka-Matsumi, J., and Marsella, A.J. (1976) Cross-cultural variations in the phenomeno-logical experience of depression: I. Word association studies. *Journal of Cross-Cultural Psychology*, 7, 379–96.

Tanaka-Matsumi, J., and Marsella, A.J. (1977) Ethnocultural variations in the subjective experience of depression: Semantic differential. Unpublished manuscript, University of Hawaii, Department of Psychology, Honolulu. Cited in Russell (1991).

Thatcher, A. (1987) Christian theism and the concept of a person. In A. Peacocke and G. Gillett (eds), *Persons and Personality*. Oxford: Basil Blackwell.

Tomkins, S.S. (1970) Affect as the primary motivational system. In M. Arnold (ed.), *Feeling and Emotion*. New York: Academic Press.

Triandis, H. (1980) *Handbook of Cross-Cultural Psychology*. Boston: Allyn and Bacon.

Turner, J.C. (1987) *Discovering the Social Group: A Self-Categorization Theory*. Oxford: Basil Blackwell.

van Fraassen, B.C. (1980) *The Scientific Image*. Oxford: Oxford University Press.

von Cranach, M. (1982) The psychological study of goal-directed action: Basic issues. In M. von Cranach and R. Harré (eds), *The Analysis of Action*. Cambridge: Cambridge University Press.

von Eickstedt, E. (1936) *Grundlagen der Rassenpsychologie*. Stuttgart: Enke.

Vygotsky, L.S. (1962) *Thought and Language*. Cambridge, MA: MIT Press.

Waismann, F. (1945) Verifiability. *Proceedings of the Aristotelian Society*, Supp. Vol. 19, 119–50.

Wallace, A.F.C. and Carson, M.T. (1973) Sharing and diversity in emotion terminology. *Ethos*, 1, 1–29.

Watson, J.D. (1978) *The Double Helix: A Personal Account of the Discovery of the Structure of DNA*. London: Penguin.

Weber, M. (1913) Some categories of interpretative sociology. *Logos*, IV. Reprinted as Appendix I in G. Roth and C. Wittich (eds), *Economy and Society*, Vols I and II. Berkeley: University of California Press (1978).

Weber, M. (1922) *Economy and Society*, Vols I and II. G. Roth and C. Wittich (eds). Berkeley: University of California Press (1978).

Wegner, D.N. and Vallacher, R.R. (eds) (1980) *The Self in Social Psychology*. Oxford: Oxford University Press.

Weiner, B. (1985) An attributional theory of achievement motivation and emotion. *Psychological Review*, 92, 548–73.

Weinrich, P. (1980) *A Manual for Identity Exploration Using Personal Constructs*. London: Social Science Research Council.

Weinrich, P. (1983) Emerging from threatened identities: Ethnicity and gender in redefinitions of ethnic identity. In G. Breakwell (ed.), *Threatened Identities*. New York: Wiley.

Wellman, H.M. (1988) First steps in the child's theorizing about the mind. In J.W. Astington, P.L. Harris and D.R. Olson (eds), *Developing Theories of Mind*. Cambridge: Cambridge University Press.

White, P.A. (1988) Knowing more about what we can tell: 'Introspective access' and causal report accuracy 10 years later. *British Journal of Psychology*, 134, 13–45.

Wicklund, R.A. and Gollwitzer, P.M. (1982) *Symbolic Self-Completion*. Hillsdale, NJ: Lawrence Erlbaum Associates.

Wierzbicka, A. (1986) Human emotions: Universal or culture specific? *American Anthropologist*, 88, 584–94.

Wiley, M.G. and Alexander, C.N. (1987) From situated activity to self-attribution: The impact of social structural schemata. In K.M. Yardley and T. Honess (eds), *Self and Identity: Psychosocial Perspectives*. London: Wiley.

Wilkes, K.V. (1988) *Real Lives*. Oxford: Oxford University Press.

Williams, R. (1961) *The Long Revolution*. New York: Columbia University Press.

Wilson, T.D. and Nisbett, R.E. (1977) The accuracy of verbal reports about the effects of stimuli on evaluations and behavior. *Social Psychology*, 41, 118–31.

Wing, J.K., Cooper, J.E., and Sartorius, N. (1974) *The Measurement and Classification of Psychiatric Symptoms*. Cambridge: Cambridge University Press.

Wittgenstein, L. (1917) *Tractatus-Logico-Philosophicus* (trans. D.F. Pears and B.F. McGuiness). London: Routledge and Kegan Paul.

Wittgenstein, L. (1953) *Philosophical Investigations*. Oxford: Basil Blackwell.

Wittgenstein, L. (1969) *On Certainty*. Oxford: Basil Blackwell.

Wolman, B.B. and Stricker, G. (eds) (1991) *Depressive Disorders*. New York: Wiley.

Wrightsman, L.S. (1960) Effects of waiting with others on changes of level of felt anxiety. *Journal of Abnormal and Social Psychology*, 61, 216–22.

Wundt, W. (1897) *Outlines of Psychology*. (trans. C.H. Judd) Leipzig: W. Engelmann.

Wundt, W. (1920) *Völkerpsychologie*, Vols 1–10. Leipzig: Engelmann and Kroner.

Wylie, R. (1979) *The Self-Concept*, Vols 1 and 2. (rev. ed.) Lincoln: University of Nebraska Press.

Yardley, K.M. and Honess, T. (eds) (1987) *Self and Identity: Psychological Perspectives*. London: Wiley.

Zajonc, R.B. (1980) Feeling and thinking: Preferences need no inferences. *American Psychologist*, 35, 151–75.

Zajonc, R.B. (1984) On the primacy of affect. *American Psychologist*, 39, 117–23.

Zavalloni, M. (1971) Cognitive processes and social identity through introspection. *European Journal of Social Psychology*, 1, 235–60.

Index

WITHDRAWN
No longer the property of the
Boston Public Library.
Sale of this material benefits the Library.